Grace Saunders was a fashion journalist and stylist at *Elle* magazine for six years before becoming a freelance lifestyle journalist and best-selling author of *The Fabulous Mum's Handbook* and *Family Life Made Easy*. She lives in north London with her husband and three children.

LIFE'S TOO SHORT

TOP TIPS AND INSIDER CHEATS
FOR THE MODERN WOMAN

GRACE SAUNDERS

headline

First published in 2011
by HEADLINE PUBLISHING GROUP

First published in paperback in 2012
by HEADLINE PUBLISHING GROUP

1

Cataloguing in Publication Data is available from the British Library

ISBN 978 0 7553 6183 0

Typeset in Palatino Light by Avon DataSet Ltd,
Bidford-on-Avon, Warwickshire

Printed and bound in Great Britain by Clays Ltd, St Ives plc

HEADLINE PUBLISHING GROUP
An Hachette UK Company
338 Euston Road
London NW1 3BH

www.headline.co.uk
www.hachette.co.uk

To Mr S, for everything

CONTENTS

THE LOW-DOWN

OK, so here's the deal. Before you shun this for being yet another self-help manual telling you how to live your life, I promise this is a girls' guide with a difference. I vow it won't preach or bombard you with over-sincere, patronising advice. It won't tell you the definitive rules to dressing for the office, how to make your partnership harmonious every day of the week or why you should embrace yoga as the key to inner peace. Come to think of it, it won't dictate how to roll pastry, wear stilettos or have an orgasm either. To be totally honest, I think we've got enough of these books to stack a bookshelf and, frankly, life's too short to be told what to do by manuals masquerading as our 'best friends'. Give us some bloody credit! What this book *will* offer busy multitasking women at their fingertips are:

- Shortcuts and top tips to help save you precious time and energy.

- Instant, expert know-how to inspire you.

- Up-to-date, tried-and-tested methods, resources and information you really can trust.

- Lots and lots of laughs.

Offer me a free Mulberry bag, an all-expenses-paid holiday to the Maldives or more time, energy and 'really-does-work' lifestyle know-how, and the latter three would win hands down every time. Admit it: aren't we all striving for that all-elusive 'perfection', a generation of swans trying desperately to swim serenely above the water while actually paddling at a million miles per hour underneath – often half-choking, spluttering and almost drowning while we're at it? The result? We feel totally and utterly frazzled. I think we'd all agree it's impossible to have it all, and unrealistic and exhausting to try to achieve it. I'm not saying life's not worth the effort, but does it have to be such hard work? Life's just too short! I hope this book will show you how to be everything you want to be, but by giving down-to-earth shortcut routes, insider top tips and useful resources on how to get there. It's the one purchase you'll make that will help you achieve (most) of what you want but taking far less time, stress, hassle, aggravation, fatigue and often cash doing it.

Because I was one of those frazzled women who never had enough time in the day and would regularly wish for some ready-made solutions to everything from 'how to work freelance without becoming a BlackBerry bore' and 'easy ideas to create an *Elle Decor* home on IKEA prices' to 'shortcuts to throwing an impressive supper party when you don't have time to mix or marinade', I *really* needed this book. Now that I have three kids, a freelance career, a bathroom full of dirty washing and even less time to work/decorate/cook/shop/groom/chill, I *really, really, really* need this book. I've tried my damndest to write it for ambitious, busy, multitasking women just like myself. I've also tried to strike a balance between what's important (career, family, ethical living, money management) and what's frivolous but still factors into our lives and makes them colourful and enjoyable (shoes, wine, lippy, beach holidays).

If, like me, you're the woman who loves hen nights but loathes the obligatory deely-boppers, I'll show you how it's possible to find easy, stylish alternatives with a click of your mouse. The same applies to getting a promotion or pay rise at work. 'Impossible in this climate!' I hear you cry. Not necessarily; it's actually not as impossible as you'd imagine. If you're also the woman who's beauty-savvy enough to know exactly where on the forehead Botox is injected to freeze wrinkles, but it challenges your morals about growing old gracefully, then here you'll find an array of respected aim-to-avoid-wind-tunnel-look doctors plus innovative ways to beat knackered, aging skin without a syringe in sight. You'll also get the answer to speedy cupcakes without the mess, fabulous investment shoes without spending a fortune, moving house without losing your sanity, eco-living without endless flat-pack boxes, managing your finances without breaking out in a sweat and my very own shortcut solution to red eyes and dark shadows after a night out or having been up a dozen times with young kids. It's not a twenty-minute mini-facial and complex make-up routine – it's simple: just wear shades! All this and, to top it off, I've got up-close-and-personal with some of your favourite celebrities and role models and asked them to drop the PR spin and tell us, with wit and honesty, *exactly* how they pull it all off.

So here it is, *Life's Too Short*, which I sincerely hope is an essential no-fuss, no-frills lifestyle guide that won't advise you on how to stuff a mushroom or arrange roses (yawn), but *will* help you survive life and all its mayhem. My ultimate aim? For us all to be less stressed and frazzled and to conjure up that extra half an hour each evening to read the first chapter of a good novel/write a card to an old friend/plan a work appraisal/

have a long bath and de-fuzz those legs/play with your kids. True, not *every* tip saves you time, but I've tried my hardest to ensure that if it doesn't give you those extra golden minutes, it'll give you the equally as golden motivation and resources. Having these at your fingertips will help you to feel more confident and glamorous, eliminating masses of guilt, stress and anxiety while you're at it. I'm not flagging myself up as a 'guru' with all the answers, but I hope that by fusing humour and honesty in equal parts, it might help us on the way to perfection. What woman doesn't need this in her life?

I hope more than anything that by sewing together all my experiences of two-day-old pesto, bad hair, morning clothes crisis, working-mum guilt, haranguing the experts, hassling some famous names and plundering my contacts book, I've come up with the ultimate one-stop-shop book of really-do-work shortcuts and top tips, guaranteed to deliver a more serene and stylish life today.

Now, forgive me while I follow my own advice, turn off the laptop, pour myself a glass of good red, change into some seriously snuggly cashmere bed-socks and get comfy on the sofa to read it. Come on, join me.

CHAPTER ONE

LOVE GODDESS

Being single and loving it

Being single is a funny old thing. On the one hand, you can master the art of bed-hogging and doing whatever you goddamn like; on the other, blissed-out, coupled-up friends stop asking you to their 'intimate supper parties' (but don't you just hate overstuffed olives and small talk anyway?). Very rapidly, the feeling that 'the grass is always greener' seeps in and what I call the 'lurve conspiracy theory' can take over – i.e. when you're single, you're made to feel like you're missing out on some big couples' secret.

Let me illustrate my conspiracy theory. Open the pages of a fabulous glossy mag and, shortly after the ad for a new-season, cult Chloé handbag, you're almost guaranteed to see some sort of girl-meets-boy-lurve-thing fashion shoot. You know the one? Blonde, skinny, long-legged girl and buffed-up, golden-brown boy lolling in each other's arms on a battered leather sofa at 'his place'. Run into Boots for that Monday morning instead-of-breakfast smoothie and – *bang!* – in your face is a similarly gloating toothpaste ad with the obligatory chiselled hunk running along a beach to embrace his Giselle lookalike partner. To make matters worse, pap snaps of single celebs scream, 'Dumped and single again' or 'Lost and desperate for a baby'. Hello? Is someone trying to tell us that *all* single women must be sad, lonely, miserable and desperate for a date?

Let's cut to the chase here. Number one, dating doesn't mean you get the key to eternal happiness. Putting up with the in-laws on a hot Sunday afternoon when you could be picnicking in the park, realising you're not free to indulge in a whole Saturday of DIY beauty rituals and instead rowing at full volume over whose turn it is to take out the rubbish doesn't sound like eternal bliss to me. Number two, single does not mean sad, psycho or forever unlovable – girlie break in the sun, anyone? I don't see sad, psychotic or unloved anywhere in this frame.

My single friend Zoe is a great example of a contented singleton. Not interested in a steady boyfriend in the slightest, she'll happily tell you she'd far rather be footloose and fancy-free, dipping into her Little Black Book of desirables as and when she fancies a flirt, than be tied down to the same man for life. Not just yet anyway. Quite frankly, she says, she loves her friends, her job and her single-girl pad, and is blessed to come home each night to a bedroom free of Will Self, crumpled-up work shirts and her expected undivided attention.

The truth is, being part of a couple isn't always what it's cracked up to be. While the comfort and security of being in a his-and-hers match can be lovely, it can be equally as limiting. I know many married women who look at their single friends with envy: some are in loveless marriages, some play out the charade of happily families but behind closed doors there is no real intimacy or kindness, while others feel they've just become invisible within the prism of so-called domestic bliss (and let's not even go down the City-boy husbands who're sleeping around/housewives who're flirting with the tennis coach route). With all these double standards going on, why should it be the single girls who are made to feel like failures?

With this in mind, let me share a few top tips for you single ladies out there who would rather donate all your designer shoes to Oxfam than spend your precious Saturday nights surfing dating websites just so you can get that 'coveted' invite to the next couples-only evening:

1. Don't believe the hype. While you're wasting time lusting after Mr Right, those with Mr Right are probably wishing they had the freedom to meet girlfriends for supper, spend any afternoon they choose browsing around a new art exhibition, swiftly followed by a cover-to-cover read of the latest hot-off-the-press issue of *Vogue* or opt to put their head back under the duvet until midday on a Sunday morning.

2. Forget 'virtual friends' and the false security of Facebook and aim to enjoy your 'real' girlfriends, being totally selfish in your exploits with them. Watch *Desperate Housewives* in oversized sweatshirts, gossip and bitch about exes while drinking Margaritas and eating salted nuts, and persuade them to accompany you to Dominic Cooper's new West End play to ogle.

3. Fill your time with all those things that become impossible when you have to visit IKEA with your other half on late-night Thursday to buy flat-pack bookshelves and a discounted loo seat – i.e. reading a good novel, going to the movies, visiting an art or photography gallery, exploring vintage fairs, starting a new exercise class (boxercise, anyone?), catching up with old friends, decluttering your wardrobe, or even heading to the sales in an attempt to refill the newly decluttered wardrobe.

4 Bin the M&S ready-meals and increase your cooking repertoire. Part of what my newly single girlfriend Willow loves about being without a boy is experimenting with cooking for one. Show me a guy who'd enjoy watermelon, watercress and feta salad quite as much as she does and not ask what's for the main course.

5 Get on a plane/train/bus and go. Just recently I upped sticks and went to Ibiza for a long weekend on my own. The EasyJet flight was as cheap as chips and I was so happy to be lying like a lizard in the sun, reading a novel without being interrupted by screaming children, phone calls or noisy neighbours having a domestic about the measurements of the half-built conservatory that I hardly spent a penny.

6 Get out there and flirt outrageously. Because you bloody well can.

Getting ready for a single-girl night on the razz *(in less than fifteen minutes)*

1 Plan your outfit before the Big Night Out. This way, you can check it's clean (no red wine stains from the last girls' night out) and you can sort out the right accessories to team it with.

2 Book a cab before you start getting ready or – better still – earlier in the day.

3 Shower and wet your hair, but don't wash it. I find clean hair has less volume and, let's face it, washing hair is a fag when you're in a rush.

4   Don't overindulge in a
complicated make-up routine.
Base, blusher, a flick of mascara
and some lip gloss is all a girl
really needs.

*Life's
too short
to lust after
romantic
ideals.*

5   Edit your handbag essentials so
that they fit into a clutch or
evening bag. You don't seriously
need wet wipes, a hairbrush, *Grazia* and a Fruit & Nut bar at
your local gastro pub.

6   Once dressed, don't analyse – just go! You'll only end
up changing a million times and getting into a frazzled
state of hysteria.

7   Drink a glass of vino. Large enough to give you Dutch
courage, but not so big that you're sloshed before you've
even left the house.

Understanding the contraception maze

when you think an IUD is the latest iPod app

- Combined Pill. Referred to by all women I know as just 'the
Pill', it combines two hormones: oestrogen and
progestogen. It's 99 per cent effective if used properly, i.e.
taken every day and not just once a week when you
remember.

- Progestogen-only Pill (POP). This used to be called the
mini-Pill and contains just a progestogen hormone. Several
of my good friends swear by it after the combined Pill led
them to weight-gain (without the fun of overindulging in

Magnums and rosé wine) or loss of libido (bad news when you may only fancy nookie once a month as it is).

- Contraceptive patch. Basically, this is the same form of contraception as the combined Pill, but in a patch that is stuck to your skin. Good if you hate remembering to take a pill, but it can irritate the skin and can be a nuisance to cover up – like we need another fashion obstacle to overcome each morning.

- Barriers – condoms, diaphragms and caps. Great because they release no hormones and protect you from sexually transmitted diseases, but how many of us find the smell of rubber a real intimacy dampener? S&M fetishists, this doesn't mean you. Condoms are ideal to keep in your handbag for that Saturday night hot date, but rubber-nausea and buying shares in KY aren't always best for long-term relationship passion maintenance.

- Contraceptive injections. Almost as high-tech as your new iPad, this injection of progestogen is given every eight to twelve weeks. Probably more reliable than any other piece of tech equipment in your house, with the only downside being that you can't undo the injection for three months. If you experience side effects, you're stuck.

- Contraceptive implants. Six little matchstick-size rods containing progestogen are implanted under the skin on the upper arm. Sounds painful? My girlie implant guinea pigs say not. The beauty? It lasts three years. Great if you're in a steady relationship and don't want the palaver of remembering to pop a pill with your morning PG tips.

- Coil (IUD). I know that for many women the idea of a copper coil reminds us of our mothers, but the coil is catching on again. It only takes a quick visit to the nurse and the T-shaped coil is placed on the uterus. Not the most comfortable experience of your week, but better than childbirth, and it lasts for five or more years. Great if you're not planning on having children yet or have finished breeding. A few of my girlfriends have complained of heavier and more painful periods, which, let's face it, we need like a hole in the head.

- Hormone coil (IUS). Not dissimilar to the IUD coil, but this version releases progestogen. One plus side of this is that your periods become lighter or may stop altogether. Note: I absolutely must make an appointment at my local health clinic to get this fitted. No periods? I'm sold.

- Withdrawal method. Think no further than the following mantra: 'High chance of a new baby and swapping Prada for Pampers'. Not a clever woman's contraception choice.

- Morning-after pill. Ideal for 'Oh-shite-the-condom-has-split' emergencies, but by no means a failsafe, regular form of contraception. You can buy it (blushing obligatory) at most chemists to take within seventy-two hours of unprotected sex, but be prepared to chuck your guts up – 50 per cent of all women do.

Being a SGBWD *(single girl boys want to date)*

I can picture her now, the ultimate SGBWD. She lounges in the centre of the pub garden, hair all glossy and tousled, tossing it back as she laughs, slim, tanned legs just long enough to be sexy, but not so long that she towers over possible prey, sipping a half-full pint of beer (miraculously SGBWD can drink beer and actually *lose* weight) and chatting in her dulcet tones about everything from football and the merits of the new iPhone apps to her super-cool job in the 'medya' and her up-and-coming girls' holiday to Vietnam. Don't you just hate her (but secretly want to know how she does it and if she ever really orgasms)?

I've attempted some pretty failed and fleeting impersonations of the SGBWD over the years. Short denim miniskirt – check. Westwood pirate boots – check. Spot in an up-and-coming underground dim sum bar – check. Large Mojito – check. Single boys to flirt with – check. The only trouble is that the flicking of the hair and false interest in iPhone apps becomes tiresome. Single-boy-with-stubble may be half-fancying a date, but could I keep up the premier league banter *and* keep down the Mojito-induced hiccups? Thought not. Here are some realistic, non-compromising shortcuts to being a SGBWD without changing who you really are or taking weeks or months of precious time to perfect it. Four words: Better Things To Do.

Be savvy, bright and confident, but not so entirely focused on your own life that there's no room for anyone else. Flourishing career and eclectic mix of hobbies? Great. Sleeps with BlackBerry and will never miss spinning on a Tuesday night for anyone? Might need to work on compromise a teensy bit here and there.

Be interested in bloke stuff and said single boy without faking an interest in things you couldn't really give a monkey's about, i.e.:

- Don't mind chatting about the World Cup, but don't let him bore you to tears or try to explain the offside rule.

- It's cool to show interest in Radiohead's new album, just don't encourage an hour-long rant detailing the intricate chord structure of track six.

- Be happy to listen to him moan about work/flatmates/ his ex to a point. Any more than 50 per cent of the initial flirt time is bad, bad news.

3 Dress for you, not for him. Men like short skirts: fact. But, by and large, we ladies find them unflattering and awkward, so why do it? Be comfortable with your style and show off your good bits. I'd go back to basics and opt for a good pair of jeans and a camisole top, teamed with a pair of Converse, Havaianas or killer heels, depending on your mood.

Note: Beware of dressing like a sex kitten in the hope of capturing your inner SGBWD. The aim is less slutty and more subtle; you want guys to be equally as keen to introduce you to their parents as they are to bed you.

4 Pare down the make-up. I've yet to meet a girl who actually loves slap that's been laid on with a trowel, so don't do it for the boys either. Who needs the hassle of getting up before dawn to reapply the mask? Forget it. Less is more, girls.

5 Get the right balance between interested and unavailable. Never, ever chase him, and if he asks you out, be busy but apologetic for his first offer.

6 Make sure he knows you have a budding portfolio of exes. However, waxing lyrical about your Brad Pitt lookalike ex-fiancé who left you for the Brazilian yoga teacher will have the opposite effect – he may then wonder if he'd be better off with a Brazilian yoga teacher too.

7 Don't get so drunk that you throw up or cry uncontrollably. Enough said.

8 Last but not least, aim to give off the air of a confident, calm Carrie Bradshaw type, not a needy psycho who may text him repeatedly throughout the night asking his whereabouts. Carving knives at dawn is such a bad look.

Mending a bruised heart *(and ego)*

No sooner have you started to relish the single-girl life (art galleries, girlie suppers, non-matching undies, pesto and pasta supper for five days in a row, no one breaking wind in bed), when along comes a cute guy who manages to steal your heart the second you take your eye off the ball. He makes you laugh, shares your fetish for Woody Allen films and actually persuades you to spend the day in bed with him instead of mooching around Top Shop looking for a bargain. For God's sake, you've even contemplated doing DIY with the guy and lovingly store every Post-it note he's left you in the back of your Filofax. It must be serious.

Besotted. Loved-up. Smitten. We've all been there. But before you know it, suddenly it all starts to go horribly wrong. He tells you he hates your friends and demands that you see them less often; you want more from him than he can give ('I'm just not ready for a serious relationship'); you catch him in bed with an ex; you start to resent his stinky gym kit regularly discarded in various corners of your girlie boudoir bedroom. All of a sudden – POW! – you're on a 'break'. Worse still, doors are slammed, contents of overnight drawers are thrown in faces, four-letter words are hurled and, before you know it, it's all well and truly over. Ah, and then comes the anguish of a broken heart. It hurts so much you feel you might actually die – either that or resort to life as a nun.

LOVE GODDESS

Rather than spend the rest of the year ploughing through endless family-size boxes of Kleenex, shortcut just a tad of the misery:

- Allow yourself a few days to wallow in self-pity then surround yourself with people you love. They bolster you up and act like a plaster over your wounded heart.

- Watch a ton of trashy movies with your girlfriends. Ben & Jerry's cookie dough ice-cream is, of course, obligatory. Once you've eaten the lot, stand on your sofa singing/ wailing along to Gloria Gaynor's 'I Will Survive' at full volume. It's a cliché, but it really does help, I promise.

- Nurture yourself by organising lots of treats – a massage, haircut, night out, visit to an old uni friend in Brighton . . . Need I list more?

- Erase evidence of your offending ex. No photos/love Post-its/sexy texts left to taunt you.

- Delete his number from your phone. If you must keep it, replace his name with 'Pain', 'Bastard' or 'Two-timing scumbag' instead. It will stop you calling him at 2 a.m. after a night of therapy with your girlfriends. If the pull to pounce is too strong to bear, write an email, spit venom at the scumbag and then delete it. A good vent for anger without the repercussions of calling his penis small.

- Write a list of all the things you hate about him and all the times he let you down (a bunch of limp carnations three days after your birthday *does* count). Read it whenever your heart lurches at the thought of how much you miss him. If this doesn't work, prepare a dartboard with a photo of his face. Bullseye!

- If all else fails, head to Westfield with your flexible friend and get a quick fix of happiness. It may only last until you get the purchase home, but it will do the trick in the short term (and receipts are good for just this reason).

Differentiating between Mr Wrong *(tosser)* and Mr Right *(swoon)*

Let me start by stating some immediate shortcuts to lurve:

1 Forget the myth built up by slushy rom-coms, *SATC* and Jackie Collins novels.

2 Banish all those teenage fantasies of romance shaped by reading *Jackie* and *J17*.

3 Ignore all couples at your local gastro pub on a Sunday, holding hands and staring lovingly at one another while snuggled by the fire.

Oh yes, it's that good old 'lurve conspiracy theory' again. The one that re-enforces the illusion that everyone but you is in unadulterated couple bliss, euphorically happy, over the moon and skipping through wild flowers at sunset, delighted to have found Mr Right. Wrong, wrong, wrong. The above are actually examples of either a) fictional escapism or b) a couple on a 'good day', post-sex and probably pre-row about whose turn it is to change the light bulb in the downstairs loo.

All in all then, you can tell I don't subscribe to the myth of finding the ultimate Mr Right. Don't get me wrong, I love my man to bits. I let out a huge sigh of contented relief when I see him at the end of a busy working day, and his cheeky, sexy texts still win hands down as the number-one method to light up my morning, but *blah, blah, blah* – you'll be sorely disappointed if you buy into the stereotype of romance as roses, satin sheets and multiple orgasms every day of the week.

Life's too short to be with a bloke who treats you like a door-mat.

Before you brand me a total and utter cynic, let's move on to the good stuff. Even with an adolescence fed mainly on *J17* boy-band fantasies, many of my girlfriends and I have found our soul mates. Mr Right feels like a best friend: easy, comfortable, good for a laugh and a sob in equal measure, who slowly but surely you fall for, like your favourite novel or over-worn cashmere sweater. Indulge me in a little reminiscing about the first flush of easy good times if you will. Believe me, with three kids and busy careers, we do bicker and hurl four-letter words an awful lot more than we used to.

I was an opinionated anthropology student earning some extra pennies as a waitress in a cocktail bar. One balmy Saturday night, my attractive boss and his girlfriend suggested a night eating Chinese food and dancing to salsa music, *and* a blind date with said boss's best friend. Enter Mr S. Some crispy seaweed, Peking duck, three glasses of wine and a sweaty samba dance later, and the rest is history. I was intrigued. He was nice, funny, could groove to salsa and didn't seem (after a first date anyway) to be a self-centred chauvinist, sex addict, stalker or gay.

The interesting thing was, Mr S wasn't at all my usual type. Previously, I'd always gone for the loveable rogues who'd fuck and then chuck (sorry to be crude, but don't we all know a few of these?). Commitment-phobes, love-avoidants, damaged goods, musicians with tattoos and dreadlocks and 50p in loose change to buy me a drink. Basically, anyone who should legally carry a warning label similar to those on Marlboro reds: 'Stay away, this man will seriously damage your health' or better still 'HIGH ALERT – THIS GUY WILL SHIT ON YOU AND LEAVE YOU FEELING MISERABLE'. I can honestly say my track record was pretty poor when selecting Mr Right. After 'hanging out' (dating would have been far too heavy a term) with a bunch of Colin Farrell/James Dean/Bob Marley lookalikes who were hard to please and even harder to get to commit to more than a pint, chain-smoke and catch-up about themselves, it actually felt very refreshing to be intrigued and comfortable with someone whom I can only describe as 'Mr Nice Guy – but with an edge'.

At first we just talked. A lot. He called when he said he'd call – something losers and commitment-phobes never do – and we regularly indulged in eating Chinese food at random places in Chinatown at midnight and going to gigs by bands no one else had ever heard of. I began to realise that, at the same time as banishing the obvious slushy myths about romance, every girl should have an essential hit list to avoid heartbreak and disappointment care of Mr Very, Very Wrong:

- If he talks about himself all the time without drawing breath, he's likely to show little or no interest in you. Crap from the start.

- If he spends vast quantities of time in your company checking out other girls or scanning his phone for texts, calls, emails or Facebook messages, he should not be trusted with your heart. I should know – I've had a few 'my mobile is more important than you' guys in my time.

- If he never initiates contact with you (even after you've left three voicemail messages, an email and a text), it's likely he's just not that into you and never will be. Never chase, just quit while you're ahead.

- If he seems to have an addictive personality (drinks, smokes, scores drugs, discusses stalking ex-girlfriends, all in the space of the first date), best ditch him before you get dragged into his downward spiral (note potential Amy Winehouse and Blake Fielder-Civil scenario).

- If he's married or dating someone other than you, *forget it*! It's likely that once he's bored, he'll replace you with a newer model. Cheating little shit.

- If he hasn't had a girlfriend in the past five years, this should tell you there're some skeletons in his closet (or a whole heap of women's clothes, blonde, glossy wigs and gimp suits).

- If he proposes on the first date (before the starter has even arrived), think desperate and not so desirable (him) and irresistible (you).

Once you've sussed the errors of Mr Wrongs (little laughter, lots of tears), you can start to work out some of the more important qualities you want in your main man. After brainstorming with my girlies, we'll share some of ours:

- A sense of humour – that will keep you from throwing the *A–Z* at him en route to a camping trip in the darkest depths of the New Forest.

- Ambition and drive – far sexier than a Maserati (although this would be an added bonus).

- Sex appeal, but not too much vanity – a guy who uses all your bathroom products and hogs the mirror in the morning is a big no-no.

- A love of good food and travel – and can drink you under the table when ordering Mojitos at the bar.

- An ability to understand you, listen to you and appreciate you without being a wet wimp. Well, sometimes. Or at least pretends to every so often.

- Family values – dogs aren't so important, but he must love his family.

- The potential to be a hands-on dad – nappy-changing promises should be included in marriage vows.

  Note: It's almost impossible to find a man with *all* of these. One or more is definitely better than none at all.

Some of my girlies insisted on adding rich/big dick/art-lover/buff body/great cook to this list – feel free to add and delete to suit your taste. Just remember your core values; you can compromise on the rest. It will save you from wasting so much time and energy on a guy who may turn around in three years and tell you that he actually never wants kids or doesn't want you to work.

Just remember: it will *never, ever* be perfect. It's impossible to sustain fireworks every single night of the week for fifty-odd years. There will always be times when even your Mr Right seems to be everything but. However, finding someone who will ride these storms with you feels pretty OK to me.

Holding out for the nice guy and bagging him

by **Denise Van Outen**, TV presenter, West End star and general Mrs Fabulous

Remember, if the basis of the relationship just isn't right, no amount of to-ing and fro-ing is going to fix things. You can't change him, and you certainly shouldn't try to change yourself either. Quit while you're ahead and stay positive. It's a myth that being single is all stiletto-wearing, cocktail-drinking fun-fun-fun; being on your own can be hard – especially when all your friends seem to be blissfully happy in smug coupledom. Still, getting out is the biggest favour you can do yourself if the relationship you're in is leading you down a dead-end street. I know it's a cliché, but you need to know who you are and what you want before you'll know who Mr Right is for you. Chances are, when you stop looking, someone great will come along.

Living with his toenail-biting and equally delightful male habits

It's a fact. The shift from flirty dating to cohabiting lovers is mammoth. One moment you're lolling on the sofa reading the Sunday papers, the next you're sharing a bathroom with his stubble crusting up the sink, a bedroom with his damp, stinky football socks lying around and a kitchen with his greasy fry-up pan forever unwashed on the stove. One moment it's 'Oh my GOD, I've finally found Mr Right. We're lolling in bed morning, noon and night and meeting the parents.' The next, it's 'Why didn't anyone tell me he'd clip (or worse, bite) his toenails while reading the In Gear section of *The Sunday Times*, insist on never washing up his cereal bowl before leaving for work and always leave his dirty clothes on the floor, ready to be scooped up, washed, ironed and returned to their rightful drawer like he's some sort of adolescent boy?' I know this all sounds rather clichéd, but who hasn't been on the receiving end of that crusted-up cereal bowl at some stage?

OK, so my friend Lucy's other half generally puts on a wash when the bathroom is overflowing with dirty washing (that's if she can leave it that long before she does it herself, muttering obscenities under her breath). He will distinguish between whites and coloureds, but doesn't think twice about putting all of her gorgeous 'hand-wash only' lingerie in with dark Levi 501s. In truth, he also cooks a mean roast beef and has been known to conjure up an Ivy-style shepherd's pie in the same time it would take me to cook cheese on toast. My other good friend Rose's man knows where the hoover lives and will use it when the dust balls are getting close to Mount Everest proportions. He will also never floss in front of the TV. Mr S even knows how to use an iron. Be thankful girls, be very, very thankful.

Having said this, there are some male habits that we were all oblivious to while we dated, but which now drive us potty. I am pretty sure they are almost universal, so we certainly need some tips to prevent us from a) leaving him for our gay best friend, who washes up wearing Cath Kidston gloves and manicures his toenails rather than biting them, or b) joining a women's commune where washing is done on a rota basis.

- To avoid toenail biting, buy him some nail clippers and tell him that if he doesn't use them in the bathroom and chuck away the remains, you'll cancel the monthly payment to Sky Sports. Should do the trick.

- Even if your other half has extraordinarily high emotional intelligence and a close connection with his female side, chances are at some stage the world will stop when the football/tennis/rugby's on or when he has a hangover. When we watch our long-awaited French art film, we enjoy it in comfy PJs, quietly nibbling through a box of Green & Black's. Ditto raging hangover. When the sport's on, the whole world knows about it. Ditto raging hangover. No conversations, no pottering about while the match goes on in the background or he nurses his pounding head on the sofa. Oh no, it's all-consuming ego time. Best solution? Avoid the temptation to scream, shout, slam doors and behave like a prima donna. Instead, compromise by asking him to watch it at the pub/handing him a box of Nurofen and a Virgin Mary with a sympathetic smile. This way, when it's your turn, you have sufficient ammunition to demand a similar response.

- Keep your interest on high and annoyance levels on low by respecting each other's space and encouraging occasional time apart. Now, I don't mean the kind of space that requires moving to separate flats, but space that allows for girls'/boys' nights out, mini-breaks with your friends, the odd weekend morning to browse Portobello footloose and fancy-free, or the time to explore intellectual pursuits you're passionate about. It's very possible that occasional nights of good pasta and even better red wine with the girls is the saviour of many long-haul relationships. As you stumble in the front door, you'll fail to notice all those annoying household habits and no doubt wake him up for a digestif.

- While embracing this space, don't forget to plan the odd 'date night' with your partner too. Supper with the in-laws doesn't count. Nor does a PTA meeting. A cocktail and sushi after work does, however, ditto the movies or theatre, where you can share a large tub of something sweet and instantly forget whose turn it was to take the Sunday papers out to the recycling bin.

All said and done, our other halves are pretty house proud (after a little bit of training, in some cases) and encourage a healthy dose of time apart and date nights. Cereal bowls aside, there'll certainly be no divorcing them on the grounds of obscene male habits. Obviously we'd all love a man to be au fait with the hoover, and who wouldn't want Jamie O cooking up a delicious Sunday lunch with four kids hanging off his legs and a crumble in the oven, but I'm happy with a few extra dust balls, a scattering of let's-pretend-we're-dating nights out, a Mr S home-made lasagne once a month and the fact that, wherever viable, we split childcare equally. My motto is: give the guys a break, minimise the male habits you can't stand, but accept some are here to stay.

> **Life's too short to start World War Three about who washes up.**

Being a sex siren in the boudoir

by **Sam Roddick**, owner of Coco de Mer
and queen of erotica

Overworked, underpaid and left with zero libido? Welcome to the world of most twenty- and thirty-something women. The first thing most of us do is tank up on booze or drugs to compensate for our lack of sex drive. A tipsy fumble is better than nothing, right? Wrong, wrong, wrong! These inhibition-loosening tonics might heighten desire, but they often rob you of satisfaction and, let's face it, who wants nothing but a blurred memory when looking back on a night of so-called passion? It's a fact that good sex works as an anti-depressant and releases endorphins; the hard-and-fast rule is to engage in it emotionally and strike a connection with your lover or partner, otherwise you may as well just masturbate.

It's very hard to ignore the social stereotypes of young women shagging all the time. But you must if you want to be realistic about sex. The projection that we're all frolicking around in lacy undies every night of the week just warps expectations and makes you feel a failure if you're in the land of slumber instead. Massively lower your expectations of quantity and raise them of quality. You'll probably find that by taking the pressure off you'll fancy sex more. The age-old phrase 'the more you do it, the more you'll want it' is so true. By going easy on your expectations, it will work in reverse: you'll probably have more sex, then – bingo! – you'll want more sex.

To recharge those sensual batteries, think about reading a few books on your own or with your partner to open up ideas of new ways to feel sexual. If you think you'll crease up by the first page, or your partner might scoff at it, then come along to a workshop at Coco de Mer and explore new ideas without having to commit to anything. Invest in a good vibrator too; you need one that stimulates your clitoris, hits your G-spot and has contour speed. I'd suggest the Ina or the Mia – the latter you can recharge at your computer!

The great news is that while you may have to work on the motto 'less is more' while work and kids eat into your time quota for intimacy, once you've been through the menopause, your libido will go through the roof. The hormones you lose during menopause are also the ones that raise inhibitions – get rid of these and suddenly you'll be raring to go. The stereotype of horny grannies is a true one! It may seem a million miles away, but it's good to remind yourself that your I'm-too-knackered-for-sex attitude won't last forever.

The L-plate-free hen night

Just the phrase 'hen night' sends shivers down my spine. I'm not sure if I'm more terrified of the forced camaraderie, the possibility of a Chippendale jumping out from behind me, or the chance that we'll have to wear pink, glittery cowboy hats alongside tight T-shirts embossed with 'Sexy Samantha', 'Busty Brenda' and 'Orgasm Olivia'. No, no, no – on so many levels. I have to ask myself why so many otherwise style-savvy women decide to abandon all sanity and embrace their hidden chavs for the sake of celebrating the end of singlehood. It's like the ritual of group humiliation is a rite of passage.

I have been known to fake swine flu prior to hen nights, but my friend Mathilda was having none of it. She was organising a gargantuan hen for a mutual best buddy and needed my help. Stop the press – here was my chance to sway the masses away from glugging pure vodka from a huge iced penis before vomiting down a club loo and opt for something less traumatic all round. I slyly suggested that instead of attacking Majorca like a mass of tanked-up football hooligans (just replace the England footie shirts with glittery banners spelling out 'Hen Piss-up'), we could hire a cottage for the night and do some civilised binge drinking instead.

Don't get me wrong, my girls and I love a re-tox holiday together in the sun and can easily indulge in staggering around until sunrise in Ibiza after throwing some shapes on the dance floor. However, most of us agree it's too much to spend a small fortune on flights and accommodation, use up precious holiday time and leave children and partners for a long week-end in the name of hen-night debauchery, especially seeing as group-shaming is often a required element of the package.

Mathilda agreed – she's not partial to iced penises or flashing deely-boppers either – so one night in a charming Wiltshire cottage it was. We could drink, dance on tables to our favourite 80's club tunes and wake up to Bloody Marys and a mean fry-up. Cheap, cheerful, straightforward to organise and perfectly polished off with streaky bacon and eggy bread. Very good research for creating a 'ditch the L-plates' hit list, methinks.

Girls, girls, girls, please don't make us go abroad. We're broke and we don't want to spend more than twenty-four hours with hen 'best friends', some of whom we may have only met once before. One night is really and truly enough.

2 Don't give yourself extra stress by having tons of different hen dos for all your specific friendship groups. Since when was it the norm to host one hen for work colleagues, one for old school friends and another for family? Who are you, the queen? Choose core friends from all areas of your life and be done with it. A small tea with mums and mothers-in-law is OK,

but having a handful of hen parties is exhausting and
unnecessary.

3   Avoid hen venues like the plague. There really is nothing
worse than sharing your hen do with another five brides-to-
be. You won't feel special, just like a conveyer-belt bride. I
know numbers can make this tricky, but there are plenty of
lovely restaurants where you can book a table for ten or fifteen
girls (try www.toptable.com or www.squaremeal.co.uk). Or
you could do a Mathilda and hire a cottage for the night. Great
websites to help you find one are www.thebigdomain.com
and www.thewowhousecompany.com. For something a
little naffer, try www.henpartyvenues.co.uk. If you're going
for cheap and cheerful, look for a quirky B&B on
www.english-country-cottages.co.uk, but do check that
they have high hen-tolerance levels before you book!

4   Delegate responsibility. Share out the hen-night roles:

- **Cocktail-maker**. Basically anyone who can make a
  mean Martini.

- **Decorator**. Someone with an eye for throwing flower
  petals, blowing up pink helium balloons, scattering
  glitter and nabbing the best cupcakes from M&S.

- **DJ**. Goes to the girl with the best repertoire of essential
  iPod tunes.

- **Prop-box stylist**. A few penis straws are fun. Even a
  tiara with flashing L-plate is a laugh; just avoid the
  blow-up groom with life-sized willy! To save trawling
  the red light district to find your penis/tiaras, buy online
  at www.gohen.com, or raise the game and get saucy
  bits from www.agentprovocateur.com.

- **Chef**. If you're away for the night, then you'll need a girlie or two who're prepared to nip to Sainsbury's en route and then fry up endless plates of chipolata sausages despite having a raging hangover.

- **Accountant**. There's always one girlfriend who loves nothing more than creating budgets and breaking down till receipts on her laptop.

- **Game organiser**. Check out www.henpartygames. com. Tacky, but some alternatives to the age-old Mr & Mrs, which begs the question: is it really necessary for all of your closest girlfriends to know on what day of the week you favour a shag and whether you go on top?

- **Memory-book maker**. Oh the delightful memory book! Take one creative girlfriend with time on her hands, one beautiful scrapbook (look no further than www.paperchase.co.uk) and ask all the fellow hens to send a note, card, poem or photo to stick into the book. Taps into the sentimentalist in all of us and saves endless time creating a multitude of diverse games, DVDs and message cards.

If you're completely sick of binge drinking and pink boas (even when done in a glorious country barn in Sussex), you could consider something totally different. Anyone for fire-eating/bread-baking/surfer-ogling/strip-teasing?

- Giffords Circus (www.circusspace.com) run circus schools (and the Brazilian jugglers make great eye candy for us girls).

- Coco de Mer (www.coco-de-mer.com) have private salons with expert lessons in everything from 'the art of love making' to 'what men really want' (the groom will be forever in your debt).

- The O'Neill surf academy offers a weekend in a wetsuit catching waves with Cornish surfer dudes (www.oneillsurfacademy.co.uk). Beats getting the night bus home from Trafalgar Square at 4 a.m.

- A delicious lunch on a floating restaurant followed by an afternoon at a sleek cookery school care of www.bordeaux-quay.co.uk/cookery-school (based in Bristol) is a seriously civilised way to spend a hen weekend.

- The London School of Striptease (www.londonschoolofstriptease.co.uk) does exactly what it says on the tin.

- Glamping is a cheap and cheerful alternative to a weekend cottage (just don't forget the loo roll or bottle opener). Check out www.canopyandstars.co.uk for your nearest cool canvas.

- Last but by no means least, request your hens don their wellies and a French Connection sundress and head to a festival for the night (www.thefestivalcalendar.co.uk). Pink fluorescent whistles hung around the neck are a must (just leave the deely-boppers at home).

I'm evidence that the 'grown-up, alternative hen' worked. Fresh off the midday train from Swindon, desperately scrabbling around for that box of Nurofen in my handbag and feeling slightly nauseous post-eggy bread, I confess I'm looking rough. Thankfully though, not quite as rough as I would look if I threw a pink Stetson, silver glittery boa and tight-in-all-the-wrong-places 'Gorgeous Grace' T-shirt into the mix. Oh hail small mercies.

Planning a wedding without becoming bridezilla

Eight years after the salsa dancing at sun-down (me badly, him slightly better) and the 'we're on/we're off, I need more space, your toenail clippings are driving me mad, I'm outta here' stage, Mr S decided to pop the question. I considered the following:

- He wasn't a) a tosser, b) a stalker, or c) more interested in my best friend.

- He made me laugh so much I considered the merits of pelvic-floor exercises well before childbirth.

- He didn't object to the fact that my shoe collection meant almost more to me than he did.

- We actually seemed to do the lurve thing pretty well and, at the risk of sounding totally soppy, I do believe (bar his strange collection of belts) we are soul mates.

Unsurprisingly, I responded with a big fat 'yes'.

I'd like to think I planned the wedding without becoming bridezilla, but it's very probable that the bride-to-be I imagined myself to be (cool, calm, collected) didn't actually meet with the almost-Mrs I was (consumed, controlling, cabbage soup diets).

Thankfully, my foray into bridezilla syndrome didn't put Mr S off entirely and seven months after he'd presented me with the sparkler, a hundred close friends and family gathered in my father's rose garden in Oxfordshire. I blubbed throughout our vows, guzzled bubbly and kicked off my shoes to enable me to dance my socks off. I may not have danced much with Mr S, but I do remember being very friendly with the makeshift podium. It wasn't a big glitterati affair and there weren't endless open bars, lavish favours for all my girlfriends, designer flowers and tiaras studded with jewels, but it was simple and charming, held great podium opportunities and didn't incur more than a few weeks on a cabbage soup diet and a handful of stressful conversations with the shoe designer ('They cost *how* much?!').

Many of my girlfriends have verged on the bridezilla: Mathilda and her enquiry into white doves, Rose and her fleeting desire for a thirty-strong orchestra, Mary and her hilarious attempts to get us all to learn a street dance routine – say no more. But, hey, it's almost part of the job description. However, here are a few ideas and shortcuts that might help you keep your inner psychopath under control:

Rings

I always think it's romantic when a man has a ring when he proposes. Do you think Prince William would have attracted quite the same ecstatic public reaction if he'd popped the question with a Pepsi ring-pull and an IOU note? Thought not. Having said that, not all men know the difference between a classic emerald-cut diamond or evocative heirloom sapphire and a gold sovereign engraved with both your initials. If you think the moment is imminent for the big get-down-on-one-knee-rose-clenched-between-teeth moment (just please don't do it in a busy restaurant), the trick is to drop hints about what sort of thing you like – cue Cartier ads torn out from your favourite glossy. Don't go for elaborate designs, but stick to classic elegance. He'll get more for his money by going to an independent jeweller, but if you take him to an f-off expensive big name first, when you go elsewhere, he'll think he's making a *huge* saving. Wherever he goes, make sure there is an exchange policy – there's nothing worse than being left with a ruby heart on a band of gold kisses for the next fifty years. When you're buying your wedding bands, go back to the same jeweller. By then they'll know who you are, what you like and there's more chance of squeezing them on the price.

Planning

1 Excuse me for stating the obvious, but if you've got the money and want to shortcut bridezilla stress altogether, hire a wedding planner. Not my cup of tea, but then I'm not made of money.

2 For those of you who can't pass the buck to a wedding planner, start by keeping a wedding notebook or file and write down all your inspirations and ideas. In a dream world it would be Smythson all the way (www.smythson.com); in the real world it may well be Ryman (www.ryman.co.uk). Stuff said notebook with tear-sheets from magazines and catalogues indicating the type of themes/colours/moods you like. It will really help you be clear and focused about what you want. If you want to go all-out you could even start a 'wedding mood board' on which to cut-and-paste all your inspiring tear-sheets/themes/ideas. A word of advice though: don't move the decks and TV in order to make it the focal point of your living room. A sure fire way to piss your other-half-right-off.

3 Work out a realistic budget and try to stick to it. I remember dreaming about vast country estates and Matthew Williamson

hand-embroidering sequins onto my dress, until I sat down and totted up the figures. Sorry, Matthew, maybe for my golden wedding anniversary . . .

Frocks, Heels and Undies

This takes me swiftly on to dresses. If I were to wed all over again and had a budget fit for a queen, I'd either a) get Matthew W on speed-dial or b) head straight for Temperley London (www.temperleylondon.co.uk) and indulge fully in my boho, sequinned, beaded, fairytale fantasy. Alas, if you're on a tight budget and the frock you love is a Temperley/Vera Wang/custom-made Matthew W, it might just be a no go. Instead, try to find a used one on eBay, look around for a less well-known designer who works in a similar vein but is likely to be a fraction of the price, buy a dress off the peg and customise to suit, or find a dressmaker with a strong portfolio of wedding frocks who can make one for you. The first dress my friend Camilla tried on was a strapless column dress by Neil Cunningham. Love at first sight. However, it was way above budget and no amount of overtime would make up for it. Instead of begging, borrowing or stealing to fund the excess, she negotiated buying the sample for a fraction of the price. A few tweaks and a dry-clean later, hey presto! Sorted and not broke. For vintage lovers who fancy something one-off and affordable, head to the Vintage Wedding Fair. It is the place of Edwardian fairytales and almost every dress is a snip at under a grand. Whatever your bridal style, remember to consider the time of year and type of venue you're planning when picking the perfect frock. That strapless, lightweight silk number might look perfect on the peg, but blue lips and goosebumps isn't the best look for a church wedding on Christmas Eve. Enough said.

2 It goes without saying that a shoe-masterpiece from Louboutin, Manolo, Gina or Choo come high on the wish lists of most brides-to-be. If you want to go all-out in the fashion stakes you could even go for a pair of YSL tributes or a wedge by Cleo B. Surely if a pair of new Converse or Top Shop courts constitute a major feet-treat, this is your time to indulge in a seriously Carrie moment? Just remember, you need to wear them *all day* and well into the evening, when ABBA comes onto the decks. Shortcut hours of foot-angst by selecting a pair you can actually walk in. Hobble, wince, lurch, fall is not the look you want to go for when walking down the aisle. If you can't justify signing a cheque that speeds past the triple figures, then check out ballet pumps (www.prettyballerina.co.uk) or a classic heel/flat by Monsoon (www.monsoon.co.uk). At the latter, you'll get a pretty vintage-style sandal for around £50.

3 If you can't indulge in seductive lace undies on your wedding day, then when can you? They certainly won't be a top priority once you're pregnant/ house-hunting/having a domestic with your 'darling hubby' in a multi-storey car park post-honeymoon. Shortcut hours of trawling naff websites that presume you lose all sense of style just because you're engaged and head straight to the pros. I'm hard pushed to suggest anyone other than Agent P (www.agentprovocateur. com) and Carine Gilson (www.net-a-porter.com). Quite simply, they are so damn gorgeous you may well decide to bed them instead of the groom. If you want something plain and simple that keeps your tummy intact, look at the nude bodysuits by Yummie Tummie at www.my-wardrobe.com. It's true, though, that Top Shop (www.topshop.co.uk) and Marks and Sparks (www.marksandspencer.com) design pretty lovely white wedding-ish undies too.

The Event

1 Before finalising numbers, resist the temptation to go OTT on guests. Are 500 'friends' really necessary? (Unless your father is Philip Green and he's footing the bill . . .) There's no point in inviting more people than you can really cater for and having to give everyone Ribena to drink.

2 Keep it simple. Some of the best weddings I've been to have been small, quirky and really straightforward to organise. Sure, the knees-up at Claridge's was a scream but, boy, it must have cost a fortune and taken an army of wedding planners to carry out. Three alternatives to the big, white, blow-the-budget shebang could be:

a) Shabby chic in the country, à la my good friend Lucie, who hosted a beautiful wedding at her in-laws' garden in Somerset. We all walked from the local church for a late lunch spread out on long trestle tables under a big weeping willow tree. White linen tablecloths, white napkins, roses in jam jars, mix-and-match floral crockery and a 'help yourself' buffet of big salads, roasted veg and a suckling pig.

b) City slicker, à la my sister, who hosted her post-registry-office wedding reception at a gallery space in south London. No stuffy sit-down meal, nightmare table plans and bored-to-tears speeches, but canapés, bubbly and tons of dance-floor tunes to move to instead.

c) Picnic and Pimms, à la my neighbour Lara, who invited a small gang of friends to a traditional English picnic in her garden. Pimm's, scones and jam, cucumber sandwiches, patchwork picnic rugs and bunting. Just as the sun and booze started to go to our heads, the

bride and groom chugged off to a B&B in a vintage
Mini. Leave on a high, and just before the best man
starts to vomit. Nice.

For easy online listings to find your very own patch of
wedding paradise try www.weddingvenues.com,
www.weddingmagazine.co.uk, www.funkyvenues.com
and www.crippsbarn.com.

3 At the risk of sounding like Martha Stewart, you could
consider a colour scheme or theme that can sew together all
the random threads of a wedding day. My boho friend Rose
went for her namesake and chose rose petals. She
embedded pink petals in the paper the invitation was made
from, scattered them on tables and had them in baskets to
throw as confetti, and gave bunches of roses to the
bridesmaid to hold and placed them loose in jam jars at the
centre of each table. If flowers seem too flouncy, you could
think about glitter, monograms, a 40s feel or even a Dolly
Parton theme . . .

4 Be really organised. Send out maps, local hotel details and
wedding list information with your invites. Don't leave it until
close to the date; it will just stress you out and encourage
your inner bridezilla to raise her ugly head. To save time and
dosh, you could consider making a smart invite on your laptop
and emailing it to guests. Another good tip is to design or ask
your printer for thank-you cards at the same time as you're
creating the invites. You could also write addresses on the
thank-you envelopes while you're doing the invites. Having
half the post-wedding job done early will help you stay super
relaxed post-honeymoon. A good place to go for classic
invites is www.wrenpress.co.uk or, for something a little
different, try www.khadi.com – I love their handmade Indian

paper, which could inspire a whole wedding theme, methinks.

5   If you're inviting tons of guests who have children, instead of fretting about highchairs, kids' menus and where to seat your buddy with three-under-three, consider hiring a crèche company. This was the novel idea of my friend Clare, who used Artfull Splodgers (www.artfullsplodgers.com) at her wedding. A team of super-nannies arrived, set up everything from ball pits to playdough in a small area of the venue and entertained the children while their parents got stuck into the Pinot Noir. Shame they couldn't stay for the morning-after hangovers too.

Snaps

When you're picking that prize photographer, make sure you check out their portfolio thoroughly first. If it's relaxed reportage you want, you'll only be pissed off when you're asked to line up with all your new in-laws for an hour of staged shots in front of that sweeping staircase. Ask yourself whether you feel comfortable around the photographer (you'll be pleased you thought about this when they're snapping you in your undies slipping into that Wang-effect number) and ask them a few questions too: will you own the rights to the images, how many prints and reprints are included in the price and do they have a back-up camera if their original decides to pack up mid-vows? It's also wise to point out key family members and important guests, to ensure you're not left with half a dozen shots of the back of your best-mate's head. If all this feels like an expensive extra hassle, just ask any snappy-happy friends to be on Pentax duty. Just don't blame them if all shots are out of focus after 10 p.m.

Pressies

Creating a wedding list in a huge department store can be exhausting. Mathilda and her other half spent three whole hungover weekends trawling round arguing about the merits of a stick-free wok over floral cups and saucers. Instead, think about setting up a list somewhere intimate, small and quirky like Graham and Green (www.grahamandgreen.co.uk) or ask for donations to buy an amazing piece of art or furniture or to go towards your honeymoon bill. By the way, that famous department store wok won and ten years later has been used all of three times.

Cake

Instead of scouring every patisserie within a twenty-mile radius, you could buy cupcakes (www.lolas-kitchen.co.uk or www.crumbsanddoilies.co.uk), macaroons (www.sketch.uk. com or www.paul-uk.com) or just a simple shop-bought wedding cake (www.ocado.com) and decorate it according to your theme. Sprinkle with petals, shower with glitter, pile on the dolly mixture.

Grooming

If you've got the money, it's worth getting a make-up and hair artist who'll come to you and give that all-over bride-to-be glow www.facetime.co.uk or www.candyandbloom.com or, for a real pro, www.jemmakidd.com. Just make sure you have a trial a week or so before. There are very few shortcuts to removing Pat Butcher make-up sixty seconds before you walk down the aisle and maintaining that million-dollar smile.

2 I never wear much more than Elizabeth Arden Eight Hour Cream on a 'dress-up day', so it seemed silly to go overboard with the lips and eyeshadow on my wedding day. For no-fuss, no-frills make-up girls like myself, DIY make-up makes sense. Just make an appointment at Space NK, Bobbi Brown or a MAC counter at a good department store at least two weeks before and ask the make-up artist to talk you through simple, easy make-up for the big day and take notes on how it's done. Three shortcuts I learnt which ensured my make-up lasted until the wee hours and didn't need constant reapplying – what a bore when there is dancing to be done – are to get your eyelashes tinted a few days before (no black-tear-stained cheeks during the vows), wear a primer before applying make-up as this helps seal your base and makes it last, and brush a super-fine, translucent powder over your T-zone and eye-shadow. It helps avoid that too-shiny-skin look in photos.

3 At the risk of sounding boring, I'd apply the same less-is-more principle to DIY hair too. Leave the crystal and diamante tiaras to the WAGs and ask your florist for some English garden flowers like sweet peas or rose buds instead. Pin them into the back of your hair or, if you're a hippie at heart like me, ask your florist to make a small wreath of seasonal flowers. If you're wearing your hair up, wash it one or two days before to alleviate fluffy-hair syndrome and help a style hold for far longer. If you have long hair, you could think about wearing it down in sexy tousles. I'm not going all beauty speak on you; I just know that this equates to damage limitation. When the bubbly flows and the dancing starts, you can then slip into dishevelled without having a major bridezilla panic. We like.

Sure, I look back at my wedding pictures and occasionally think, 'Ouch, big faux pas!' Would I really wear those slightly naff kitten heels today? Would I honestly do those haute cuisine starters (all that quails' egg nonsense now seems rather pretentious) or just serve up couscous in big Moroccan bowls? But,

Life's too short for tacky meringues and tiaras.

by and large, I wouldn't change much. The main thing was my bridezilla alter-ego stayed away for the big day, and I can't say I've seen her since. Well, that's my story anyway, and I'm sticking to it.

Belle of the ball wedding guest glamour

- Clarify the dress code with the bride. 'Smart/casual' is just too vague and will give you endless worries about being over- or underdressed. Go straight to the source and work from there.

- Go for quirky and cool as opposed to the obvious high-street choice – there's nothing worse than having two other guests in the same Monsoon frock. Even if you don't have time to hunt down a vintage find, team a simple floor-length maxi (not white) or well-cut slip dress with a chic cover-up, cape or bolero. Nothing beats a simple purple maxi dress with a silver sequinned cape and fab wedge shoes or flat gold thong sandals.

- Accessories, accessories, accessories. Clutch bags, high heels you can dance in (or wedges if you're going to be on grass for canapés), chandelier earrings, jewelled/corsage headbands and great chunky bracelets – this is your chance to enjoy all those items that stare longingly at you from your wardrobe on a wet Monday morning.

- If you're stuck for ideas, steal inspiration from red-carpet coverage such as the Oscars. This is great for on-trend dress shapes and hair and make-up ideas.

- Remember the legs or chest rule. Don't flash both at a wedding, unless of course it's Jordan's wedding, in which case you can probably get away with exposing all.

Overcoming a marriage wobble without shredding shirts

Anyone who's been married for as many years as I have and hasn't had a 'marriage wobble' of some description must be either dosed up on Valium or seriously deluded. Mr S has vowed to have my suitcases packed and my favourite frocks torn to shreds if I go into too much detail, but, simply put, we've had our moments and I've learnt a few things that might help you shortcut some inevitable marriage aggravation and save your beloved frocks from the shredder.

Talk things through. Maybe I talk too much (highly probable) and some would say you should keep your cards close to your chest (and, in hindsight, giving full details of my major flirt on the dance floor in Ibiza may have been a mistake). However, I do feel that open and frank discussions about everything from toenail clippings to school choices and dance-floor flirts is the healthiest and most positive way to avoid issues becoming entrenched as resentment.

2 Tolerance and forgiveness. Need I say more?

3 Accept imperfections. I know I've harped on about manufactured 'lurve' before, but the same applies here. If you expect Brad Pitt, rip-roaring sex, footballer's wife wealth and the ever-elusive 'happiness' all in one neat package, you'll be seeing divorce lawyers before the end of the honeymoon.

4 Give each other space. It's impossible to be absolutely everything to one another all of the time, and if you're going through a rough patch, your girlfriends, work colleagues, hobbies and own autonomy will be even more important. Drown those sorrows with a gaggle of girlfriends and a strong G&T. Works every time.

5 Don't be too proud to ask for help. Seeing a couples' therapist or attending Relate for counselling is almost as common as shopping for food online these days.

Fertility

by **Jools Oliver**, author and super-mum

It's a fact: if you're trying to conceive and someone with kids comes along imparting morsels of advice, you're likely to think, 'Blah, blah, blah. How the hell does *she* know what it feels like?' I may have four children, but not all of their conceptions were a breeze – far from it. So, believe me, to a degree, I get it. For what it's worth, here are a few of my coping strategies.

I know it's a cliché, but the more you worry about getting pregnant, the higher the chances you won't. I always knew I wanted to be a young mum and I lulled myself into a false sense of security that it would happen instantly. At the time, I didn't realise that it takes the average couple over seven months to conceive. In actual fact, it took me much longer to conceive Poppy, and a similar length of time for Petal.

Anyone who is trying to fall pregnant month in, month out knows it can become a chore of fertility cycles, 'positive' days of the week, sticking your legs in the air after sex and calling your other half at random hours saying, 'Get home now!' While inevitably succumbing to *some* of the above, I found a few other secret weapons to assist in getting pregnant. I'm not sure how much of it was down to them, lots of practice or just fate, but they're worth a try if you're hoping the stork might pay you a visit anytime soon.

- Eat well. 'Easy for her to say,' you'll no doubt be thinking, while imagining Jamie chefing up creamy fish pie and apple crumble every night of the week. Ha! In fact, most of the day-to-day nutrition is up to me. I always try to minimise the amount of processed food, salt and sugar we eat as a family and include as much fresh produce, whole grains and oily fish as possible. When trying to conceive, I up my intake of green leafy veg (an excellent source of folic acid), avocado (a rich source of vitamin E, an essential fertility nutrient), lean red meat (packed full of B vitamins and iron, which prevent anaemia and ovulatory infertility), honey (rich in minerals and amino acids that are widely believed to aid fertility) and oily fish (salmon, mackerel and sardines are the best source of essential fatty acids).

- Make sure you're taking in enough iron in your diet, as being iron-deficient can contribute to fertility problems. You may need to consider taking daily supplements to boost iron levels.

- Consider acupuncture, massage and nutritional therapy, which are all helpful for fertility and a great excuse to indulge in some serious relaxation too. How many of us are going to turn down the chance of an hour-long massage after a stressful week at work?

- Get your dates straight and have sex as much as possible! I know it sounds obvious, but having sex as much as you can around your ovulation dates (usually around fourteen days before your period) will increase your chances. Once you're throwing up from morning sickness each day at 6 a.m. you'll look back at this as the fun part.

- If you've been trying for months, go to your GP for a check up, express your fears and get yourself referred to a good gynaecologist. Mr Geoffrey Trew, my gynaecologist from Queen Charlotte's and Chelsea Hospital, is a hero. If you can afford it, a fertility health check at Zita West is worth it. It costs £185, but this covers tests into everything from vitamin D levels to an analysis of your other half's sperm. Having a greater understanding of your fertility will make you feel less helpless and more empowered. Polycystic ovaries (which I suffer from), endometriosis and irregular periods can all impair fertility, so it's good to know where you stand. Don't be downbeat if tests reveal things aren't entirely straightforward; there are amazing drugs like Clomid available on the NHS that can really boost your chances.

Good luck!

Working a look while heavily pregnant

by **Baukjen De Swaan Arons**, director of Isabella Oliver and mistress of dressing bumps with style

- Celebrate your pregnancy curves rather than hiding them. Even if you've never owned a wrap-top or rouched dress in your life, this is the time to get one. You may feel rotten, but at least a flattering silhouette will make you feel immeasurably more like your old self.

- Forget giving your whole wardrobe a pregnancy overhaul (who has the time and money to do this?). Instead, create a versatile capsule wardrobe of basic staples. Maternity camisoles, tank tops and tees are perfect for layering, while maternity skinny jeans are a failsafe option for day and night. You'll literally be sleeping in those comfy T-shirts by month nine. Just you wait and see.

- When you're pregnant, comfort is key. Go for good-quality, soft and stretchy fabrics so they'll last throughout your pregnancy.

- During my first pregnancy I committed the cardinal sin of borrowing clothes from my other half's wardrobe. Tragically, I also kept buying a cheap item one size up from my normal clothes every six weeks. Two words. Not. Flattering. The clothes may fit around the bump, but will hang on the shoulders and almost every other body part, making you feel horrendous. During my subsequent two pregnancies, I opted for Isabella Oliver dresses day in, day out, which were a million times better for feel-good factor *and* flattering silhouette.

- If you've the energy for parties and weddings, congratulations! Now go forth and invest in a LBD that is versatile. For this very reason, I've designed dresses that can be wrapped and tied differently, making several looks with one purchase: a halter-neck, choker, asymmetric, cap-sleeved dress all in one design. Just vary your accessories (hello, favourite vintage clutch and your mum's diamante brooch). A pregnancy no-brainer.

Surviving pregnancy without strangling your other half *with the elasticised waist of your maternity jeans*

Forget radiant, blooming and serene. Generally, pregnancy means bored, fat and tired. You feel sick, you can't drink and the only excuse for not being able to wear anything but stretchy tops is not because you've been devouring deep-crust pizza, chocolate éclairs and buttery king-size croissants stuffed with almond paste, but because you're expecting. Anyone who tells you otherwise is still in the blissful hormone bubble that is serotonin overdose or trying to sell you something related to pregnancy. I'm sorry, but it needs to be said.

After three pregnancies, three labours and years and years of broken nights, I think I'm OK to advise on being up the duff without strangling your other half with the elasticised waist-band of your maternity jeans. I've done a great impression of Marge in *The Simpsons* and I've slammed doors with vigour, but death-by-Top-Shop-maternity-jeans is yet to go on my CV. A few top tips to achieving this are as follows:

1 Stock up on vitamins. Zita West are the best (www.zitawest.com). At least this way, even if you eat Wotsits for nine months, you know you'll be getting some nutrients along the way.

2 Abandon the idea of being a Yummy Mummy. This means, stop looking at snaps of A-listers looking drop-dead gorgeous at eight months pregnant, kitted out in a vintage Yves Saint Laurent caftan and Prada thong sandals and thinking it's a viable reality. Viable for millionaire mums with fleets of staff – to include a nutritionist, personal trainer, nanny and beautician – and who eat nothing during pregnancy. For the rest of us, it's cast-off maternity jeans, voluminous tops and scuffed-up ballet pumps. In an attempt to upgrade slightly from feeling like a sack of potatoes, you could treat yourself to a wear-it-every-day maternity look (www.topshop.com) and some ballet pumps that will see you though pregnancy and those buggy-walking early days (www.frenchsole.com).

3 If you can't face the thought of splashing out on clothes that will be stuffed into bin bags and shoved to the back of the loft post-baby, invest in some luxurious mum-to-be body cream instead. You'll smell like a garden in full bloom and reduce the risk of stretch marks at the same time. Renew Rose, a nourishing body oil by Aromatherapy Associates (www.spacenk.com), is so delicious, it's almost better than sex. Pricey at £34, so use sparingly, or buy some equally as delectable cocoa butter at your nearest Boots or any cream with added vitamin C or peptides, which stimulate collagen therefore reducing stretch marks. Slather on while eating a Galaxy and you'll forget all your pregnancy woes.

4 Expect to be knackered the whole time, so cut down on social obligations (especially those where all your friends will

be rip-roaring drunk and smoking out the back door) and sleep as much as you can. You'll still feel exhausted, but at least you'll be trying.

Life's too short to kill yourself attempting to snap back to a size ten in ten weeks.

5 Prepare yourself for the birth by keeping an open mind. If you get lucky and manage au naturale, then it's a bonus. Sure, embrace the alternative and read up on weird and wonderful birthing methods, but spending months focusing *entirely* on acupuncture, hypnotherapy, homeopathy, private home births and Amazonian chanting gurus will only lead to the feeling that you've let the world down when you scream for an epidural or you're rushed in for an emergency C-section.

6 Save yourself a weekend of trawling around Mama & Papas with hoards of other bumps just to buy that newborn car-seat and a changing mat. Log on to www.johnlewis.com and use their nursery advice service instead; it will help you work out your essential hit list of must-haves. Yes to a Maclaren lightweight buggy, no to a Disney nursery-wall freeze. A quick click and it'll be delivered to your home without you having to change out of your Sunday PJs. If you've got cash to splash, opt for www.babylist.co.uk instead. It's a VIP baby concierge service that will have your baby kitted out like an A-lister in no time.

It's true what they say: you're likely to love your baby more than you ever dreamt possible, but avoid the fear of failure in the nine-month lead-up by cutting yourself some slack.

Riding the emotional white-knuckle roller-coaster of those first few mummy months

Once you've completed your thirty-six-hour labour (slightly less, if you're lucky), you are likely to feel one of the following towards your bundle of fleshy, creased up, milky newborn:

- A textbook lump-in-the-throat, primeval, I-would-die-for-you rush of love. You may well find yourself weeping at regular intervals at the enormity of this new emotion.

- The not so openly talked about 'I know I should love you but feel nothing but lonely, helpless and isolated when you cry for the fiftieth hour in a row,' which is usually a combination of post-natal depression and utter exhaustion.

- Something in between, which combines euphoria and adoration with panic and desperation, often in the same sixty-second timeframe. Normal, totally normal.

I'd be on to a million-pound-mummy-fix money deal if I could offer you a failsafe route to overcoming this avalanche of emotions entirely. However, there are a few things you could try to prevent yourself glugging a whole bottle of Calpol in the hope of keeping them under control.

Take the pressure off yourself by having little or no expectations of those first few months. Don't plan boot-camp diets, strict feeding and sleeping routines and excessive brunches/lunches/teas to show off your baby. You're likely to find that just having a shower will take you until four o'clock in the afternoon, and even that will be a major achievement.

If you're breastfeeding, try to place getting the hang of it as your foremost priority. Avoid the temptation to feed from only the nipple and shove as much of the areola part of your breast into your newborn's mouth as you can. If all else fails, drive the midwives mad, call your mother at three in the morning and turn on all the lights in the ward to see what the hell you're doing wrong. Cracked nipples, a screaming newborn, mastitis and the desire switch to Aptimel and Avent within days will be inevitable if you don't get the hang of breastfeeding at the beginning.

3 Unless your emotions have an on/off switch, you have a major hearing defect or your newborn was built with the over-developed gut of a five-year-old, you can forget the idea of sleeping for more than a few hours at a time throughout the night. My three children would wake every two to three hours, and almost all my girlfriends have relayed similar tales. Have your baby in the bed with you, or in a Moses basket close enough to reach – at least for the first few weeks. You'll be delirious with sleep deprivation and sore from the labour, so ease and intimacy has to come before Gina Ford for now.

4 When the four walls of your home are driving you to despair (day six), bundle your newborn into that Baby Bjorn (after five failed attempts to work out how the damn thing goes on) and walk to your local corner shop. Buy every trashy magazine on the shelf, a tub of cream cheese and chive Pringles and a king-size Snickers. Consume all together when you return home while watching *Ricki Lake*. Re-sult!

5 Lean on your other half and nearest and dearest for everything from midnight nappy runs (why doesn't anyone tell you newborn poo is yellow with the consistency of really bad diarrhoea?) and cooking (even if it's baked beans on toast and a boiled egg for the first week) to emotional meltdown hot-lines ('I just can't cope'/'Will she ever stop crying?'/'Can

new mums have colic too?'/'Is it OK to breastfeed after a medicinal stiff brandy?') and taxi services. Standard stuff.

6 Make life easy and stock up on a few delicious ready-meals for those first few weeks. (www.ocado.com). There's nothing like a creamy moussaka delivered to your door ready to pop in the pre-heated oven when you're delirious and have piles from pushing out a 9lb baby. No one has time to be layering mince and mozzarella while breastfeeding a newborn and surviving on three hours of sleep (on a good night).

7 By all means send your friends and family occasional pictures and updates – 'Lily in her new snow-suit'/'Alfie has passed his hearing test today' – but don't become a new-mum bore. 'This is Chloe in all fifteen of her summer dresses'/'Leo has sneezed twice today and it's only 9 a.m.' are classic examples of too much information, unnecessary and boring for everyone other than you. There's a fine line between heart-warming anecdotes and being well and truly over it already.

I can't say I managed those first few months with anything more than black rings and neurosis, but I survived them. *Just!* I was never very good at white-knuckle rides anyway. Always opted for the carousel.

CHAPTER TWO

BOARDROOM STAR

Find your perfect working niche

Wouldn't it be nice if we all owned our very own career crystal ball? Every time we had a crap Monday at work, we could peer into it on the 106 bus journey home and see with total clarity whether all the hassle and deadlines were going to be worth it in the end. You'd be able to decide with ease and confidence to either a) stick out the long hours and stifling commute safe in the knowledge that you'll have your own glass-fronted office and top-dog title within a few years, or b) write up your letter of resignation that night, safe in the knowledge that you'll be headhunted by the end of the week and all will be rosy once again. You'd know whether to follow your heart and do what you love, follow your overdraft limit and do something that pays top spondoolies, or find something that does a little bit of both with a peppering of deadly boring admin on top. Sadly, it's rarely that easy.

This may find you on said bus route home wondering desperately if all the training and odd jobs are ever going to find you that dream career, or it may well even find you wondering if the dream career is all it's cracked up to be after all. Whichever side you're coming from, there are a few career questions you should ask yourself to help you get closer to that crystal-ball wisdom and further from shoving the fax machine up your boss's backside.

- I left university with a first-class degree in anthropology. Only about half the people I've ever met know what anthropology is (a study of ants?) and even then they tended to ask, 'And what are you going to do with *that*?' Good question. While I loved the idea of throwing myself into work abroad, my desire to be part of the glossy world of magazines and weekend supplements was stronger. Not very PC, but true. The crux of this was my passion to succeed in fusing glamour, creativity, fun and frivolity with more serious concerns about women's identities and desires. OK, a shoe collection to drool over wasn't an overwhelming 'aspiration', but being a creative lifestyle journalist, challenged and stimulated by my job and resident within a one-hundred-mile radius of Mr S was. Focusing on these goals helped me step into the world of journalism, even if it was as an unpaid intern making tea and filing press releases, instead of diluting my passions somewhere else. Writing a list of your long-term aspirations is a good tip and might help you become clearer about what you want and how you're going to get there.

- If the years are rolling by at an alarming rate while you pass time in 'pay-day vocations' as opposed to a career, consider seeing a career advisor. My friend Willow harps on endlessly about how this saved her bacon. She was miserable in her job as a waitress and had spent longer than she cared to admit waiting for a big bolt of lightning that would indicate what direction her life would take next. Alas, lightning didn't strike, so she sought help from an online career consultant instead. They helped her produce

a self-assessment of core values and linked her
up with a host of relevant companies. Two years later,
she's happy as Larry working as a trainee fashion
buyer and is no longer boring us all to tears with stories
about the damaging effects of day-to-day cappuccino
machine use on cuticle quality. Try Career Consultants
(www.careerconsultants.co.uk), Milk Round
(www.milkround.com) or Career Site Advisor
(www.careersiteadvisor.com).

- If you can afford it, dipping your toe into the water of a new
or intriguing career can be the best way to find out whether
it's a lurve or loathe thing. After my stint interning on a
national newspaper, I had a fleeting foray into fashion PR.
In truth, the money wooed me and I fancied a change to
the humdrum of filing, taking phone messages, writing the
odd headline (as a treat) and watching like a forlorn puppy
as all the other journo girls went off to interview big names.
PR and GS – let's just say we were most certainly not a
match made in heaven. I *wanted* it to work, honestly I did. I
just had an annoying habit of insisting I write copy *for*
journalists. Not very popular. Or good for business. I began
to get the reputation of being an RP (repressed pain) rather
than a PR. Back to taking phone messages and writing up
the odd headline then . . .

A decade on from writing captions as a Christmas bonus, I
must confess I bloody love my job. I feel I've finally nailed that
elusive fusion of the creative and good fun, and I earn enough
to cover my half of the mortgage and the occasional sun-
drenched holiday. Having said that, there are days when I
stumble over my words, or get feature ideas rebuffed, or have
to write a duller-than-death advertorial to meet the steep
nursery fees. It makes me wonder if anyone ever feels they've

found their perfect niche. As inspirational, modern women, we'll always strive for more, better, further. We'll always wonder 'What if?' Even though I was an RP fashion PR, I do have fleeting moments when I wonder whether, if I'd stuck at it, I would be living in glorious splendour with an open-top vintage Porsche and Louboutins for every day of the week. The annual sunny holiday would seem like a drop in the ocean. On second thoughts, best to admit career perfection doesn't exist and resign oneself to being more productive than pain. The fashion PR world can breathe a big sigh of relief.

Following your creative calling

by **Savannah Miller**, creative director of Twenty8Twelve, doula, amazing mum and, quite frankly, one of the most inspiring women you're likely to meet

I'll cut to the chase here: if you've got talent, you're prepared to work your arse off and you really, *really* want something, it's possible that you'll make it happen. Don't be fooled into thinking that even with this formula there's an easy-street option; to follow your creative calling, you must be prepared to work all the hours God sends, and often for less than the price of a travel card and a loaf of bread. It took enormous courage for me to stray from the academic path my parents had expected of me. Although I'd always secretly known my creative medium came from my hands, my schooling was steering me to a destiny of academia, and when I left for Edinburgh University, I was firmly on the trajectory of very conventional job prospects.

After a year studying at Edinburgh, I was miserable (and cold). To be honest, I'd just had enough of trying to be someone I wasn't, and after a lot of soul searching, I decided that instead of risking many lost years working in jobs that stifled my creative talents and filled me with dread, I'd do everything in my power to be accepted on a fashion course, literally anywhere, anyhow. I remember scribbling down the names and numbers of almost every art and fashion tutor across the country in the hope of finding an opening to study women's wear. By some stroke of luck, almost the only person to answer the phone (admittedly after about fifteen consecutive calls) was a teacher at St Martin's and, even without an art GCSE to my name, I was determined to prove I was worth a place on a course. I turned up to see her with a book crammed full of sketches and an attitude crammed full of enthusiasm. That same year, I was accepted by St Martin's.

Changing direction is never going to be easy and, trust me, you'll probably have to embrace tons of random odds-and-sods jobs along the way to fund things while you re-train (I took out plenty of grants and overdrafts and worked every single weekend in a crystal shop on the Kings Road), but, simply put, I reckon life's too short not to have a stab at doing something you love.

I confess, once at St Martin's I set my sights high. As 'not in your wildest dreams' as it sounds, my secret ambition was to work for Alexander McQueen. Again, we all know no one just walks into these paid jobs, so it's worth thinking outside the box and trying to source small openings you can capitalise on. I blagged my way in as a free extra pair of hands ushering at his fashion shows. It may not have been design or personal assistance, but it opened up the door for the possibility of a paid job later on. It worked, and I ended up as his PA before going freelance as a designer for Anya Hindmarch and Shanghai Tang.

All those long hours, hard graft and dedication set me up for the launch of Twenty8Twelve in 2006. Along with my sister

Sienna and the backing of Pepe Jeans, our label was born. I'll be honest, I've not looked back. I relish what I do and although the market's tough and silk prices have risen, I'm still driven by the desire to design clothes I love that are both innovative and cutting edge while still being commercial and wearable. Although I work Tuesday–Thursday in London, the rest of the time I'm with my children in the countryside, balancing work calls with collecting them from school and making them supper. I'd never imply that I have the perfect work–life balance. Ha! You must be kidding – any working mum knows that juggling a career and kids comes with a bundle of ready-made guilt. Having said this, even though I long to kiss my children goodnight on the days when I'm away working in London, I'd miss the glamour, excitement and creativity if I lost it. So, for now, I try to make it work as best I can.

Recently, I decided to add a new string to my bow and have trained to become a holistic doula. I've just supported my first birth partner through labour and although I missed the *X Factor* final (gutted!), it was the most empowering, uplifting experience I've had in years. My aim now? To balance my three passions: my family, my fashion label and my desire to help women achieve a calm and liberating birth. All this and earn enough to pay the mortgage. Tough, but not impossible. I've never been one to shy away from a challenge, so why start now?

Writing a CV that stands out from the 968 others that land on employers' desks

Making your CV the perfect length is a fine art. Anything more than two pages and you'll be submitting a mini-novel (and most bosses couldn't care less about your four-month stint as a dog-sitter for your neighbour's greyhound). Anything under two pages and you'll look like a loser. If you haven't got enough to fill two sides of A4, cheat. Larger spaces and increased font size are genius solutions for just such scenarios.

2 Save the poncy prose for Valentine's cards and use active verbs and bullet points to get your point across in short, sharp hits. I'll never forget going for an interview on a national newspaper and being told, in no uncertain terms, to cut the Jane Austen effect CV. Obviously I didn't get the job. I'm probably lucky I even got the interview.

3 Stretch the truth, but don't lie. All her working life (so far), my good friend Chloe has got away with calling her first job 'party and events organiser' when in actual fact she was Chloe the Clown – on hire for children's parties, a snip at £150 per afternoon. However, stating an outright lie, as opposed to flowering up the truth and adding a bow on top, could get you into trouble.

4 Pepper it with personality. Anyone can download a CV from the net and formulaically recreate it. Add a little information on your personal interests (what novels you read, not what vodka you drink), so you'll stand out from the crowd.

5 Still lacking in inspiration? Pinch ideas from an array of mock-up CVs at CV Masterclass (www.cv-masterclass.com).

Getting that dream job and being the blue-eyed girl once you've got it

by **Charlie Miller**, Grazia's executive fashion and beauty director and proud owner of serious fashion booty and a hard-working ethos in equal measure

I spent ten years working as a fashion and beauty PR, and decided from day one to always treat every editor I met with the same courtesy and respect, irrespective of whether they were on a tabloid paper or a super-glossy mag. It's worth abiding to this principle in any career you choose: snobbery and only prioritising political friendships are such unattractive traits. Seeing as you never know who's going to end up where, it always pays to be genuine and down-to-earth so you don't burn your bridges.

When I was approached by *Grazia*'s original editor in chief, she'd already seen me 'on the job', so to speak, so I didn't have to endure a very conventional job interview. Having said that, in this economic climate, we all know that just being professional and nice to be around doesn't often equate to landing you that dream job – so you need to do your homework too. In my case, 'homework' consisted of giving examples of projects and situations I'd undertaken in the past that could be relevant to the *Grazia* job. I explained how I could add value to the team and expressed my honest desire for the position. You'd be surprised how many people fail to offer up real energy and desire for the title, so it's a good way to stand out.

Getting your dream offer is only half the task of job satisfaction and success. The moment you step foot into a new role, make sure you know your stuff, anticipate situations and are a good team player but also work well on your own. In any job, it helps to have a large dose of humour and a great attitude to hard work (believe me, life on a weekly magazine might be lots of fun, but it's no easy ride!). Be ready to give everything a go and get out of your comfort zone. A challenge should be seen as a positive spin of any job. Beats being bored hands down.

Get a pay rise without falling asleep at your desk every night

Being summoned into your boss's office to be offered a pay rise only happens in American sitcoms. I always pined for a pay rise on my measly wage as a fashion writer at a women's glossy. The reality is that pay rises rarely just 'happen' and when they do it's usually only to those who seem to work until midnight every night and lick arse all round to prove they're worth the extra pennies. Having said this, 50 per cent of all company bosses admire workers who fight for money, so there must be a few shortcuts to getting the extra wonga you deserve.

An essential quick tip is to dig out your original job description and note ways in which you're now working above and beyond your original role. The chances are, your responsibilities will have increased and evolved without your contract doing the same. It's also worth logging onto www.paywizard.co.uk in your lunch break. Here you can compare your wage with those of others in the industry, giving you a good benchmark position for upping your salary. Fix up a meeting with your boss and pepper your case with these facts. Impressive ammunition is surely far less exhausting than relentlessly slogging a ninety-hour working week to prove you're worth that extra few grand?

Earn a promotion without losing your dignity in the process

Getting a promotion was a golden nugget of a question when I was working my way up the ranks of the weekend supplements and eventually to a prestigious fashion magazine. It took almost a year of steaming clothes, filing press releases and making tea as an intern to earn myself even a small nod of recognition when bumping into the editor in the lift. I'd almost gone grey and qualified for a free bus pass by the time that nod turned into a real job offer. Thank God I was closer to the free bus pass; my wage would just about cover travel expenses and some Tesco own-brand instant coffee. No wonder all fashion juniors look anorexic – it's not because they're trying to emulate the catwalk, they're just not paid enough to eat.

Sorry, I digress. In short, I'm trying to convey that in almost any desirable job these days, it takes forever to move up the ranks. My girlfriend Hannah is in her early thirties and even after years slogging away as a TV runner (fetching sundried tomato ciabatta sandwiches and Americanos for her boss), then moving up to researcher, she has only just got her break as a producer. It took my other gal pal Kat almost five years to get a decent promotion in her City job. She says that staying at her desk until past midnight and returning before daylight relentlessly for the last few years is the only reason she's now got the job she needs to pay her top-whack London rent. Never mind that she's got a worrying addiction to caffeine and confesses that her 4 p.m. espresso is occasionally the fifteenth of the day.

I confess that when my job promotion prospects seemed bleak, I got itchy to move on. At said fashion mag, I felt that if I organised one more pair of designer stilettos by colour order, I'd have to walk out and re-train as a yoga teacher, and there were more times than I care to remember when my unread feature ideas ended up crumpled in the bin, leaving me to fantasise about sticking two fingers up at my boss and getting a job with an opposing title. Kat even considered making a dartboard out of her boss's face. There are, however, a few tricks and shortcuts to getting where you want to go faster.

- It's a cliché, but doing the best you possibly can in your current position should get you noticed eventually. Good attendance, punctuality, willingness and affability will all put you in good stead. No one likes a brown-noser, but keep in contact with your direct bosses and subtly let them know what you've been up to. You can't always expect your merits to speak for themselves, so make sure people know you're doing a good job.

- Put yourself out and go that extra mile. If you can go above and beyond what's expected of you, you'll show you can manage everything within your job remit plus new experiences and challenges beyond it. Many years ago, I went to New York to assist a senior fashion editor on a shoot. My job description was, in short, to be a dogsbody for all and sundry on the crew (dressing six-foot, stroppy models in the Meatpacking District in torrential rain and steaming clothes in a location van that stunk of Marlboro reds). What I really wanted from my job was to write, so while my fashion editor analysed Polaroids from the shoot (remember, this was pre-iPad downloads), I escaped the shared hotel room to explore the niche boutiques of Greenwich Village, wrote it up as a trend feature and made sure I emailed it to my editor once I returned home. I confess, my 'Village Chic' article was never published, but I proved I could do it and that got me noticed. Eventually.

• Always own up to what you want and where you want to go. How many of us go to formal appraisals, smile and keep our fingers crossed for a promotion? Never be scared to say, 'Look, I love my job but want more.' It could save you years of hoping your boss reads your signals, when actually you need to vocalise what you want. Just remember to be clever when choosing a time for the big meet; asking your boss when she's frantically busy or rushing out the door is more likely to be rebuffed with a tut than welcomed with a hefty bonus.

• Kat eventually found that living off fifteen espressos a day and slogging away in her current job wasn't going to get her anywhere fast (terrible for the skin too). It was when she began to apply for other positions within the company and went through the interview process competing with candidates outside the company that she got where she wanted to be. The trick is to take it seriously and sell yourself like the new Chloe Green range for Top Shop. In short, be versatile, value for money and like nothing else on the high street.

• You may have to invest a little time in gaining new skills to give yourself that extra edge over others. Hannah enrolled in a short film-making course and even picked up a diploma in camera skills just to impress her boss. Check out Hot Courses (www.hotcourses.com) and School of Everything (www.schoolofeverything.com) for ideas. If you're showing a range of skills and qualifications way beyond your current job description, you can back up your case that your current job is a waste of your talents.

- Whatever anyone tells you, it pays to be popular. I hate office politics with a passion, but I know when I have to play the game (and, believe me, the game can get really nasty when it's played with a bunch of *Devil Wears Prada* divas all vying for that front-row seat at Balenciaga). Focus on being kind and helpful to those you work with, go to all the office shindigs and build relationships that show you're professional yet fun to be around.

- Getting a work mentor is a good way to shortcut a whole load of internal hassle. Anyone who's in a senior job to you and knows the company well will have the insider scope on how to get ahead. My eccentric Italian fashion editor Claudia still goes down in history as the most fabulous mentor I know. Although she worked me like a dog, she took me under her wing and gave great advice on how to get noticed and win over the right people to get the job I wanted. 'Do the job you're in to perfection, never imply a task is beneath you and be ridiculously nice to be around,' she'd tell me. 'Keep submitting those feature ideas and make them so fresh, sharp and inspiring they're impossible to ignore. You'll see,' she'd say with a wry smile. She may have hated my fetish for boho maxi skirts and demanded exhausting late nights in the lead-up to 'show-time', but she gave me great insights after a few post-work glasses of Pinot Noir.

- It may be that even if you can't get that promotion upwards, you could get it sideways or even expand the role you're in. My job title was changed several times, purely because there wasn't a more senior position free and my editor could see that my role had diversified and grown. Sometimes even a small shift in working title, responsibilities and pay can satisfy your itch to move on.

- You may find that even though you've been early for work every day for months, exhausted your array of 'I mean business' wardrobe essentials, performed like Deborah Meaden in every strategy meeting in recent memory and applied yourself with total professionalism to an array of internal jobs, you're still not getting noticed. Alas, after all this hard graft there are few shortcuts left to force your boss into a corner. I wouldn't even recommend seducing them as a last, desperate resort. Your best bet is to keep smiling and playing the game while looking elsewhere for a more suitable job. It may well be that if you get a job offer elsewhere a promotion will miraculously appear from nowhere in a last bid to keep you. If not, say farewell and remember to take your Rolodex and soft-nib pens with you.

Luckily for me, no dignity was lost and eventually, after more months than I dare confess, I got the promotion I so desperately wanted. To this day, clothes rails and safety pins give me the heebie-jeebies. However, I had to saturate myself with them to get that break. No pain, no gain. I can't tell you how many mugs of PG tips I made and how many scrunched up feature ideas I had to discard in order to get that lusted-after title on the magazine masthead, but, at the ripe old age of twenty-five, I got it. I'm pretty sure it was worth the countless late nights and billions of double-sided-sticky-tape multipacks.

Life's too short to stagnate at work.

Not sure about the vast overdraft I incurred while I climbed the ranks, but it could be worse – I could still be steaming clothes in the back of an airless fashion cupboard, only able to afford Tesco coffee granules as my staple diet. Great for the waistline, shocking for just about everything else – including breath.

Forging ahead fast

by **Deborah Meaden**, TV presenter, career guru and the one person you'd love to have on speed-dial prior to a pow-wow work meeting

If you are seeking promotion and you believe you are ready, then you need to bring this to the attention of everyone, but in a subtle way. Being obviously pushy rarely wins allies! Dress, speak, act and take responsibility as if you are already in the next job and it should become obvious to everyone that that is where you should be.

Unsticking yourself from that career rut with nerd-free networking

Midst recession, my good friend Zoe calls me. 'I'm in a career rut,' she says, 'and I need unsticking.' Now, I love Zoe dearly, but even she confesses she's an adrenalin junkie. She craves new challenges and gets a huge buzz from pressure and new hostile environments (I know, go figure). Routine, continuity and the same humdrum job for anything more than a few months and she starts to feels itchy for the next hit. I hate to be the one to remind her that in the current climate no one's going anywhere at a great speed and she'd be a madwoman to hop off into the void of the unknown, especially when new job opportunities are so thin on the ground. My words of wisdom are met with a sigh. She hates staying put.

A good way to diffuse the career-rut jitters is to broaden your working community, and online is the perfect way to do this. I'm the first to admit I'd rather undergo slow torture than succumb to the world of Facebook, but here are a few alternatives to making your work and home life feel more supported and empowered:

- www.140women.com. A brilliant site dedicated to empowering women. Careers are top of the agenda, alongside human rights, sex, parenting and health.

- www.linkedin.com. Many working women I know say joining this has given them a huge amount of working support and guidance with professional issues.

- www.seednetworkingforwomen.com. Set up by Lynn Franks to promote an online working community of women. You'll find this helps build a real local network of like-minded working females.

Zoe is still in her job but is far too busy networking on LinkedIn to comment further.

Be a finance whizzette with your wages

by **Sasha Speed**, senior private banker at
Coutts and seriously fabulous wealth manager

You may not consider yourself a financial whizzette *yet*, but in the modern, fast-moving world there really is no excuse not to be savvy with your finances and work income. Here are my basic fundamentals to get on top:

- Work out how much money you have coming in (x) versus how much money going out (y). For pure peace of mind, y should not exceed x – well, at least not on any consistent basis. A good discipline is to sit down and draw up a simple spreadsheet with a summary of total income versus total outgoings. In this way, you will be able to see what surplus there is each month, once you have covered your basic fixed costs – accommodation, utilities, travel and food. If you're a creative and this sounds like torture, then use colours! With any luck, there will be a surplus – if there isn't, it is time to a) reign in your costs or b) ask for that pay rise or find some other way to increase revenue. As much as those new wedges or high-waisted Acne jeans may be calling out from the pages of your favourite glossy, try not to let this tempt you into getting yet another credit card, which is momentarily rewarding but potentially extremely dangerous for long-term financial health.

- If you do need a loan or an overdraft facility to see you through a cash-flow squeeze, then you could start with your existing bank to see what rate they would be prepared to offer you. Take note: don't take their first offer; instead, mentally take this quote and use it to compare and contrast rates and prices across the industry. The easiest way to do this is to nab a financial paper when you're buying your weekend read and look up the comparative rate charts at the back of the finance sections. The price of a debt can be analysed using its APR (Annual Percentage Rate), which is the total cost of the loan, including interest, fees and any other charges over its lifetime, expressed as an annual percentage. The idea is that it gives the buyer a level playing field to assess the total cost and, broadly speaking, the lower the APR, the better.

- Used cautiously, credit cards can be extremely useful and, with reward points, travel insurance and other fringe benefits, some of the total packages offer great value. However, do try your damndest to pay your debt off in full each month in order to avoid hefty interest charges and NEVER use your card to take out cash from holes in the wall. Trust me, you'll be debited immediately with a fee for the privilege and interest will be charged from the moment those crispy notes are in your hand.

- One other small point of good financial discipline is to take two minutes when statements arrive in the post, or when you are looking online, to check your bank and credit card statements. Not only do banks make mistakes with your money, but there's a whole underworld out there trying out cunning schemes to take your money away from you. If you're not even checking what's going through your account on a weekly or at least monthly basis, their chance of success is so much higher. While you're glancing at your statements, it's a good idea to monitor whether bank fees and charges are appropriate or not and to keep an eye on direct debits and standing order payments that are no longer relevant.

- If you're a tax payer, look into the advantages of an ISA (Individual Savings Account). It's attractive because the interest you earn isn't taxed. The current maximum amount of cash you may save each tax year into an ISA is £5,200 and this can be topped up with a further £5,200 in shares, or you could put the whole £10,200 into shares potentially.

- We all know that there is big anxiety over the nation's future pension requirements. As independent women, unless we start taking responsibility for our own pension needs, we'll be facing the question: just how are we going to fund our own retirements? Many of you will probably be on company pensions, but don't just switch off and rest in a false sense of security – find out the terms of this pension and what it actually means to you. You may wish to top up your company pension and look at the alternatives that are open to you. Your employer, depending on its size, should have an individual or HR function that can talk to you about this. The bottom line is: don't ignore pensions and fob yourself off until you hit mid-life, do something about this now! You'll be grateful in the long run, I promise.

Embracing success without becoming a total BlackBerry bore

The phrase 'work–life balance' has been discussed to death in recent years. However, anyone who still finds themselves answering emails at midnight is likely to seek a few extra top tips for swapping the BlackBerry for a glass of Merlot and the latest Adele Parks novel. I, more than most, could do with a reminder of how to be disciplined about work time, me time and family time. At present, I seem to be constantly sending emails while in the sandpit with my toddler/supermarket with my recycled bags/school playground with my umbrella and the kids' library books, and have even been known to lean over the rim of the bath to punch an all-important message into my iPhone.

Life's too short to sleep with your iPhone instead of your other half.

At 11 p.m. On a Sunday night. Not great for exuding that weekend chilling vibe and not at all ideal for iPhone maintenance, I'm sure you'll agree.

- Try, if at all possible, to leave the office at least twice a week with enough time to do something you enjoy. Don't stress if this isn't anything as high-octane as you'd imagined. I know that in an ideal *SATC* world it's all about Monday night book clubs, Wednesday night yoga groups and Friday night glam cocktails, but in the real world doing 'something you enjoy' is more likely to be vegging out with that Adele Parks and some pesto pasta, wearing nothing more spectacular than your Gap sweatpants and granddad slippers. Believe me, this is a totally normal mode of relaxation for most frazzled working women and doesn't warrant guilt or explanation. End of.

- The words 'lunch' and 'break' were almost never said together in the same sentence when I worked on the glossies, but it's worth trying to put them together in the same universe sphere a few times a week. A Prêt sandwich at your keyboard doesn't count. Sitting in the local park (weather permitting) with said sandwich and flicking through the first half of *Harper's Bazaar* does.

- Turn your phone off. Occasionally. I'm the worst person in the world to advise on this, but I do try. I recently turned my iPhone off for a whole afternoon *during the week*. I came out in hives and had to keep the damn thing clenched in my fist the whole afternoon, but I rode through the fear of loss and failure, coming through the other side unscathed. Almost. Until 6 p.m. at least. Oh iPhone, come home, all is forgiven.

- If all of the above seem impossible, ask yourself the following question: On your death bed, would you wish you'd worked longer hours, or spent some more time lavishing attention on other aspects of your life? If the answer is the latter, then try and do something about it. If it's the former, you're obviously a femme fatale and destined to rule the world. Go forth and conquer – just don't leave your BlackBerry charger behind.

Working freelance and actually getting a teensy bit of work done each day

I really don't think it was the office bitch that did it. I don't think it was the measly pay that did it either. I don't even think it was the annual conferences that took a month to detox from that did it. What finally made me decide to do 'it' and jump into the unknown void of freelance work was twofold. Number one, I'd had two kids in the space of eighteen months and rusk-smeared blouses seemed more common than pointed stilettos in my day-to-day working life. Number two, after working on staff for almost seven years, I just didn't see anywhere else to grow. My fashion features editor was so shit-hot she'd never be needled out by a rusk-smeared writer and taking on more responsibility seemed impossible when I had to be home for bath time at 7 p.m. every night.

To be honest, I had absolutely no idea how much I'd miss all the office politics and fashion cupboard mayhem when I marched, all guns blazing, into my editor's office, convincing her (and myself) that I was off to bigger and better things. I didn't have a clue how much I'd pine for the rhythm of a working day in the office (Starbucks at 11 for a latte and skinny blueberry muffin is so much more appealing than a cup of PG tips and a mouldy old Custard Cream in front of your laptop). And no one ever tells you how much you'll miss getting dressed for work. Yes, simply put, you only ever wear a tracksuit and Uggs when you work from home. Fact. I read an article in one of the Sunday papers recently which gave examples of women who worked from home and got dressed up each and every day for themselves. They must have unearthed the only three women in the UK who actually put on a vintage sundress and deco sandals to sit at their kitchen table and send emails. Surely there can't be more than three? I am certainly not one of them. Baggy jeans, a white Gap T-shirt and unwashed hair. On a good day. Oh how I miss well-cut dresses and stiletto courts.

I suppose, ripped denims aside, I can now viably live life without double-sided tape. This is a bonus. The trick is not to lose your sense of self or, worse, fail to do any work whatsoever if you opt for the freelance/work from home route.

- After the honeymoon period of the first few freelance weeks, pay-day arrived. Or should I say 'pay-day for the rest of the world' arrived. Alas, suddenly no paycheque, no guaranteed income, no steady stream of bills paid off for moi. Oh shit. Rather a wake-up call, really. The only way to nip the temptation to switch on *Loose Women* and eat

Digestives in the bud was to attempt to be very organised about my working week and aim to put in similar office hours at home. Time to do some bloody work.

- Keeping up contact with industry folk is a massive part of making a freelance career work for you. If commissions dry up or the flow of money isn't fast enough, I panic, so being seriously proactive about keeping my finger on the pulse is part of the job description. My worst fears mainly came true when I went freelance. PRs and commissioners can forget you instantly and without the backing of a big working title, you become less visible. You need to keep contacts up and work on building strong relationships with specific employers. My friend Rose is a freelance graphic designer and she makes one day a week her 'meet-and-greet' day. She uses it to pack in meetings with clients and possible employers. A great way to get out from under the Rich Tea selection and the ideal opportunity to switch from Uggs to stiletto boots. She swears it's 'meet-and-greet' in pointed Russell & Bromley stilettos or deal with the bailiffs at the door.

- Rose swears that the key to getting any productive work done is to carve out a space that feels like an office. She's utilised her thirty-foot garden and roped in her brother to build a shed-come-office, which she swears is her salvation. My friend Kim sourced a retro caravan in order to run her quilt design service. If no one remotely related to you is a dab hand at DIY, lust after offices at home on www.cotswoldshepherdshuts.co.uk and www.shedworking.co.uk. No such garden luxury here, and a small desk in the corner of my living room with an armoire stuffed full of floral filing systems is as close to a 'study' as I'm going to get. I swear, with my next paycheque, I'll look to Flujo Home (www.flujohome.com) to design and organise a cubby-hole office space for me.

- I hate support groups – they make me feel like I've joined AA. However, linking up with freelancers in the same field can be a good source of work contacts. Try www.freelancer.co.uk or www.freelanceadvisor.co.uk.

Over the years, I seem to have overcome my rather alarming cravings for daytime TV and, thanks to a half-decent laptop, 'meet-and-greet' days and a trusty black book of contacts, have kept the flow of income intact. I am absolutely not a freelance role model – I attend far too few press events, have a massive fear of failure when pitching new ideas to editors and have put on a half a stone since swapping a mid-morning skinny latte for Digestives – but I do get my work done eventually. I'll confess too that even though I relish the freedom and flexibility of working at home, I'm also a success-seeker and workaholic.

Life's too short to banish your dream of one day starting the next Net-a-porter.

Even if I were a millionaire, a life without work wouldn't be a life I'd want to lead. Tennis lessons, cake-baking and mums' coffee mornings after the school run sound nice. For about a day. Two at max. Thanks anyway.

Starting your own business without losing your sanity and your dosh in the process

by **Serena Rees**, co-founder of Agent Provocateur and Cocomaya and general creative visionary genius.

We've all read tons of glamorous stories about women starting up their own businesses and making an overnight fortune. Magazines are stuffed full of case studies pedalling the idea that you dream up a concept one morning and then – POW! – after a few easy steps, you'll be a millionaire. Well, let me tell you something, it's a lot harder than that! Firstly, you need to be realistic about what you want to do and why you're doing it – working on a whim just won't cut it. When Joe and I started Agent Provocateur, I not only had a very clear vision of what the concept was, I also had to be realistic that my role wouldn't just be that of a creative visionary. I'd have to turn my hand to everything from number-crunching, budgets, packaging, marketing and PR. If you're a one-trick pony and find diversifying your roles a challenge, be very wary of starting your own business – the ability to multitask is key.

Of course, you need to do market research by investigating the competition both online and on street level, but even if you do all the research in the world, you can still fail miserably at launching an innovative concept. Relying on a strong sense of intuition is just as crucial. I'll tell you straight, our original business plan for AP was a pile of crap, but I had a very strong intuition of how and why it should work. When you combine this with total and utter commitment, damn hard graft, optimism and a good sense of humour, you've a better chance of success and keeping your sanity intact. Of course, almost every new entrepreneur needs funding, just don't spend more than you've got. If you're heading to the bank for a loan, shop around; many are unsupportive, so if you find one that backs you, fabulous.

Before presenting that cupcake and macaroon tea-shop to investors, banish all illusions that starting your own business will a) make you rich fast and b) give you flexible working hours. Sure, if your business is your passion, it's likely to feel like a labour of love as opposed to relentless, mind-numbing hard graft but you *will* work 24/7 and you're unlikely to make money fast. Chances are, any bucks you earn will go straight back into the company anyway. I didn't draw a salary for the first ten years at AP – I may have owned 50 per cent of the company but, bar my living expenses, everything else was tied up in the brand. This isn't such a bad thing because when you're living and breathing your work, you don't have much time for long holidays, lavish suppers out with friends and retail therapy! As for flexible working hours – pah! At seven days old, I strapped my daughter Cora to me and went back to my desk – taking a six-month maternity leave would have been business suicide. I'd have morphed into a raving loony from boredom anyway. My business and family life merge on so many levels – those boundaries need to be fluid if you're going to plunge your heart and soul into a concept.

After grafting hard for twenty-seven years, I admit I've finally learnt to switch off on holiday. Having said this, I can still be found jotting down ideas in a notebook or gleaning inspiration from my surroundings. While I value quiet holiday times and lazy Sunday lunches at the weekend, my brain never really stops. Working hard runs through my veins.

Have a career and children without being demoted to part-time office tea-maker

It's a fact – the hardest challenge I've ever had to face is navigating the fine balance between my career ambitions and my desire to have children and be a hands-on mum. I must confess, I hadn't planned to face this challenge quite as early as I did. When I married Mr S, I was thoroughly enjoying my footloose-and-fancy-free career on a fashion magazine. Although the instant coffee wages were an issue, I'd managed to graft my way to a good position and I was thoroughly enjoying the fusion of girlie office banter and presenting new trends, even if it was black and camel *again*.

I vividly remember lying on a day-bed on our honeymoon, having a conversation with Mr S that went something like this:

Mr S: 'When do you think we should have kids?'
Me: 'Oh God, in ten years' time?'
Mr S: 'You're mad, I'll be forty. I'm not waiting that long!'
Me (sitting bolt upright on lounger, sunnies falling off my head): 'I'm sorry, but there is *no way* I'm having kids just yet and sabotaging my great career and all the fun I'm having at work. *You* are mad . . .' And on and on and on . . .

Eight months later. Easter. I'm looking decidedly fatter than on my wedding day, my breasts are huge and I'm vomiting down the loo in Costa between cries of 'Why does that coffee smell so bad?!' At least eight pregnancy tests, twenty-four hours of disbelief, insomnia and a dating scan later, and I'm told I'm almost twelve weeks pregnant. 'OH MY GOD! WHAT THE F***?!?!'

So you see, 'planned', 'organised' and 'scheduled' don't instantly spring to mind when I think back on my first pregnancy some ten years ago.

- Step one: Feel immense remorse at the many boozy weekend suppers that had been undertaken when ignorant about pregnancy.

- Step two: Marvel at my new Jordan-esque, page-three boobs. How could I have failed to notice them?

- Step three: Get on with it.

I absolutely convinced myself that I'd have this baby and return to all my fashion-girl fabulousness unscathed and without a stretch mark in sight. What I hadn't bargained for, as I fumbled along ignoring all baby manuals and maternity trousers, was that despite the cracked nipples and flabby tummy, I'd fall head-over-heels for my new baby. Though AquaBaby would never be my thing, leaving her five days a week, with almost eight weeks away every year when the fashion shows came around, wouldn't be either.

For the first year, I juggled it all – breastfeeding with fashion shows, shitty nappies with writing copy, teething with press launches – but I was torn. All the time. Never able to give 100 per cent to either camp, I felt I was letting both sides down. And I was knackered and covered in baby poo and vomit. So what was my answer? Fall for the exhaustion-inducing insanity, of course, and decide on a whim to have another baby! Why not? I must have been totally off my rocker. Eighteen months after my daughter was born, along came my son, and then we were four. Five, if you consider my career too. Eight years and a third blonde minx added to the mix later, and I think I'm still in shock.

Juggling it all was inexplicably hard, but it was also sometimes pretty wonderful. I was exhausted and run-down, but I was also, on a really good day, focused and inspired. I felt mad and brilliant all at the same time. It would be totally misleading to say this was all due to my wonderful ability to multitask. Ha ha ha! The truth is that more than half my wages went to employing great childcare. I begged favours from friends, neighbours and godparents and twisted the arm of my boss (almost right off, and certainly to the detriment of her new Lara Bohinc bangle) to convince her I could do the same job in four days a week.

Eventually, after living at a high level of panic and stress most of the time and down to my last 'pretty please' favour from good friends, I went freelance. I also tried my damndest to ensure my family time remained just that – family time (although, as any working mum knows, this can be a total joke and there are many occasions when an iPhone or BlackBerry gets almost as much attention as the kids).

I suppose the question I have to ask myself is, would I wait that extra ten years to have kids if I were to do it all again? I'm pretty sure the answer would be no. It is a sad fact of life that if you want to get to the top, you should think carefully, *very carefully*, about taking a career break to have children. (Although, I must add that a man must have invented the term 'break' when discussing caring for a newborn. More like 'running a marathon backwards on one hour's sleep'.) I know too many women who've had to rush back to their desks weeks after a C-section for fear of motherhood diminishing their career prospects to believe that having children doesn't affect your status at work at all.

However, while I may not have that New York, glossy-magazine super-job I could have earned if I'd devoted 24/7 of blood, sweat and tears in my twenties, I don't allow myself regrets. While most of my friends in their early-to-mid thirties are just getting round to having their first babies, my third and youngest is gearing up to go to school. I've done the sleepless nights, double-buggy mayhem and 'will we ever go on holiday or have sex again?' conundrum, and I can now strive to find a work–life balance that will suit me as I rise up my thirties.

Sure, this scenario isn't possible for many women. Trust me, I know how lucky I was to find Mr S when I was a mere whippersnapper (and, believe me, I see enough women in their mid-to-late twenties who'd love to have kids but are dating immature idiots who won't commit to know I'm in a minority). Trust me, too, when I tell you that having a baby 'young' can have many downsides. Paying off a vast student loan while saving for a buggy and babygros, for one. Dealing with a screaming newborn while your peers are island-hopping in Greece, for two. Worrying about surviving in a shrinking job market, for three. However, right now, I just can't imagine being one of my fast-approaching-forty-plus friends who are finding all the colic and chaos debilitating. Different stages, different challenges. What I will say is that while I couldn't afford newborn designer booty, I can now afford to feel occasionally smug that I've waved goodbye to nursery-rhyme time and pureed butternut squash. Oh the boredom and desperation! I can now return to the working world not too far from where I left it, even though half my wardrobe is rusk-stained and too small to fit past my ankles.

In an ideal world, we'd plan careers and babies to sync up perfectly. Stage 1: you climb the career ladder to your dream spot. Stage 2: you meet Mr Right at the click of a finger and over breakfast in bed plan the perfect window in which to take a year out to have a baby. Stage 3: you get pregnant immediately. Stage 4: you return a year later to exactly the same job, three days a week, on the same money as before.

D-R-E-A-M ON! It isn't ever going to happen like this. Not in a million years. The only thing you *can* do is accept that if you do want children (and I'm not suggesting that this is a given for all women), when the time comes, the career balance will never feel ideal. Whether you're in decision mode about whether to have kids and when exactly to have them, or trying to juggle the ones you've got with a demanding job, resign yourself to huge amounts of guilt and to the fact that you'll have to compromise in both camps along the way. Just do one thing for me, if you will:

- Stop waiting for the perfect window.

- Stop listening to other people's narrow opinions on careers, babies and work–life balance. Everyone is different.

- Stop beating yourself up in search of the dream 'balance'.

- Stop with the GUILT.

- Start seeing that your best is enough.

- And if the stork does pay you a visit, start turning off that BlackBerry at weekends and laughing with your children more. And realise that you can't 'have it all' but that having a grubby kitchen and imminent deadlines is normal for working mums and is not a life-threatening condition.

Good. Can we all eat macaroni cheese while watching CBeebies now?

CHAPTER THREE

DOMESTIC DIVA

Understanding the crazy-hazy business of buying your own place

I look back at my flat-sharing days with a mixture of delight and horror. Let's deal with the delight first. Three bottle-blonde girlies, the top floor of a shabby house on the corner of a busy road, a collection of shoes to give Office a run for their money and a stash of CDs ranging from hardcore drum 'n' bass to Joni Mitchell classics. The laughs, the high jinks, the swapping of clothes, the endless glasses of Pinot Grigio consumed while sitting on the window ledges, the bike rides, the boyfriend stories, the hungover wet Sundays watching children's TV and eating buttery toast thick with Marmite, followed by cookie dough mixture straight from the bowl. We had some serious fun.

Now for the horror. The landlord chasing us for rent, the bath with a built-in dirt rim that not even Mr Muscle Super Concentrate would shift, the constantly empty fridge ('But it was your turn to buy milk!'), the unsuitable boyfriends hanging out for the weekend on *my* spot on the sofa, the never-seen-again Top Shop sequinned cape, the new issue of

Elle with all the best pages torn out, the smelly dog we looked after for a fortnight, and so on.

Admittedly, I don't miss my Top Shop sequinned cape (much) and, really and truly, the boyfriends weren't particularly unsuitable, so undoubtedly the delights far outweighed the horrors. But in every girl's life there comes a time when you feel emotionally and financially ready to face money-borrowing hell and attempt to be solely responsible for the semi-skimmed-milk-buying. Failing that, you'll chance swapping girlie leg-hair stubble around the bath rim with boys' stubble around the sink. My time to embrace the latter came after years of renting with a handful of girlfriends and a sprinkling of unsuitable flatmates (male model with a fetish for my Speedo swimming costumes/MA anthropology graduate who only ate bird seeds). At a scrimp and a save, I was close to being able to stump up my share for a first deposit; just as long as it wasn't anywhere remotely trendy or desirable, I may just be able to blag it. After a particularly bad day, when I'd had to wade through Speedo cossies to get to the bathroom, I decided that it was time to beg, borrow and steal (literally), abandon Marlboro Lights and white wine on the window ledge and step cautiously onto the property ladder with Mr S and his array of dodgy Caribbean wooden artefacts (these would have to go).

After bed-hopping between my girlie flat and Mr S's place for years, losing toothbrushes like odd socks and never having the right clothes in the right place for that Monday morning meeting with my editor, I found myself rejoicing at the thought of some stability. Sure, the prospect of a huge deposit scared me shitless, but I dulled this real fear by embracing 'property porn' with relish.

Hours were spent drooling over Victorian maisonettes with wooden floorboards and original period fireplaces, salivating over top-floor studio flats with views over the heath and built-in Smeg ovens, and literally breaking out in a sweat over tiny cottages still in the N postcode area, with roses climbing over the front door and jasmine dripping over the window boxes. Until – suddenly – warning bells chime, snap you out of your fantasy world and force you to address the issue of finance. Oh yes, the crucial point in house-hunting: finding a property you can realistically afford and beginning to navigate your way through the crazy, hazy world that is buying your own place. Please note: the stress of all this will age you drastically (bad), but possibly enable you to lose half a stone in weight without even trying (good). A few shortcuts to help you cut through the maze of jargon and assist you on your way:

1. Talk to the mortgage advisor at your bank to find out what you can borrow and what you can realistically afford. There is absolutely no point in doing anything (even property porn) before you've worked out your budget. Instead of making several appointments with the bank, use this one appointment to discuss exactly what type of mortgage you require and how you can get your finances in order so you can prepare for your mortgage offer. Prepare a breakdown of your salary, plan a suitably professional yet style-savvy look and take a notebook. Two reasons for these: a) part of this chit-chat will be deathly boring – by taking notes you'll eliminate the desire to fall asleep; b) if you can look charming yet brainy and give a pow-wow breakdown of your earnings, you may be able to borrow up to five times your salary. For easy online financial advice check out www.home.co.uk/guides/buying and www.buyassociation.co.uk.

2. Now for the property porn bit. Yes, yes, yes! First things first, decide on your area. Check out said area for shops, transport links, parks and open space and good places to eat and

drink. If a good local school is high on your priority, check you're in the catchment area of at least one. Don't trust agents' spin on this – call the local council or the school in question for a more impartial answer. It's also a good move to ask friends or family who live nearby what the low-down is. You may have to split an area or postcode into grades, depending on your budget and what's available: first choice, second choice, third choice and possibly even fourth, i.e. 'Oh stuff it. If I absolutely have to live here just to get on the property ladder, I bloody well will.'

3 It's a good idea to drive around your preferred area to suss out the location properly. The property details of one flat or house won't tell you if the others in the street are derelict/ there's a noisy main road at the end of the street/your potential neighbour has built a huge plinth with life-size stone lions on either side. If you want to save time log on to http://maps.google.com and get an instant zoom-view of the hood.

4 Register with two or three reputable local estate agents and charm the pants off them on the first visit. This is better than blanket-registering with every estate agent in town (exhausting) and works on building up a relationship where you'll get the nod before a property even goes on the open market. If you're clear about your budget, where you want to live (you can even be specific about the roads) and what style of property you want, you can then be direct when they try to fob you off with a new-build that sits directly on top of the overland rail-link. Remember, estate agents are salesmen extraordinaire who will give even a squat with dead bodies under the floorboards a positive spin, so make your own mind up before falling for the masters of spin.

5   Once you've registered, save time by viewing properties via the internet – www.findaproperty.com and www.primelocation.com are perfect to browse on your iPhone while on the bus to work in the morning.

6   Although opting for a fully renovated property with nothing left to do except change a light bulb will shortcut time, it will no doubt cost you more and mean you'll have to compromise on your own individual style and flair. It's a fact: the best shortcut to a good deal is to buy a wreck. Obviously, major structural damage is a no-go unless you can afford to take on the full-time job of property developer, but try to see beyond the floral lampshades, yellow carpet and 1920s kitchen units and visualise what you could do with the space as an empty shell. If it's in an area you're happy with and you instantly feel 'this is my home', trust that gut instinct. It's never failed me.

7   Never buy the best property in the road – the best investment for the long run is to buy the worst and upgrade it. Ideally, find somewhere you can expand and improve. Look for loft spaces that can be converted later, kitchens that can be extended out and walls that can be knocked down to create open-plan areas.

8   If and when you see *the* property, it's now time to get that super-whizz-irresistible-I-mean-business offer on the table. This is where the heartbreak begins. The offer is too low/there is a counter-offer (or several)/the buyer is pulling out. My advice is to make the best offer you can afford, stay calm and (most importantly) drink lots of good wine to abate the nervous energy.

9   To shortcut heartbreak, make it a condition of your offer that the estate agent takes the property off the market while you

get surveyors and builders in for quotes. Never mind that you're just planning to repair the staircase.

All being tickety-boo, you should be older, greyer, addicted to Pro Plus and half a stone lighter by now, and ready to exchange and complete (same day, please). Quick tip: Forgive all stray dog and crusted-up bath rim sins and move in with your best friend while you tear up the vinyl floors and knock the tiny kitchen and dining room into one. You don't want to be totally grey by the time you move in.

So I could finally see why people say that buying a place/ moving is one of the most stressful things you'll ever do. There's the heartbreak of knowing what you love and then the realisation of what you can actually afford. Yes, that sinking feeling of falling for an area, only to realise you may be able to see the green, leafy streets lined with Victorian houses from your top-floor window, but you'll actually be next to a Wimpy and directly opposite the off-licence where teenage boys love to loiter on a Friday night. Then (like we need anything further to put us off buying altogether) there's the stress of finding something you're happy with and losing it to someone who managed to offer a few thousand more than you and will install that Smeg fridge you've always dreamt of.

Still, stress and envy aside, buying your first place will feel liberating. My single pal Zoe says she'd opt for her small but totally self-funded basement flat over a shared penthouse any day. The freedom to come and go as she pleases, to stick whatever naff holiday snaps she fancies on the fridge door, to cook up a big, garlic-fest pasta supper without worrying about the smell and to play cheesy iPod tunes, very loudly, while she does all of the above feels worth her random, new-found grey hairs.

Our first flat (also known as 55b) had peeling yellow wallpaper, horrid swirly green carpets and a teensy-weensy postage-stamp patch of grass that, once weeded, we could call a 'garden'. Now that I think about it, there was one summer's afternoon when we lay down in our 'acreage', pulled up our knees at a specific pins-and-needles-inducing angle and caught a few rays. That was 55b – small, sweet and admittedly in the wrong part of town, but ours all the same.

Be a mistress of the mortgage process *(ensuring that you don't need your dad or boyfriend to lean on)*

by **Jasmine Birtles**, director of Moneymagpie and endless source of novel finance advice

Step 1: how much money do you earn?

Mortgage companies base their lending on the amount you earn, either on your own or as a couple. So before you start applying for loans or contacting any banks or brokers, you need to calculate how much money you make each year. When you do your sums, remember to add in any extra cash that comes in regularly (like investments or alimony payments). Generally speaking, in the current climate, a single-income applicant can borrow about 3.5–4 times their salary. Couples are able to borrow about 2.75–3 times their joint income. If you're self-employed, you'll need to calculate your net profit from the last three years. If you don't have three years of accounts, it will be harder to get a mortgage, but not impossible.

Step 2: get a deposit together

The next step is to get a decent deposit together. A deposit is the actual cash that you provide upfront as part of the payment for your home. This is your own money, not money you have borrowed. In the days when mortgage providers offered 100-per-cent-plus loans (i.e. if you wanted to buy a house costing £100,000, the mortgage provider would be prepared to lend you all of it – sometimes even more), some homebuyers used to be able to get away with putting down no deposit at all. Not any more; the deposit is now more important than it has been in several years. Most providers won't lend you any money until you've put some cash on the table. You'll normally need to put down a deposit of, at the very least, 5 per cent of the value of the property in order to get a mortgage – this is the minimum that any lender now requires. Even then, deals with this 95 per cent loan to value (LTV) ratio are rare, and the interest rates are usually high. Ideally, you should put down the biggest deposit you can to get a mortgage with a good, low interest rate. To get the very best rates on offer, you should have a 20 per cent deposit, or as near as you can get to it.

Step 3: make sure you have some extra cash

Unfortunately, it isn't just your deposit money that you're going to need upfront – there are a few other fees involved as well (oh joy). You'll need to have extra cash put aside to cover:

- stamp duty

- surveying fees

- legal fees

And if you opt for a mortgage broker who charges, you'll also have to fork out for brokers' fees too.

Step 4: shop around

You can go to your bank and ask them for a mortgage – it's a good starting place. But remember that they're not the only ones offering deals. They may well offer you the best deal because they know you, but it's also worth shopping around. Try London and Country (www.lcplc.co.uk) and John Charcol (www.charcol.co.uk) for complete mortgage comparisons.

One of the important factors in nailing that mortgage offer is to improve your credit rating. *Simple if you know how*

Make sure you are on the electoral roll. It sounds odd, but if they can't find you on that, credit referencing agencies put a black mark against your name. If you're not on the electoral roll, write to your local council, who will send you the registration form.

Make your bill payments on time (particularly credit cards, loans and any existing mortgage). If you can't do this, contact the lender as soon as possible to discuss what options are available to you. You may be able to change your repayment schedule, or make a minimum repayment instead.

If you have paid a fine because of a court judgment, make sure it is shown as being settled on your credit record. If it isn't, contact the court to get it put right on your record.

4 If a bankruptcy order has ended or been withdrawn and this is not shown on your credit report, send a copy of your certificate of discharge or annulment to all credit reference agencies and ask for your report to be updated.

5 If you have paid off a credit account but your report doesn't show this, contact the organisation concerned and ask them to make the necessary changes.

6 Avoid credit repair companies. If information on your credit report can be removed or altered, Experian or Equifax (the two main credit referencing agencies) will do it for free. The Office of Fair Trading has issued a warning that the advice and information given by credit repair companies may be wrong and unhelpful and can even make your situation worse, not better.

7 Build a good credit history. If you've no real credit record to speak of, it's obviously hard for companies to judge your reliability and they don't usually give you the benefit of the doubt. So how do you build a good credit history? Borrow money and pay it back religiously, on time, every month. If companies won't lend to you, there are credit cards aimed at people with poor credit records. They have whopping interest charges though – so only use it a small amount every month and then pay the bill DURING the interest-free period. Capital One does a very high-interest credit card (34.9 per cent) which it will offer to people with poor credit histories, as does Vanquis. ONLY USE IT IF YOU CAN PAY IT OFF! If you're struggling to repay your bills now, don't take out this card.

8 Always check your credit report. It makes sense to get a copy of your credit report before you apply for credit. It gives you the chance to clear up any wrong information that may stop you getting better financial products. Just as importantly, it will help ensure you don't get rejected for what you apply for.

9   Don't let rejection lead to rejection. If you are rejected for a loan or other type of credit, find out the reason why. Examine your credit record – it may be that it's got false or out-of-date information on it. If you just apply somewhere else without investigating your first rejection, you're even more likely to get rejected the second time around. And it's not just rejections that harm your credit score – every time a company searches your credit record (i.e. every time you apply for something), it's logged. If you have a number of searches in a short period, it will affect your credit rating adversely.

Let's face it, a mortgage is just one very, very big loan. Just as with smaller loans, the longer you have a mortgage, the more interest you end up paying because you pay interest for every day you borrow that money. So paying it off quickly – certainly a lot quicker than twenty-five years – will save you a lot of money. Here are the main ways to do it:

Overpay

If you can easily afford your mortgage payments right now, a good way to discipline yourself and pay off your mortgage quickly is to ask your mortgage company to reduce the number of years you have left to pay. If you can reduce the term by, say, ten years, your monthly mortgage payments will go up significantly, but the amount you could save in interest payments over those ten years is enormous. Be warned, though, not everyone can do it as quickly as they would like. If you have a fixed mortgage, you will probably only be allowed to pay off up to 10 per cent extra each year. However, there's nothing to stop you doing that *and* setting up a savings account on the side and building up savings which you can put into your mortgage at the end of the fixed rate.

Get an offset mortgage

It's not right for everyone, but if there are two of you paying the mortgage or you have a lot of savings, an offset mortgage can help you pay your mortgage faster. I had one and it certainly worked for me. Basically, how an offset mortgage works is by lumping together your mortgage with your current account and savings account. Any money you have in these accounts is *offset* against your mortgage, so the bank assumes that you owe less than you really do. So, for example, if you have a £100,000 mortgage but you have £20,000 in savings, you will only be charged interest on £80,000. In short, this means that although you pay the same amount into your mortgage each month, less of it will be wasted on interest and more in paying off the capital. Offsets are also very flexible, so generally you can overpay as much as you like each month.

Cut down on outgoings

It's not rocket science. Freeing up money to put into your mortgage involves cutting down your spending in other areas. Start with the easy stuff first:

- Reduce your bills. One of the easiest ways to save is to spend less on your everyday household bills. Go to www.moneymagpie.com and use the comparison services to switch to the best deal for energy providers, insurance, phone and broadband providers and your bank account (stop paying so much in overdraft rates).

- Change your mortgage. If you have enough equity in your home, now could be a very good time to switch, as there are many good mortgage deals on the market for those who don't want to pay a high loan to value ratio. Shop around first and speak to some brokers to see what you could move to. However, don't forget the cost of switching, particularly as exit and set-up fees have rocketed in the last few years.

- Downsize your shopping. Now is the time to slash your supermarket bills by buying some generic items from cheaper shops like Lidl and Aldi or ignoring them altogether and doing all your food shopping at your local market. Street markets tend to be 30 per cent cheaper than supermarkets.

- Pick up bargains. Sign up to voucher sites and the Birtles' Bargains weekly newsletter on www.moneymagpie.com for the latest bargains and money-off vouchers.

- Get as much as you can for free. Join a mystery shopping agency like TNS Global (www.tnsglobal.com) to get free meals out. See if you've got any forgotten-about money in an old bank or savings account with www.mylostaccount. org.uk. Sign up to freebie sites (with a separate email address from your usual one, so that you don't get spammed) and pick up the odd good bargain that comes your way.

- Have fun on the cheap. Budgeting doesn't mean you can't have fun – there are lots of ways to have a good time without a big price tag. Go out for dinner for half price with www.toptable.com. Use shopbots to get the best price on everything you buy. Try www.kelkoo.co.uk, www.mysupermarket.co.uk, www.pricerunner.co.uk and www.groupon.co.uk.

- Use your home to get free holidays. You don't have to forego holidays just because you're saving. Join a house-swap agency such as www.homeexchange.com or www.intervac.co.uk and you can swap your place for the homes of families in the UK and around the world for weeks at a time. All you have to pay for is your travel and food.

Make your home pay its own mortgage

Rent out a room

This is the most obvious, and tax efficient, way of cashing in on your home. If you have a spare room, you could make up to £4,250 a year tax-free under the government's Rent a Room scheme. If you can't stand the idea of someone permanent, rent it to a foreign student from a local school – check www.languageschoolfinder.co.uk. Or you could put someone up for just a few nights a week – try www.mondaytofriday.com.

Rent out your whole house

If you have somewhere cheap you could stay for six months or a year, then move out of your home and rent out the whole place to get some serious income from it. It might sound drastic, but quite a few people have done it and you can remind yourself that it's just a temporary situation in a good cause!

Rent your driveway

If you live near a station or in a popular part of town and you don't use your driveway or garage, you could make money from it by renting it out through www.parkatmyhouse.com or www.parklet.co.uk. You could make £20,000 a year if you have a great space in the middle of London.

Hire out your home as a film set

Not everyone can do this, but if you have a large home in or near a major city with good parking and light, you could make £2,000 a day by hiring it to film companies. Get in touch with locations agencies and see if your home is the sort of place they could use.

Get connected *without spending a full day queuing at the post office or listening to Bach while waiting to talk to the telephone company*

- TV, phone and broadband. Make your life easy and use one major provider for all three (Sky, BT, Virgin). Simply put, this means that even if you're kept on hold for a couple of hours waiting to order the services, at least at the end of the excruciating wait you'll be totally and utterly sorted.

  Note: to keep the cost down, be specific about what TV channels you want. All-inclusive deals can cost up to £70 a month, but if you're selective, you'll pay much less. Let's face it, do you really need CBeebies if you're single, or sports if you can't stand the sight of testosterone-fuelled men in tight shorts?

- Gas and electricity. Before moving into your new place, ensure the old occupiers have notified the gas and electricity provider(s) of their move date. They'll then contact you to come and read the meter. If you feel unhappy with the existing company, then get in touch with uSwitch (www.uswitch.com). They'll be able to tell you the cheapest alternatives if you're paying over the odds for the gas and electric bills and allow you to make an informed choice.

- Council tax. When you've unpacked your array of back-dated *Vogue*s, call your local council to notify them that you've moved and they'll amend your council tax accordingly.

- Insurance and home security. Log on to www.moneysupermarket.com to get a good selection of home insurance quotes. Remember, if you invest a little more on home security, not only will you feel safer, but your cover price will be lower. Chubb (www.chubb.co.uk) and ADT (www.adt.co.uk) are two of the most respected names.

- Post. Log on to www.royalmail.com for re-direction of post.

- Driving licence. To let them know you've moved, just send off the detachable slip at the bottom of your existing licence.

- To save you hours of time re-directing your *Grazia* subscription and Tesco Clubcard mail, make one click of the mouse onto www.iammoving.com. They'll notify almost every company you belong to about your move and stop any unwanted junk mail cluttering up your doormat.

- If you're feeling flash and flush, order some change of address cards from Heritage (www.heritage-stationery.com). Failing that, Moonpig (www.moonpig.com) will send them out for you, saving you the stamp hassle.

Achieving that *Elle Decor* look on an IKEA budget

I don't know about you, but I have what can only be described as 'schizophrenic home syndrome'. On the one hand, I have the realistic home I actually live in – reasonable size, small garden, IKEA kitchen, too many raincoats cluttering up the hallway, felt-tip pen marks on the kitchen walls. On the other hand, I have the alter-home I dream of living in – large, double-fronted Victorian abode, six glorious-sized bedrooms, open-plan kitchen/living area, Conran kitchen, huge cream sofas, no raincoats in the hall (in a dream world it never rains, of course, and if it does, a Burberry mac appears as if from nowhere).

Life's too short to spend Sundays in IKEA/ Homebase. A dash on late-night opening, yes. Every weekend, get a grip.

My good friend Emma confesses to suffering from the same syndrome. Her real home is a two-up-two-down in north London with a pebbledashed front, twenty-foot patio and interiors fitted entirely by Magnet. Her alter-home is a 1920s, free-standing number with a glass back, hundred-foot garden and interiors by Philippe Starck and Eames and scented candles by Diptyque. Don't get me started on Mathilda's fantasy abode, which involves a walk-in shoe wardrobe and sheepskin rugs laid out beside roaring open fires.

Never mind the lurve conspiracy theory, the homes one is just as potent. Here we are, a bunch of successful thirty-something women who have managed to claw our way onto the property ladder. However, instead of feeling delighted with our patch of semi-detached glory, we secretly feel we should be entitled to that sprawling, modernist, glass-backed pad on the cover of *Wallpaper*. We feel that if we could just work that little bit harder, that extra bedroom/loft conversion/ leather coffee table/Smeg fridge/Aga would be ours, and oh how happy we would finally be. For ever and ever – even with a hangover *and* PMS.

While 55b was my proud and much-loved home for a good few years, it wasn't long before schizophrenic home syndrome set in and I got itchy to move. Practical restrictions made the itch turn into full-blown scabies in no time at all: we'd had our first baby, who was sleeping in our bed due to lack of space – adorable for the first few months, claustrophobic once she was topping the scales at 25lbs and crawling. Plus, I was taking on more and more freelance writing, which was proving impossible to do while sitting on the loo seat with my laptop – the bathroom seems the best option when you don't have a study or spare room, but is obviously not ideal when your other half needs to do a seated performance.

The raging scabies soon became impossible to ignore and, within months, the whole property porn, mortgage-advisor schmoozing and offer/exchange/complete palaver began all over again. I should add here that unless you're totally loaded or prepared to exchange your existing abode for an itsy-bitsy shoe-box, moving onwards and upwards will be impossible unless you move onwards and *outwards*. A shoe-box flat somewhere remotely central/hip/desirable might be just about viable for some, but if you're looking for more space, I'm afraid the chances are you'll have to compromise on the postcode. Sorry, but it's true.

I don't want to bore you to tears, so I'll cut a long story short. Several years after buying our patch of independence at 55b, we saw, we bought, we conquered and we moved to number 65, a few miles further out of town. It may not have been a mega-bucks, double-fronted Victorian legend straight from the front page of the Foxtons brochure, but it was a cosy family home, with potential to strip a few floorboards and host more than two very small people for supper. The main obstacle to overcome was not avoiding the dust fumes caused by Mr S with a sledgehammer or deciding where to fit the slightly musty, paint-chipped cot on loan from my most generous and stylish friend (is it really essential to be able to shut the baby's bedroom door?) but to make the house quirky and stylish enough to keep schizophrenic home syndrome at bay. Surely if you can make your home look like a shoot from *Elle Decor* (even if it's a two-bedroom flat in Willesden), then you'll be less tempted to drool over your fantasy alter-life and feel like a failure because you haven't achieved it.

Now, unless you a) earn an absolute fortune in your own right or b) have family money that allows you a town house in Knightsbridge and a vast acreage in Somerset (meaning your house(s) can instantly be transformed into a vision of *World of Interiors* gorgeousness), you might just need a few tricks and shortcuts to achieve a great look. Most of my girlfriends have home-envy periodically, so at least a few ideas to achieve *Elle Decor* style on an IKEA budget are required to keep the green-eyed monster at bay.

- Before you even pick up a paintbrush, log on to www.thehousedirectory.com, the ultimate online bible for everything from interior design tips to where to buy your door knobs. Thanks to this site, property porn will be instantly replaced by interior porn.

- When you're doing up a kitchen, opt for Magnet or IKEA units and spend a little extra on the appliances. You can get really stylish and simple shelves and cupboards from somewhere cheap and then invest in granite worktops (www.cotswold-granite.co.uk or www.boniti.com have all you'll need) and a fridge, cooker and dishwasher from somewhere a little flashier. Try www.buyersandsellerson line.co.uk for range and value for money. My friend Rose has a plain wooden kitchen that was a reduced flat-pack IKEA number, but by adding grey granite worktops and a stainless steel Bosch fridge, oven and hob, she managed to upgrade it.

LIFE'S TOO SHORT

- Go to John Lewis for your appliances (www.johnlewis.com). My friend Emma found her oven, fridge and washing machine online at faithful JL, and all came with a five-year guarantee. They even delivered and installed them. It's such a ridiculously competitive market that department stores like John Lewis will offer you appliances with a guarantee that if you can find them cheaper elsewhere, they'll refund the difference.

- Don't hold back on lighting. If you create clever lighting, the whole room will look more expensive. I always go for lamps in various corners and have up-lights on the floor of my living room. Opt for low-watt bulbs or a dimmer switch, which give the effect of subtle lighting and will hide a multitude of sins.

- All that needs to be said about cost-cutting on curtains is 'Curtain Exchange' (www.thecurtainexchange.co.uk). Buy those desired sash curtains; they may be used and abused, but a quick dry-clean and they'll be as good as new.

- Think about using stripes when decorating rooms. My friend Rose swears by them and waxes lyrical about their 'architectural power to give a room more depth and space'. She's used cream and beige vertically striped wallpaper on one wall of her small-but-perfectly-formed living/dining area and, without a doubt, they make the low ceiling feel higher. Horizontal stripes are a good idea too and instantly make a room look Art Deco, meaning you need to fuss less about the fixtures and furnishings within the room.

- Mix and match your bog-standard Habitat sofa and IKEA rugs with some quirky retro or antique pieces. I'll never forget a very hungover Sunday morning on Portobello

Road (post venomous argument with Mr S about whether we could park on a double-yellow line on a Sunday or not) when I stumbled across two hand-painted cabinets from Rajasthan (think washed-out blue with tiny ornate flowers painted all over them). We paid sixty-five quid for both, lugged them home along with our bacon butties and didn't get a parking ticket in the process (OK, Mr S was right about the Sunday double-yellow parking rule). I can't guarantee you'll find an antique or retro gem for precisely sixty-five spondoolies, but Lots Road Auctions (www.lotsroad.com) is a great place for bargains, as is Alfies Antique Market (www.alfiesantiques.com), where you'll find everything from vintage textiles to twentieth-century furniture that could take centre stage in any room. Failing this, search for bargains online at the huge auction house Dorotheum (www.dorotheum.com) or, while you're grabbing the Sunday papers, pick up a copy of the *Antique Trade Gazette* and look up listings for local antique fairs and auctions. Go with a hangover – I promise, it'll help you to be more spontaneous (the Rajasthan cabinets are testimony to this).

- My friend Sarah utilised all her issues of *Vogue* (she's a self-confessed fashion whore and has over a hundred copies) by making them into table legs. She bought a thick piece of glass from a local window supplier and put her stacks of *Vogue*s under each corner. *Voilá*, a fabulous coffee table! And being a slave to style, she reckons there's no better place for a glass of wine at the end of a long day than perching on the pout of cover-star Ms Moss herself.

- Get your hands on a Victorian (or mock-Vic) armoire with glass doors. I found a collection of really battered-up ones (splinters and lost legs) at an antiques fair in Bath. They're so versatile, look bloody fabulous and cost less than a generic storage unit from MFI. I have one in my daughter's bedroom (I took out the shelves, replaced them with a rail and hung all her pretty clothes behind the glass); one in my living room (I kept the shelves and display art books, scented candles, photos and anything that isn't plastic/ didn't come from Ryman); and one in my kitchen (great for my mix-and-match crockery, cake stands and anything else I imagine I'd use if I had the tea parties I never have the time nor inclination to organise). I may have had to sacrifice seating space and the weekly food shop to house them, but we all sat on each other's knees and ate Tesco value pasta for a few months without too much bother!

- If you have room in your bedroom to swing more than a cat, invest in a dressing table. A good place to look for inspiration would be Graham and Green (www.grahamandgreen.co.uk) or Brissi (www.brissi.co.uk). Then you can nip to Laura Ashley (www.lauraashley.com) or M&S for a cheaper version. I love my Deco, mirrored 'dress-up table' with a passion. While all the other areas of my home are polluted with football socks and ground-in Cheerios, my dressing table is sacred. I opted for 1920s boudoir chic (think of that alter-life, where weekends are spent at Claridge's sipping Kir Royales) and pile my glass dressing table with old photos, postcards, perfume atomisers and flowers in jam jars (when I can be bothered). Sarah hates girlie boudoir chic ('So bloody Laura Ashley') and instead found a perspex dressing table which she uses to stack her array of red lipsticks and ultra-modern framed photos of her other half.

- Instead of forking out thousands on a hi-fi, go for an old record player instead. A 1980s set of decks and a stash of classic vinyl make a mega-bucks, flash-your-cash stacking system look positively footballer's wife. Check out www.decks.co.uk for the decks and www.retrovinyl.co.uk for the tuuuuunes.

- Start a collection of arty coffee-table books. The *Pucci* books by Vanessa Friedman are pricey but have such fabulous covers they'll steal the whole room (www.taschen.com). If you don't fancy remortgaging your house to fund them, just buy any good second-hand art and photography books from Amazon (www.amazon.co.uk). The more battered, the better.

- My friend Camilla works a seventy-five-hour week and says she'd rather drink petrol from a pint glass than re-vamp her living room on her quarter-day-off weekends. She gave her white and grey living room an *Elle-Dec* update by adding retro cushions to the (grey) sofa. In an ideal world, she vows she'd make them by hand from vintage fabrics sourced at Paris flea markets; alas, in her real world, she bought a handful of Union Jack polyester-mix cushions online in the Marks & Spencer sale. They pass as Conran to anyone who doesn't work for a sleek interior design firm.

- Hardly any girl I know can be bothered to visit a florist once a week, spending her well-earned Whistles fund while she's there. I'm the first to swoon over fresh flowers, but the best way to get from oh-no-the-lovely-pink-roses-have-died-and-it's-only-the-ninth-of-the-month to pay-day is to invest in good-quality can't-believe-they're-not-real silk flowers. Sally Bourne sell amazing ones (www.sallybourneinteriors.co.uk) and if you display them

Life's too short for major home-envy. A little passing lust for Wallpaper *chic*, yes. Stalking of double-fronted neighbours, no.

individually in a quirky, vintage green bottle or soda siphon from Bottle Green Homes (www.bottlegreenhomes.co.uk) or a vintage metal vase from Niki Jones (www.niki-jones.co.uk), you'll save on cash and no one will be any the wiser. Genius.

It goes without saying that if I win the lottery, I shall be heading straight for Liberty's homes department without stopping at any red lights. Until then, I shall continue to fill my shabby chic armoires with mix 'n' match floral cups and saucers sourced from my local branch of Oxfam, and store my gravy granules, olive oil and Dorset Cereals in cupboards from IKEA. My fingers remain crossed that if the art director from *Elle Decor* calls in for a cuppa, he'll be none the wiser.

Instant girl-about-town interior glamour

by **Audrey Carden**, director of Carden Cunietti interiors and God's gift to drab living rooms

- Buy a fabulously comfortable sofa in a classic shape. It will serve you well. It can be dressed up with throws and cushions that can be changed inexpensively to give you different looks. Make sure there is good access for the sofa and save hassle by choosing a company that will make sofas that can be assembled on site. Avoid sofa beds if you can; they are never comfortable as a sofa nor as a bed. A lose–lose situation.

- Hallways and guest WCs are good places to add a bit of drama. The hallway is an area that you merely pass through as you rush out to catch the bus, so you can afford to go over the top a little. A dark hallway can make the other rooms feel lighter, so experiment with muted tones if you dare. If you have a guest WC, this can be a good room to have a bit of fun with. Add a chandelier, patterned wallpaper and a feature basin made in stone or glass, or from a found object.

- Buy one large dramatic piece of art or frame a beautiful textile or dress; this can bring colour and texture into a room. Mirrors are also good for creating drama and hanging art on a mirrored wall is great for making a drab room come alive.

- Curtains in a neutral fabric are versatile and can have borders added if you move house. A shiny fabric always adds glamour in bedrooms. Roman blinds are always specific to the property, so not a good long-term invest-ment; however, if the room is small, a Roman blind is a cleaner window treatment and will give the illusion of space.

- Buy the best mattress you can afford. You spend at least six hours of every twenty-four in bed, so this is not an area to scrimp on.

- There are different pillow types for different sleepers. If you sleep on your side, then a baffle-edge pillow will be more comfortable. Silk pillowcases and sheets are cooler in summer, and silk is reputably better for your hair than cotton. Just make sure your blow-the-budget silk sheets

can be machine-washed. There's no fun in hand-washing
sheets after a long day in the office.

Storing clutter without resorting to worryingly organised perspex boxes

Storing clutter is one of the banes of my life. Where does all
this stuff come from? Piles and piles of paperwork, clothes
with no home, keys, stamps, magazines, toys, toys and more
toys, just endless tat. I hate it all. When on a declutter mission,
I have been known to throw away essential bank statements
(sometimes unopened) and even on one occasion a stray
passport. I'm like a living Dyson vacuum cleaner – nothing in
my path is safe.

It goes without saying that chucking out Mr S's passport,
my daughter's limited-edition Sylvanian fox cub and a letter
from my bank informing me of my exceeded overdraft limit all
within the space of a week wasn't a decluttering highlight for
me. Mr S still bears his grudge.

You could do what my friend Sylvie does and admit defeat.
She's resigned to the fact that her twins and home-working
partner treat the house like a tipping ground and is happy to
leave it that way. Pop over for a cuppa and you're likely to
wade through piles of magazines, umbrellas, recycling which
is 'on its way out' and beeping and moving children's toys,
like a vision of Hamleys' basement. I'm not exaggerating when
I say that the quantity of clutter would make walking through
quicksand feel like a breeze.

An alternative to the 'total surrender to clutter' ethos is
illustrated by my friend Hannah. She isn't a clutter-nutter
Nazi like me, but doesn't quite resign herself to total chaos
and destruction either. She won't bin passports, but is famous
for organising anything and everything in boxes (she's known

for being able to retrieve filed bank statements from the 1980s in under sixty seconds). Plastic, colour co-ordinated boxes are her friends. I think she may even have shares in a perspex production company. Surely there must be storage solutions that fall somewhere between rubbish dump and 'I will sterilise your hands and fleece you of any paperwork/possible waste prior to entry'?

I promised Mr S that if he'd forgive me for making him endure the six-hour queue at the passport office, I would investigate and implement.

The Kitchen

I confess, as minimalist as it is, it's not really viable to cook with only one saucepan now I'm married with three children. Believe me, for some time now I've tried. I'm at pains to admit that it's also pretty tough to feed breakfast to said family of five with only three floral Cath Kidston bowls. If I *must* store all this 'necessary' kitchen equipment, I'll opt for a stainless steel saucepan rack hung from the ceiling. IKEA and the Holding Company sell them as cheap as chips, and they keep pots and pans up and away (www.ikea.com, www.theholdingcompany. co.uk). I'm also experimenting with extra shelves in my cupboards for all those 'essential' items, like cheese graters and kitchen scales, that you may only use occasionally but I'm told are a rite of passage for family cooking (thanks, Nigella). While hiding away the grater, I've taken out any crockery that's remotely pretty (hello, vintage bone-china rosebud bowls from Florence & Florence – www.florenceandflorence.com) and stacked them on a new shelf above the toaster. They look lovely; just, please, kids, don't ask to use them for your Shreddies – it will ruin the display.

The Living Room

All hail those sixty-five-quid Rajasthan cabinets. At first I wasn't sure what the hell we'd keep in them, but once fitted with some brackets and plywood shelves, they became a brilliant way to store paperwork, documents, wrapping paper and postcards. Admittedly, not everyone will stumble upon Indian gems on a hungover Sunday morning (it's happened to me once in my life and never again since), but you could do the same with any interesting cabinets or one-off free-standing cupboards.

For all those excess piles of paperwork, I'd head for Paperchase (www.paperchase.co.uk), Kate Forman (www.kateforman.co.uk), Muji (www.muji.co.uk) or Cath Kidston (www.cathkidston.co.uk) for pretty organisers. They'll save you succumbing to those plastic organisers that still smell of polystyrene even after a year's use.

If you're a hoarder of ornaments, give yourself the challenge of shedding some and displaying others, or at least putting some in storage. Don't get me wrong, I'm a contemporary and flea-market gem junkie and, although I find bank statements easy to bin, would be hard pushed to part with my collection of porcelain flowers and silk butterflies. Instead, I set myself the task of selecting my favourites. The flowers I put under different-sized bell-jars on the coffee table (www.twenty twentyone.com), the butterflies I framed in eclectic frames and picture-hooked onto one wall. Decluttering with a twist.

The Bathroom

My single, chrome-obsessed friend Zoe came up with the bloody genius idea of using metal gardening shelves from Homebase in her bathroom. She stacks up all her flash lotions and potions on them and keeps the less-fabulous Tampax boxes and cheap two-for-one nail-varnish remover in small pound-shop white-wicker boxes. I've done a similar thing with a frosted glass cabinet that I spotted in the kitchen department of IKEA, being touted as an ideal place for storing 'special' dining plates. I put it up in the bathroom (admittedly with much cursing at the mother-f***er Black & Decker drill). Add those useful pound-shop baskets, and it's made perfect storage for my bath salts and cotton wool pads.

The Bedroom

Stylists and celebrity fashionistas are always advising us mere-mortal women to store our shoes in shoe-boxes and stick Polaroids on the front, but honestly who has the time? I took the cheat's route and invested in perspex boxes for my favourite, most-used shoes. Sadly, the rest remain in their original shoe-boxes or heaped up at the bottom of my wardrobe, but at least I'm trying.

The Stairs

My friend Rose made good use of the three flights of stairs that connect her very tall and skinny, size-zero town house in Brighton. Instead of cursing loudly every time she had to climb forty steps when she needed a pair of socks from the bedroom (top floor) when she was making a cuppa (bottom floor), she fished out the number of a local carpenter who turned her stairs into drawers. You almost need to see it to believe it, but each step pulls out to reveal organised drawers of bank statements, old photos, Pac-a-macs and spare bedding. Her house really does look like a shoot from *Elle Decor*, but hidden beneath the clean lines is a collection of clutter that makes you realise that even in *Elle Decor* world, you need a vast collection of easily accessible warm socks.

All-over extras

Whenever I go to a hot country that sells the obligatory authentic baskets for the same price as a London travel card, I bring a few home for hoarding clutter (alas, no passports here, but a consolatory stash of napkins in the basket above the kitchen broom cupboard and a surprisingly vast array of odd gloves in the basket under the coats beside the front door). Useful for storing everything you can think of, even recycling. No beach break on the horizon? Do not fear; browse the net for cool baskets at www.basketbasket.co.uk or www.baileys homeandgarden.com for alternative storage solutions, most of which don't have 'plastic' anywhere in their descriptions.

I confess, my clutter-tolerance levels have been raised and I feel slightly less like a Dyson and slightly more like a super-efficient PA, plus I've managed to avoid *almost* all plastic storage solutions. But, in all honesty, I still hate all this stuff with a passion. Wouldn't it be far easier to persuade my bank manager to inform me of my exceeded overdraft limit over the phone and to ask Mr S to keep passports in a secure safety deposit box with the same willing bank manager? This should ensure I'm free to nurture clear shoe-boxes and floral teacups to my heart's content.

Keeping your nest clean when Mr Muscle brings you out in hives

I often hope that a natural progression for my clutter phobia will be an allergic reaction to dirt and grime. I tell myself that surely if I can't stand the sight of piles of discarded toys and paperwork, I should have the same aversion to dust and dirt. Hey presto! I'd become a dab hand with the duster and au fait with all the different nozzle attachments on my Dyson. Alas, there seems to be no correlation here and I am, simply put, the type of woman who'd like to kick dust-balls under the sofa instead of hoovering for fifteen minutes before the school run/attacking an article for a glossy magazine. Pop round for a cuppa and move my sofa an inch, and you'll see what I mean.

Life's too short to turn your house into a Stepford wife show-home.

Although I'd love a cleaner to arrive at 8 a.m. every morning to help me de-smear the Weetabix and milk from the kitchen floor and lovingly hand-wash my favourite M&S cashmere roll-neck, it's just not a viable option for me, or for most of the women I know. The snag is, I do feel better about life when my home exudes an illusion of cleanliness and calm. I therefore reluctantly resign myself to that fact that a *small* daily commitment to cleaning is probably a necessity. Getting up-close-and-personal with my DC26 Dyson's array of detachable nozzles, emptying the bins, making the beds and loading/emptying the dishwasher have begrudgingly become part of my endless list of 'Must Dos'. On a good day, that cashmere-mix jumper may well get a wash too and the Cheerios are removed from underfoot. On a bad day, the contents of bins will just be squashed further down and the dust kicked under the sofa. Hey, no one's perfect.

Whether you're a junkyard junkie or from the field of fully staffed fabulousness, every woman needs the following:

- The big stuff. Surely juggling a career and three children would be near impossible without a washing machine and dishwasher? Many women do it, just not me if I want to remain sane. Also essential are a decent hoover, dustpan and brush, kitchen broom, feather duster and hand-held dusters, J cloths, tea towels, ironing board, iron, toilet brush and Marigolds. Look no further than John Lewis for all of the above and invest in a Cath Kidston ironing-board cover to jazz it all up a tad.

- The products. Ecover (www.ecover.com) cover all the basics and by using plant- and mineral-based ingredients you'll be doing your bit for the environment too. Cleanliness and eco-consciousness in a squirt – we like.

Here are a few helpful hints to ensure using it all is just that little bit more manageable:

- When hoovering stairs, use the nozzle. Unlike rooms, which can generally be hoovered mindlessly and while day-dreaming about more important issues, the stairs need to be done one-by-one, generally on your knees. Glamorous: no. Essential: I'm afraid so.

- I can never see the point in rinsing crockery before loading the dishwasher (surely speed and cleaning are the point of dishwashers?) Alas, my continual stacking of ketchup-smeared plates and bowls encrusted with Dorset Cereal left my Bosch caput and me with sky-high washing-up during one of the busiest weeks of my working year. Take note: forget to rinse at your peril.

- It's a good idea to clean out your fridge once a month to avoid the mouldy strong cheddar taking on a life of its own. Chuck out any foods well past their sell-by date and mop up any spills using a light washing-up liquid and cool water mix. Replace all your items as if they're going to take part in a 'What's in Your Fridge' shoot (joke) and endeavour to buy the Heinz beans fridge-pack from now on: the only sure-fire way to eliminate the risk of your beloved Pinot Grigio being covered in a delightful orange sticky stain.

- Even if you can't bake to save your life, stock up on baking soda as a cheap and useful cleaning product. Mix with lavender or rose oil and sprinkle on carpets before hoovering to add fragrance and get rid of nasty odours, add to water and use to clean glasses made cloudy from the dishwasher cycle and sprinkle on oven spills to ease the effort of cleaning. Genius.

- My friend Cath cleans her floors and marble worktops with a DIY mix of two cups of vinegar and two litres of hot water; she swears it's a miracle cleaner for giving her tiles shine. She goes on to add that the same mix is ideal for shifting carpet stains too. I tried it at home, but couldn't get rid of the niggling feeling that I was living in a chippy, so resorted back to pinewood Flash instead. Vinegar may be cheaper, but I think I'd prefer to channel a forest vibe as opposed to a fried-fat one.

- When using your oven, put foil on the baking tray and base. It will speed up the cleaning of spills and washing-up of trays.

- If your kids have been getting busy with felt-tips on the walls or your leather upholstery is marked, look no further than baby wipes to remove. Not just handy for poo, you know.

- To ease the hot fluster incurred when making beds, always opt for fitted sheets instead of flat ones. End. Of. Bed. Fluster. Misery.

- My friend Lily's only tipple is red wine and even she admits her animated post-third-glass conversation causes regular staining of her American Apparel long-sleeve Ts and beige carpet. She tells me the answer is not to give up booze for eternity, but to adopt a failsafe stain-illumination trick: sprinkle with salt, rinse in soda water and wash ASAP (the top in the washing machine, the carpet with Fairy Liquid and water). I promised her I'd try this the next time I have a Merlot-down-frock horror moment.

I will go on record and say that I absolutely don't follow these tips daily, just some of the time, when I can be bothered. Or my home is looking in danger of morphing into a squat. I'm certainly no super-housewife and generally have far more pressing things to do than shove an Alka-Seltzer down the loo. Having said that, Mr S and my three children are unlikely to do much to de-grime the oven or rid the toilet of stains anytime soon. With this in mind, it's good to know how to do it quickly and efficiently, leaving me to get on with more pressing things, like earning some money.

Washing and ironing with minimum hassle and maximum efficiency

True, I'm pretty indifferent to the household task of washing clothes. Load, switch, leave. Easy. I wish I could say the same about ironing, but in fact I hate it with a passion and am about as good at it as I was at algebra at school. Basically crap. However, here are a few shortcuts to doing both without throwing the iron at your other half while trying to de-crease your work-blouse.

- My friend Tilly substitutes Fairy tabs with neat bleach and runs her machine on a 90°C cycle once a month to stop her washing machine smelling of skanky old football socks.

She also sprays two tumble-dryer sheets with her favourite fragrance and keeps one at the bottom of her laundry basket to counteract the pong of sweaty clothes and pops one in the dryer to make clean, dry clothes smell delicious.

Life's too short to iron your undies.

- Don't tumble-dry your knitwear unless you want it to fit a toddler when it finishes the spin. Instead, dry it flat, preferably between two towels, in a warm room.

- You could invest in a super-sleek, work-of-art Laurastar Evolution G4 steam iron in the hope that it will capture your inner domestic diva, though at around £400 it's almost too precious to use on your much-loved, much-used GAP white Ts. With this in mind, I suppose you may well prefer to buy a cheap version from Tesco and use what you've saved on a mini-break in Rome. Or to pay your very overdue mobile phone bill.

- Laurastar or not, always iron clothes when they're still slightly damp. It makes those stubborn creases disappear in a flash.

- Blast a hairdryer at the creases. They come out in an instant and you don't even have to plug in the iron.

- Unless you're a total crease-freak, never iron your children's clothes. They will spend most of their time trashing them in the park or school playground, so why bother making them look like Little Lord Fauntleroy before leaving the house? Brushing hair is a much simpler solution to looking semi-groomed.

Nailing the shabby chic look

by **Alice Temperley**, to-die-for designer of
fashion and interiors and expert on all things exquisite

I'd be lying if I said living in Notting Hill wasn't brilliant, and
Portobello Market is one of my weekly pleasures. It's a great
treasure trove for lapping up inspiration for both my home
and collections. I must also confess to a fetish for antique
markets in the countryside, where you can pick up anything
from a beautiful old chandelier to a dining-room table. They
beat mainstream matchy-matchy interiors hands down. The
trick is to root around as much as you can and keep an eye out
for gems no one else will have. My shortcuts to navigating
your way through the junk to reach shabby chic loveliness are:

- Try not to see collecting inspiration for your home as a
  chore. When you can squeeze in the time, it can be great
  fun and a good way to kill some time on a weekend. When
  browsing, just keep an open mind and don't let
  mainstream home trends dictate what you buy. If everyone
  else is doing the modern minimalist thing, dare to be
  different.

- Make your pad stand out from the run-of-the-mill crowd by
  evoking a little individuality. I'd pick statement pieces, like a
  chandelier or an ornate antique French mirror. I'm also very
  bold with my colours. One of our bedrooms in the
  countryside is black and, as spooky as it sounds, people
  actually say they get the best night's sleep.

- I know sometimes just framing a photo can feel like a
  hassle. We all have that feeling most of the time. However,
  once you've finally managed to frame that holiday snap,
  spare a moment for making your home a place you can

entertain and socialise occasionally! A great shortcut is to look for bits and bobs that ensure your guests are as comfortable as possible. I hate too many formalities and prefer houses to look lived in. You don't even need the flash guest bedrooms to make this work; just cooking up a pasta supper (bring your own bottle) does the trick. Wild flower arrangements, beautifully scented candles, plenty of drinks flowing and good fluffy towels and goose-down pillows in case people end up crashing at yours.

- Find key interior items you just can't live without and make them the centrepiece of your home. We have a thick wooden kitchen table, a very large 8 x 8ft bed and a collection of old chandeliers that have become a bit of a feature. We even have one hanging in a tree out in the field.

- Even if you can't afford flash designs, you can still use insider tricks to give your home flair and style. Mixing up old and new, sourcing from markets, playing with lighting and trying out different colour schemes that might not seem obvious at first are all worth a go.

- Don't be scared of storing clutter – you can still do it while maintaining style. I try to be very organised and throw out quite a lot on a fairly regularly basis. Out of sight Muji drawers are great stacked up; my cellar is full of them. Otherwise, baskets for kids' toys, old trunks and plenty of shelving are great for busy homes.

- Utilise your fashion eye in your home décor by using old props in the house. We have some foxgloves and giant apples from a shoot we did years ago with Tim Walker in our orchard. I am also very keen on the Union Jack, as you might have noticed, so this is often a feature. Classic but playful sums it up.

- If you want to stumble on a few great talking-point pieces, make a day trip to west London. Head straight for Alice's on Portobello Road for Union Jack luggage and old perfume bottles, the Façade on Lisson Grove for beautiful lighting, and Portobello Market and Golborne Road on Friday mornings.

Investing in art when you don't know the difference between a Rothko and a Rembrandt (oh, and only have the dosh equivalent of a pair of designer wedges)

If I knew tons and tons about art, I probably wouldn't have my toddler's splash-prints-with-appliqué-glitter framed as master-pieces in my kitchen. Oh, and tear-sheets from back-dated French *Vogues*. My friend Leigh, however, is a totally different kettle of Sam Taylor-Wood. Her house is a hubbub of eclectic art that gives the Tate Modern a serious run for its money. Absolutely no toddler's hand-prints on show here. I turned up at said chic address armed with expensive chocs to pick Leigh's brains for quick-fix, glamorous girls' art know-how.

According to Leigh, the only golden rule when it comes to buying art is to purchase something you love. It doesn't matter if it's a ten-thousand-pound masterpiece or a five-quid Picasso print from the National Gallery shop; if you love it, you'll make it work in your home.

Everything looks better in a frame. Silk butterflies, a page from your favourite art book, a metre of flock wallpaper, a black and white print from the Photographers' Gallery, frame it and you'll upgrade it.

3 Avoid the art-snob trap by mixing and matching eras and styles. You want a home full of personality, not a house so interior-designed it makes you feel you're sleeping in the Saatchi Gallery.

4 Looking for something around £100? The Print Club (www.printclublondon.com) sells prints from £35, or at Nelly Duff (www.nellyduff.com) you can buy big screen prints from a whole host of art names including fabulous fashion illustrators such as Natalie Ferstendik. I'm loving her illustrations of 'Pearl' and 'Florence' so much I wonder whether Mr S would mind if they slept next to me in bed.

5 The Affordable Art Fair is widely known as 'the Oddbins of the art world'. It does what it says on the tin – sells a cross-section of art at affordable prices (www.affordableartfair.com).

6 If you've got a few hundred pounds plus, head straight to the degree shows. Central St Martins, the University of the Arts, Slade and the Royal Academy of Arts all have BA and MA shows where you can pick up a gem from £300.

7 Can't face the leg work? Log on to Amazon and buy *The Catlin Guide* by Justin Hammond. This annual gem brings together the crème de la crème of BA and MA artists and, at £11.99, it's your essential one-stop shop for sussing who's who in the contemporary art world.

8 Art dealers such as the Contemporary Art Society (www.contemporaryartsociety.org), Hannah Barry (www.hannahbarry.com), Degree Art (www.degreeart.com), Keep Calm Gallery (www.keepcalmgallery.com) and Pertwee, Anderson & Gold (www.pertweeandersongold.com) are also worth a shout if you're hoping to end up with the next Tracey Emin. I'm totally inspired. Down come the framed

pink-splattered hand-prints and up goes Ferstendik's 'Pearl' girl transforming my home in a flash. Love that.

Grooming a jungle-free garden

I have the least green fingers of anyone you're ever likely to meet. Don't get me wrong, they're not manicured fingers – they're just not green. The closest I get to gardening is filling up my toddler's watering can and asking him to go outside and sprinkle it somewhere. Only a few months ago, Mr S asked me if I'd noticed how nice the jasmine plant creeping up the front of our house was looking. I stared blankly and asked what he'd like for supper. It's a shame really, because I'm sure, somewhere deep inside, there is a green-fingered goddess waiting to be unleashed. It's just there are so many other things that need doing that gardening – with all that dirt and digging – seems about as appealing as eating Ryvitas for a week.

I must confess that, post-jasmine comment, I finished cooking supper and went outside to inspect said plant. My God, it was gorgeous, and the smell? WOW! How could I have not noticed it before? Tunnel vision? Colour blindness? Blocked nasal passages? I may not have green fingers, but even I could appreciate how lovely it was. I decided that once I'd finished filing copy, hanging out washing, helping the kids with maths homework, and so on, and so on, I'd brainstorm a few gardening tips with any green-fingered folk I knew. No thanks to complicated horticultural techniques – what I needed were simple shortcuts to gardening for a novice. Let me share a few with you:

Life's too short for striped lawns.

- To save you changing your flowerbeds every few months, plant reliable and interesting evergreen shrubs such as photinia, ceanothus, choisya, phormium and pittosporum with long-flowering perennials such as euphorbia, penstemon, anemone and ceratostigma. Guaranteed to give interest all year round.

- Water your flowerbeds twice a week instead of every day. It will encourage the plants to grow and gain strength (and watering twice a week somehow feels more manageable than the daily drag). Go for the roots and base, not the leaves.

- If you weed twice a week too, it will keep your flowerbeds manageable. A tangled-up jungle is far too intimidating to be pleasurable.

- Window boxes are a good cheat's way of embracing your inner green-fingered goddess without getting out the lawn mower. Paint plastic window boxes pastel blue or grey to give them an edge, fill with soil and add a few roses. Easy.

- Add pots of seasonal bedding plants to give the garden a boost of colour without incurring weeks of complex bed-planting. In winter, go for brightly coloured cyclamen and winter pansies; in summer, geraniums fed with Miracle-Gro are great. If your delightful potted plant looks half dead (oh sorry, major garden neglect wins again) submerge the whole pot in a bucket of water and then place in the shade overnight. It might just save those dahlias – this time round at least.

- Sprinkle Pro-Grow lawn conditioner on your grass (www.pro-grow.co.uk). It's like a vitamin supplement for your lawn and will keep it looking healthier for longer. Goodbye, dried-out wilted patch; hello, Wimbledon lawn!

- Bring some glamour to your acres by adding tea lights in pretty jars, sticking thick candles into the flower pots or throwing a quilt on the grass and scattering cushions around. Oka (www.okadirect.com), Habitat (www.gardentrading.co.uk) and Meggymoos (www.meggymoos.co.uk) are all worth a peek. A Deco planter or children's vintage cloth playhouse are great distractions from your not-so-perfect flowerbeds.

- If you still can't face the idea of weeding and watering, then just clear up all the plastic junk – watering cans, hosepipes, the kids' paddling pool filled with leaves and dead snails. Your garden will have the appearance of looking a little less tragic and your nails will still be clean.

Note: If I'm honest, the ultimate gardening 'cheat & treat' is to enlist a trusty local gardening firm to pop by in late spring and give your patch of green some TLC. It doesn't have to cost a fortune and you may well be so inspired with the results that you go forth to sow runner beans. Try Joe Stubley Gardens if you live in London (www.joestubley-gardens.co.uk), Jonnie Wake for beyond (www.jonniewake.com).

Green living when you have an aversion to flat-pack boxes

by **Sheherazade Goldsmith**, author, eco-campaigner and green goddess.

'I haven't got the time' is the usual excuse I hear from women when chatting about how to lead a greener life. That and 'recycling units are so ugly'. You know what? I'm not going to argue. We are all very busy. Almost every woman I know is juggling several things at any given time, whether it is work, children, home, travel or a major emotional crisis. Basically, *life*. The brilliant thing is, you don't have to change much to make a small impact on your carbon footprint. Just think of your efforts as tweaks rather than life overhauls.

- When you're next in the supermarket, buy energy-efficient light bulbs. They may be slightly more expensive, but they last eight times longer than normal bulbs, so over the course of a year, you'll actually be making a small saving. If every household in the UK took on this tiny task we could light two million homes for a year, free. Still not convinced? Well, it seems the government plan to make non-efficient light bulbs illegal in the future, so be a step ahead of the game and switch now.

- 8 per cent of electricity in a home is lost by leaving appliances on standby. This is huge! I know it's hard to get out from under the duvet when you finally remember that you haven't turned your TV off properly, so I invested in an energy-efficient multi-plug from John Lewis. These genius plugs will automatically turn all appliances off standby, so you can stay in bed.

- Wash all your clothes on forty degrees instead of sixty. You'll save a third of all your household electricity and clothes still get clean, I promise.

- Turn down your thermostat by one degree and you'll save another 10 per cent of your household's energy.

- If you're doing up your kitchen, look for appliances with a A+ grading (A++ is even better). This rates the overall energy efficiency of the product. Just opting for a A+ fridge-freezer will save you 33 per cent more energy than your ancient model and you'll feel that saving when you get your fuel bills.

- Equally, if you're doing up a home or looking for ways to make long-term impact and savings, think about double-glazing and solar panels. Not for everyone, so maybe just consider insulating your loft space – 40 per cent of all household heat is lost through the walls and roof, so you'll see a reduction in your gas bill. Don't you love the sound of that in the lead-up to Christmas?

- I've invested in a recycling stacking bin, and I love it. I hear lots of complaints about how ugly and big recycling units can be, but a stacking system is streamlined and non-bulky. Shove it in the corner of your kitchen, and sorting rubbish for recycling will feel like much less of a chore.

- When you're shopping, quick switches to recycled paper products makes a huge difference on eco-living. Loo paper, kitchen towels and paper for your home printer should all be made from recycled paper.

- Food is a massive issue for carbon footprint. Why do we need all that packaging? OK so the fruit looks like a work of art, but at what cost? I'm not saying buy everything loose and from local farmers' markets; just be a conscious shopper. Ask yourself these three questions:

  1 How did it get here? If you're checking out strawberries in January, chances are they've flown halfway across the world.

  2 How many chemicals have been used? Commercial farmers can use up to 450 pesticides on products. That's a lot of junk to make a peach look appetising.

  3 How much packaging has been used? Twelve rasp-berries in a huge plastic box? A ready-meal with endless cardboard and plastic dishes? Come on, be wise.

Cheap, easy kitchen updates *(when you can't afford to move)*

Every year it's the same: kitchen upgrade versus summer holiday abroad. The smell of Ambre Solaire fused with anchovy-stuffed olives wins every time (I know, not the perfect aromatic mix for some, but for me it nails it). Back copies of *Homes and Gardens* and *Elle Decor* destined for the recycle bin and a Sunday morning trip to IKEA's kitchen department handed over to some other weary, pasty family. You're free to try one of the following chic kitchen shortcuts. Trust me, they absolutely work. Now, come hither, anchovy-stuffed olives; I love you.

- Hide away no more your late grandma's pretty cups and saucers or those Moroccan glasses you tenderly carried back in hand luggage from Marrakech last summer. No need to labour over a complicated storage system either – you'll only divorce your other half when he can't work out which bit goes where. Instead, paint an old bookshelf, making it look a bit different by painting the gaps between shelves in different colours or covering them with a selection of wallpaper.

- Got a blank wall with peeling wallpaper and unsightly boiler pipes? Head to Homebase for blackboard paint and use the wall as a memo chalkboard. Great for late night, post-fourth-cocktail-and-dim-sum games of hangman too.

- Make a boring kitchen splash-back into a talking point by framing some garish wallpaper or some bold floral fabric and filling the space. Sekon Glassworks (www.barrettsgroup.net) will laminate your choice of fabric in two weeks flat.

- Instead of laboriously tiling that small 'what can we do with this' space between the kettle and breadbin with matchy-matchy tiles, buy a collection of mismatched printed tiles and lean them against the wall instead. Moroccan-look navy and white tiles are my favourite (www.tilesbytextiles.com or www.habibi-interiors.com). If even this sounds like too much hard work, buy a roll of wipe-clean vinyl wallpaper and be done with it.

- Fill a blank white wall by hanging up interesting oversized bowls or plates. The Four Seasons plates by Rob Ryan come in blue and white and are almost too lovely to eat off (www.bloomsburystore.com). I can't imagine how modern art can fuse with baked beans and not look tragic. Save the chipped white plates for the Heinz and make these plates into treasured wall hangings instead.

- A gallery of black and white photos arranged in a montage can make any kitchen look interesting. Cover them with a perspex sheet to protect them from grease and grime. It transforms a kitchen far quicker and is cheaper than re-fitting all the IKEA units and squabbling with the other half over Dulux swatches.

- If you can't even squeeze in the time to tile your splash-back and want an instant new-kitchen, feel-good-factor update, then invest in a high-end appliance instead. Ideal if you don't even want to leave your desk to do it. Magimix and Dualit design stylish chrome toasters and kettles (www.selfridges.com), as do Bugatti Volvo (www.bodieandfou.com). Now I think about it, an uber-chic yellow Bugatti Volvo toaster may well give equal satisfaction as new cupboard doors. It's hard to believe toasted granary won't taste better made in it too.

Designing a nursery that isn't yellow with duck-themed wallpaper edging

Generally, I love children, but what I still have a real problem embracing is the nursery-decor dichotomy. On the one hand, you have this semi-stylish nest, an impressive collection of fabulous shoes and a pretty decent understanding of cool art and what restaurants are hot. In short, you do a pretty good impression of someone who has this style thing sussed with a capital S.

Fast forward a few weeks, months, a couple of years, and suddenly, with the appearance of that thin blue line, stylish with a capital S becomes 'Seriously Suspect'. What I mean by this is: the growing baby bean, soon to be a squidgy, pink newborn, seems to drain any creative juices from the new mum-to-be. Not only are those Kurt Geiger stilettos discarded for an ancient pair of Birkenstocks (yes, the closed-toe variety and worn with socks), but suddenly a viable choice of nursery decor is wallpaper with duck-themed edging and a night light that reflects teddies all over the wall. All of a sudden, it's out with the Victorian grey armchair, Venetian mirror and collection of 'Moroccan interior' books, and in with the Disney duvet, pink plastic storage crates and yellow gingham changing mat.

I should know – I've been guilty of SS myself. Before my second child was born, I not only toyed with various designs, but actually *bought* a white 'feeding chair'. Now, I'm not talking distressed antique rocker; I'm talking cumbersome feeding chair which slides along tracks and comes with arm rests, head rest and footstool. Yes, footstool. Think BA economy class seating in your own home. Fine for flights to the USA; really not fine slap bang in the middle of your teeny-tiny box room.

Now, I'm no advocate of going all grown-up luxe when decorating your nursery. However, I do think there's a fine balance between naff nurseries with yellow ducks/Barbie bridal carriages/primary-coloured wall friezes and some short-cut alternatives that offer up a little charm and individuality. The latter will hopefully be ideas to prevent you (and me) from becoming 'Seriously Suspect' on the home interior front, leaving only the crime of the closed-toe Birkenstocks to contend with.

- Four walls: Dulux, lead-free off-white. Too simple to try to argue with.

- Paint a couple of white shelves with the remaining Dulux dribbles and use them to put up a collection of wooden toys from Mulberry Bush (www.mulberrybush.co.uk), novel toys (think Deco printed paper animals by Mibo – www.mibo.co.uk – not stuffed Pooh Bears) and any vintage children's bits you can get your hands on. A good time to ask your mum for any old books/toys/shoes that once belonged to you, or cruise www.toyday.co.uk and www.jesters.com for mock-antique goodies.

- Instead of a wall frieze, nail a few hooks below your shelf and hang up a piece of vintage children's clothing. I hung my old christening dress in my daughter's nursery, and she still has it in her room today (right next to her posters of Alvin and the Chipmunks and Bratz). If your parents were atheist or that beloved christening dress has been long binned along with your school reports, try www.antiquelinen.com or www.vintagekit.com for a mini-frock that would easily pass as your own.

- If whitewashed walls remind you of the NHS, you could consider hanging a watercolour of your baby's

name, some painted letters spelling it out (try
www.thewoodenletterscompany.com or
www.poshgraffiti.com), a vintage print of a classic
children's story (Babar, Peter Rabbit, Tintin) or a pretty
nostalgic print (I love the Lila Freedom picture at
www.belleandboo.com). Cue the perfect opportunity
to delegate creative responsibility to godparents or
grandparents and slip them the details of a watercolour
artist (email Judith at jadudart@sky.com).

- When you're buying a cot, make your life easier and
  opt for a cot-bed. It will save you forking out another few
  hundred quid as soon as your baby is walking and ready
  for a 'big bed'. Check out www.mothercare.com and
  www.kiddicare.com for a huge range of styles at
  competitive prices.

- Unless you've got a nursery the size of a palace, you will
  want to be clever with space, not to mention cash. Instead
  of buying a changing station, opt for a simple chest of
  drawers and put a changing mat on top. The White
  Company (www.thewhitecompany.com) sell white
  changing mats with changeable white towelling covers that
  beat yellow ducks hands down on the style front.

- If you want to design something totally different, even
  bypassing the vintage Babar vibe, then why not get a
  mural painted on one wall instead? Now, I'm not talking
  Disney's Sleeping Beauty, oh no, no, no, I'm talking
  modern wall graphics, such as spins on the Russian doll or
  even butterflies in neon colours. Super Nice is your place
  (www.supernice.co.uk). You may well love this company
  so much you bypass the red balloons for the box-room
  nursery and choose a modernist limited edition wall
  graphic for your staircase instead.

Trust me when I tell you that your baby will grow up faster than Usain Bolt running the 100m, and they will do to your beautiful nursery what children do best. Trash it, stick up Arsenal/Cinderella/Girls Aloud posters and use the back of the door for glow-in-the-dark stickers. Suddenly those Birkies will seem the least of your problems. It's a good idea to start off on the right foot and then discard all sense of style and charm once you have no choice.

Preparing your home for sale

by **Sarah Beeny**, property guru and the last word on practical yet fabulous interior design

Want to sell your house fast and for a higher value? Well, apart from first logging on to my site (www.tepilo.com), the rest is relatively easy. You need to ensure it stands out from the rest.

How your house is presented, inside and out, is crucial to influencing buyers. Don't be fooled into thinking that an amateur lick of paint here and there and a quick shove of your clutter under the bed will cut it; in this market, it won't! I'm not saying you need a diploma in interior design or a huge pot of cash to achieve this; you just need to be clever with space and detailing and you'll stay a step ahead. A few helpful hints you might want to consider:

> Remember that doing any home improvement job badly and then having to get someone else to sort it out is expensive and time-consuming. However handy you think you are with a Black & Decker, make sure you do the job properly in the first place and you'll save yourself masses of unwanted DIY hassle.

2 Before you plunge yourself into re-painting your bedroom, replacing that broken toilet seat and fluffing the pillows on your favourite armchair, think carefully about the state of your roof. If your roof is showing signs of age (a common problem in properties that are eighty-plus years old), mortgage surveyors will flag it up, potentially holding up a promising sale. Re-roofing is a good way of boosting a good price, especially if buyers are nervous.

3 Remember that you never get a second chance to make that first impression, so think about the initial snapshot buyers will see when arriving at the house. An air of TLC is definitely a plus. Trim that hedge, do some simple, low-maintenance planting, paint the front door and polish the letterbox. All this will soften the look of a home and make it more attractive.

4 Stained carpets are a big no-no and can put people off straight away. Would you relish the thought of a grubby carpet when visualising your dream home? Thought not. Any carpets that are long past their sell-by date and have seen the worst of the spilled Merlot should be replaced or cleaned by a professional cleaning company.

5 If your house is crying out for a lick of paint or re-paper, opt for neutral shades. OTT colours and wallpaper covering all four walls will just make buyers wince. Contrary to the popular myth, you could consider dark shades for smaller rooms: dens, toilets and dining rooms can look striking in dark hues. Websites such as www.seemydesign.com offer interactive room planners where you can upload pictures of your room and play around with colours. The best way to avoid 'Oh no, what have we done?' paint-job mistakes.

6 A well-lit home will add to its value, so why not fit dimmer switches? It's the cheap, easy and effective way to create an enticing mood. Trust me, you don't notice good lighting, but bad lighting screams out at you.

7 Your bathroom mantra in the lead-up to selling should be 'simple luxury'. Buyers generally favour something sleek and minimal, so if you're redecorating, think natural tones and natural materials such as wood, stone, slate and marble. No time or cash to do an overall? Ridding those bulging cupboards of out-of-date bubble bath and editing those excess towels piled high in the corner is a good start.

8 Ignore all that designer nonsense about 'ergonomic work triangles' (do we seriously need to be told exactly how many metres to leave between the fridge, hob and sink? I mean, come on!). Clever kitchen storage solutions are a much bigger plus when showing off your home for sale. You could consider investing in a butcher's trolley for excess appliances or installing an over-the-sink wooden drainer, so crockery, pots and pans can drip-dry out of sight.

Now go forth and keep your fingers crossed for the asking price!

Moving house without having a nervous breakdown

I have a nervous breakdown when packing for a long weekend of family 'glamping' (and still forget the loo roll and tin foil), so I dread to think what I'll be like when I eventually move house again. Valium? Morphine? Divorce proceedings? This may well mean we stay put in our snug Victorian semi until I'm admitted to a care home with my favourite patchwork quilt. As much as I love the idea of renovating a new home, and still enjoy the occasional escape into property porn, the cost and effort of actually doing it puts me off until the next year. Every year. Nine years in total, so far.

Life's too short not to drink a double vodka at midday on move day.

While the rest of my friends are upscaling to bigger and better things to contain growing families, downscaling to pay school fees and beat the recession or escaping it all and retreating to thatched cottages on the Norfolk coast to make jam, I've so far resisted the move-mania by reorganising my chintzy teacups and saucers and adding a lick of paint to the staircase. But just in case I win the lottery and am forced to accept defeat, I thought I'd better dig around for some shortcuts to stress-free moving.

Selling without Sudafed

My dear friend Cat is the queen of house-selling. The handful of times she's sold up, she's managed to make her family home clutter-free, oozing with *Elle Decor* charm and filled with the aroma of baking carrot cake and freshly cut sweet peas in time for viewings. It never fails to prompt a frenzied bidding process and, in no time, a lucrative offer on the table. I can't even make carrot cake, let alone do it at 7.30 a.m. with children running around like banshees prior to the 9 a.m. viewing slot.

She swears by a few shortcuts:

- If you don't have time to do a massive declutter, make sure the house has an illusion of order instead. Get rid of papers, coats slung over banisters, clothes hanging on wardrobe doors and old plants.

- Hide away knick-knacks and souvenirs that you might love but will look like clutter to everybody else.

- Give the house a good clean, or even hire a cleaner just before viewings. I love the sound of www.maid2clean.co.uk and www.timeforyou.co.uk. Plump up those cushions and lay your most stylish coffee-table books out to view.

- Get rid of odours and burn that scented candle you've saved for special occasions.

- Buy fresh flowers for every room.

- Hide children and animals.

- A Betty Crocker muffin mix in the oven, Ocado-delivered cupcakes displayed on a pretty plate in the kitchen – both great for creating the image of domestic goddess extraordinaire.

All being well, this illusion of calm homestead bliss will work its magic and you'll be on your way to selling up in no time (it's amazing what banana bread and throwing your Crete holiday knick-knacks under the bed can do for a place). Don't put the Valium on hold just yet though; as I mentioned at the beginning of the chapter, completing the sale and buying-up is when you seriously start to look emaciated. However, should you still be a) in one piece and b) talking to your partner/children/house-sharing companion/dog enough to move with them, then here are a few failsafe ideas for surviving the move.

Moving without morphine

Rivalling Cat as the queen of house selling my girlfriend Lesley is vying for the title 'Queen of Moving House'. She's done it with style and grace several times in recent years and still hasn't resorted to dying away the grey hairs or seeking therapy for anger management. Her tips:

Before the move

1. Declutter, and be really ruthless. Chuck, chuck, chuck, give to charity or sell on eBay or at boot sales. It will save you so much time packing items you won't really want or need in the new place.

2. If you need to use a storage facility while you're doing up your new place, consider a company outside the city. By going out of town, you can save up to 70 per cent of the storage price. We like the sound of this when saving for that new Aga.

3. If at all possible, budget for professional movers to pack and ship bulky items. It will ensure furniture and electrical goods are up and running when you arrive. Look into www.bishopsmove.com and www.uk-removal.co.uk. Or try Anyvan (www.anyvan.com) which is a delivery auction website that matches vans with customers going in the same direction, saving you a lot of money.

4. Get boxes dropped off a week before and make sure you order a ton of bubble wrap, paper and tape too. Label or colour-code boxes for each room, and you could even prioritise them with numbers to remind yourself which boxes need unpacking immediately and which can wait. It's also a great idea to set aside boxes with fragile goods and stipulate where and how you want these moved on the day.

Pre-arrange for these boxes to be collected 3–5 days after the move – the last thing you want is to be tripping over empty boxes a week later, and they can't always be collected on demand.

5 Buy some transparent coloured boxes from Really Useful Products (www.reallyusefulproducts.com). You will probably need:

- one for moving essentials (loo roll, dustbin bags, tape measure, kettle, mobile charger, parking permits, TV remote controls, cash for tipping movers, PG tips, Digestives, bottle of vodka . . .).

- one for leaving at your old house (keys, appliance instructions, alarm codes, window lock keys, takeaway menus).

- one for key paperwork and valuables (bank/mortgage details, solicitor's papers, jewellery).

6 Arrange for an electrician or handyperson to take down all light fixtures you are taking with you and replace them with basic pendants or caps, so there are no live wires. Look no further than www.020handyman.com.

7 Buy some cheap knives or some retractable extractor blades to fit in your back pocket (www.stanleytools.co.uk). If you only have one, you'll lose it and only blame your nearest and dearest.

8 Invest in a bottle of your movers' drink of choice. They'll look after you better with the incentive of a bottle of Grey Goose at the end of the job.

On the day

- Ask for mattresses and light-coloured upholstery to be bagged or covered in plastic wraps (hand-print on your cream armchair, anyone? Thought not).

- Focus on getting one room ready and liveable before you start getting busy with the whole house. This will act as a perfect retreat when the rest is in chaos.

- Settle kids and animals first, or rope in grandparents or friends to provide sleepovers so you can get stuck into unpacking, uninterrupted.

I shall refer to this handy hit list when my time comes. Until then, let me reorganise some floral teapots in the kitchen and chronologically file my back issues of *Vogue* beside my coffee table. Easier, cheaper, much less chance of incurring divorce proceedings and should keep me satisfied for another year. At least.

Heading to the sticks without alienating yourself and resorting to a dodgy Pac-a-mac

by **Pearl Lowe**, designer, resistant rock chick and very probably the most glamorous gal in the sticks

If you'd told me ten years ago that I'd be living in rural Somerset, swapping YSL wedges for Hunter wellies and wild rock 'n' roll parties for a good bedtime novel and 10 p.m. lights-out, I'd have told you to take a hike (straight over those Somerset hills). However, to the surprise of all our cool

London friends, we're now so ensconced in country life that fetching kindling for the fire seems as normal as popping to Oddbins for a few bottles of wine. Moving to the sticks has led to both a professional and personal metamorphosis. I'm a totally different person from the one I left behind in Primrose Hill.

I must confess, though, while reigniting my zest for living, it's also very hard work adjusting and making life in the country work for the whole family. Don't be seduced by the romance of roaring fires and thatched roofs; it can be cold, lonely and a real test on emotional and financial resources. Not to mention posing some serious style challenges for any semi-cool city-chick who values popping to Selfridges on a whim or browsing in Top Shop on a Saturday afternoon.

A few of my top tips to making sure you end up happy in those Hunters (and not slinging them in the mud and running back to the Big Smog with your tail between your legs):

- If you're a social person, think very carefully about what part of the countryside you move to. Choosing an idyllic isolated spot on a whim can be a recipe for disaster, and the loneliness and lack of social life can drive people back to a city. Equally, opting for a location on the commuter belt might feel cosmopolitan at weekends, but by Sunday night many of those people will have jumped into their four-by-fours and be heading back to London. This was the problem with our first country pad in Hampshire. Fabulous fun at weekends; a desolate void when our friends went back to their main bases during the week. Our new home in Somerset ticks all the boxes. We have a community of like-minded people, most of whom live here all the time, easy access to great creative galleries and shops and proximity to places like Glastonbury and Bath.

Just remember, this is a huge decision, so don't be hasty and prioritise an intensive recce of the area first. Renting almost ruined us financially. I wish instead we'd spent a few weeks in a local hotel or with friends, sussing out areas. This way, you can get the low-down on local schools, shops, restaurants, pubs and community life.

- Great country houses are *really* hard to come by. More often than not, locals with an 'in' nab the best properties before they hit the market. You really need to invest in a property finder to find you something special. Pricey, but worth it to find a gem.

- Once you find your dream pad, succumb to vintage interior decor. Rock 'n' roll goth looks totally out of place in a thatched cottage. I have become totally obsessed with antique quilts and Venetian mirrors.

- I used to think I'd never tap into my inner welly-wearer, but I honestly couldn't live without my Hunters here. The trick is not to turn into a beige-cord-wearing Sloane (however much my kids beg me to 'blend in'!) and team those boots with vintage dresses and thick tights and throw a Burberry Mac on top. There's no reason you can't maintain an element of your own unique style. Sadly, heels and rural living never mix (they always get stuck in the floorboards or mud), so save those Manolos for rare nights out in the city. It's actually a great excuse to start a huge collection of ballet pumps! I wear mine to death and wouldn't survive here without them. Internet shopping in general is a godsend. You'll start off imagining you'll grow, source or buy everything locally, but this is expensive and bloody hard work. Lovefilm, Amazon, Ocado and www.my-wardrobe.com are essential quick-fix, country-girl sites.

- To get that shopping fix without resorting to a click of your mouse, explore local vintage fairs and boutiques. Poot is a firm favourite of mine in Frome and I've actually sourced better clothes there than I'd ever find in the maze of Harvey Nics. I also love the Bath vintage fair for home decor and fashion fixes.

- I'm crap at attending 99 per cent of the London parties and launches I'm invited to, but I do make the effort to go and see friends whenever I can. Having my daughter Daisy in London is a good incentive; she nags me to see her on the catwalk at London Fashion Week, so this is the time to make an extra effort. What I love most of all is inviting old friends here for a good party. Light a fire, cook tons of food, fill the fridge with wine, lay on some extra wellies, and they're all happy to escape the rat race.

If you nail a good country community, there's no reason you can't make it work for you. Just remember to pack those thick jumpers and Wellington boots. Oh, and that Burberry Mac, just for good measure.

CHAPTER FOUR

MICHELIN-STARRED CHEF

Be a domestic goddess when really you only 'cook' instant Smash and Pot Noodles

I've always *tried* to embrace my inner Nigella. The truth is, I'm usually far too lazy or in too much of a hurry to get anywhere close. At university I lived off Alpen for three years straight. As a treat, I'd add a chopped Granny Smith and some dried apricots. A can of Diet Coke and slice of strong cheddar would qualify as a major mid-week treat. My shopping basket was incredibly dull. If friends came over for supper, they were asked to bring semi-skimmed milk and their own bowl. Once I moved back to London and began my job in the heady world of fashion magazines, my Alpen-only diet was replaced by coffee and sandwiches, with a Friday Crunchie and a hungover Sunday supplement of bagels with cream cheese and Marmite. Weekend dinner guests were asked to bring wine and eat before they arrived.

As a mum of three who now spends most of her day cooking endless rounds of meals for grumpy, post-school under-tens ('I'm staaaaarrrvinng, what's for breakfast/elevenses/lunch/tea/supper/bedtime snack?') and hosts the occasional supper party on a Saturday night or Sunday lunch for friends, my careless, not-so-fussed, life's-too-short-to-slave-over-a-hot-stove attitude has been seriously challenged. I've had to expand slightly on the Alpen/coffee/bagel repertoire. Sadly, none of my children like any kind of muesli ('What are all these *bits*?') and Mr S gets rather narked if I pour him a mug of instant granules when it's my turn to cook. I have reluctantly been pushed into a culinary corner.

Mastering a few meals you can cook well and which look semi-impressive on the plate is the crucial trick of any kitchen bluffer. Here are some I've mastered over the years and use often enough to buy Parma ham in bulk. Always heat the oven to 200°C. Why the appliance offers a choice on this, I don't know . . .

Pesto chicken, sweet potato mash and sugar snaps

Roast some pine nuts in the oven, but take them out before they go very dark brown or they'll taste really bitter. Dollop a tablespoon of pesto on top of chicken breasts and then spread it like butter on toast. Heap some nice strong cheddar on top and load up with the roasted pine nuts. Put in the oven for around twenty-five minutes. Peel and chop a few sweet potatoes and carrots, boil until nice and soft and mash up with butter, salt and pepper. Steam a bag of sugar snap peas or mangetout, then sprinkle with sesame seeds and soy sauce. A total no-brainer.

Pizza

Brush a pitta bread with olive oil. Lay some mozzarella, grated cheddar, cherry tomatoes, olives, sweetcorn and Parma ham, pepperoni strips or leftover cooked chicken over the top. Season to taste. Put it in the oven until it's crisp at the rim (about ten minutes) and then garnish with any fresh herbs you have lying around (have I really reached an age where I just happen to have fresh herbs lying around?). Serve with a green salad.

Parma cod with salad

Wrap some cod loins in a few strips of Parma ham. Put them in the oven for about twenty minutes. Slice a few large plum tomatoes, a mozzarella and an avocado. Dress with olive oil and balsamic and a handful of chopped basil. Serve with good bread warmed up in the oven and a glass of wine.

Lamb with feta, couscous and watermelon and cucumber salad

Flash-fry some lean lamb steaks and the moment they're cooked to your taste (pink and bloody for me, please) sprinkle with feta and chopped rosemary. Steam some couscous, add raisins and chopped dried apricots, and mix together in a haphazard fashion with a glug of olive oil. Sprinkle with fresh, chopped coriander and chopped almonds. Roughly chop a watermelon and some cucumber and add a similar glug of olive oil. Serve together and puff your chest out with pride.

Versatile burgers with sundried tomatoes and fries

Use your hands to mix up a packet of minced beef, a finely chopped onion, a teaspoon of Dijon mustard, a heaped teaspoon of coriander seeds, a pinch of cinnamon, two eggs and a large handful of breadcrumbs (make your life easy, buy Paxo). Season with salt and pepper. You now have two choices: 1) make the mince-mix into burgers, cook for around 20 minutes and serve in a bun with cheese, mayo, ketchup, mustard, fried onions and some sundried tomatoes, with a green salad and oven fries on the side; or 2) make the mince-mix into small balls, cook for around 10 minutes and add to already heated Ragú pasta sauce and cooked wholemeal spaghetti.

Nutty salad and cold meats

Roast a bag of pine nuts in a splash of olive oil until they're toasted. Slice an avocado while they're browning. Add to a bag of chopped herb salad and dress with olive oil and balsamic vinegar. Serve with a plate of cold meats and some good strong cheese. Merlot obligatory too.

Don't take my recipes as gospel, but use them as a guide. I'd advise any novice chef to avoid becoming a slave to recipes per se. I always find, when I'm trying to conjure up a complex Nigella number, that I'm so busy following the ounces and grams and working out how the hell to sieve flour while whisking the egg that I feel the stress levels rising and end up a frazzled grump, retreating straight back to the comfort of toasted bagels in front of a DVD. Instead, play around with recipes and experiment a bit. If you've got eggs in the fridge, scramble them up with some stray parmesan, ham and pepper and serve on toast. If you've had a crazy week with no time to click onto the Ocado website, mix up a tin of tuna, a tin of sweetcorn and some mayonnaise and stir into pasta. Who hasn't got these essentials lying around somewhere in the back of the food cupboard?

My newly married friend Carla swears that cooking should always be teamwork to prevent it becoming a chore. She failed Home Ec at school and pre-wedding dined out after work on dim sum and Martinis almost every night of the week. She added 'shared cooking' as part of the informal pre-nup and has morphed into the new Tana Ramsay. Together, this surprising new uber-chef couple have conquered Ibizincan tomato gazpacho, chorizo-infused lasagne and crème brûlée, and have vowed to experiment with pigeon pie next week-end. Thankfully, they are also embracing their expanding waistbands with pride.

Some of my best cheats' meals have been inspired by dishes I've eaten at friends' homes or in restaurants. I love the teriyaki chicken squares they serve at Wagamama, and often improvise a similar recipe by stir-frying chicken chunks and adding a slather of honey, teriyaki and soy sauce. It will never taste *quite* as good as the chef at Wag's, but I'm game to give it a go. It's easy and tasty, and that's just the way I like it.

We all have weeks when we don't seem to leave the office before all the lights are turned off and can't even be bothered to take our mascara off before we hit the sack. Marinade, roast and toss seem about as likely as winning the lottery jackpot. In your dreams. This is where girl-about-town, failsafe foodie shortcuts come into the fore. Although they won't save you cash, they will save you time and effort. My favourites are as follows:

- Rotisserie chicken. Cooked, piping hot and ready to be accompanied by a handful of new potatoes and some steamed broccoli. The other half will be convinced you came home from work early and have been basting the chicken ever since.

- Couscous selections. Waitrose, Tesco, M&S, Sainsbury's – you name it, they'll provide it. A variety of cold couscous salads that, once decanted into large Moroccan-style bowls and served with grilled salmon steaks, will give you top marks from none-the-wiser, mid-week supper guests.

- Deli divine. Make a small diversion to your local deli to scoop up an array of fresh salads, cold meats and ready-made pastas. Straight out of a *Vogue* food shoot, and without even rolling up your sleeves. Some firm favourites include Forman and Field (www.formanandfield.com), The Natural Kitchen (www.thenaturalkitchen.com) and Carluccio's (www.carluccios.com).

- Door-to-door delivery. If your favourite deli doesn't deliver and money is no object, log onto Chef on Board (www.chefonboard.com) or Ottolenghi (www.ottolenghi.co.uk) and take your pick of to-die-for 'ready-meals'. Expensive food with buckets of style that, once decanted, will look and taste like you have just completed a year-long course in cuisine. Bloody love the idea of that.

If, even when you don a pinny, chuck a few strips of Parma ham around and add a deli salad, you still seem to serve up a meal that's just average, do not fear – appearances can add a few Michelin stars in an instant. My friend Alice swears that pretty crockery and fresh flowers on the table always make her 'just OK' pasta Bolognese that little bit more special, and our mutual friend Carla agrees. She'll garnish her simply roasted sea bass with fresh parsley and lemon and serve with a bag of rocket salad and olive oil, all of which make the meal look far more River Café than bung-in-the-oven-blind-folded-after-a-hideous-day-at-work. Dim the lights, and you could easily feel you'd popped to Sophie Dahl's for supper.

> **Life's too short to sweat an onion. Come to think of it, soaking chickpeas is up there too . . .**

I do love the illusion of being a domestic goddess. Somehow, serving up a hot supper for friends and family makes me feel I'm slightly more of a culinary whizzette than I really am. Tea lights – check. Sweet peas on the table – check. Pretty pink glasses full of cold white wine – check. Chicken roasting in the oven – check. Lovely, happy family vibe expected of a thirty-something mum of three – check. Good.

Basic nutritional know-how without resorting to mung beans

by **Jane Clarke**, acclaimed nutritionist, author and the final word on accessible healthy eating

Even if your typical day is a crazy whirl of dash-for-it buses, work deadlines and young children, the one nutritional tool that will help you feel better is hydration. Keeping hydrated influences your mood, skin and energy levels, so it doesn't take a genius to work out that slugging back the caffeine and sugar-packed fizzy drinks all day will leave you feeling shocking. Carry a bottle of mineral water in your handbag, pour a jug full of tap water to keep at your desk or make a flask of chamomile/peppermint/fennel tea to sip on the commute to work. So many women are caffeine-sensitive; a quick succession of espressos may well give you an immediate jolt of energy, but in the long term it leaves many of us feeling destabilised. I'm not saying eliminate caffeine altogether (believe me, my morning cup of English breakfast tea is sacrosanct), but try switching your second or third cup of dehydrating coffee for rehydrating herbal tea instead. You could always carry fresh mint leaves in a small sealed bag in your clutch – add hot water and you're away.

Many of us have the best intentions of starting the day with fruit, but wake up to nothing more exciting than a drop of milk and almost-empty box of Crunchy Nut cornflakes instead. If you keep frozen berries in your freezer, you'll never be caught short and you can add them to porridge oats, yoghurt or any chopped nuts and dried fruit you have hanging around in the back of your cupboard. If you've time on a Sunday night, peel and core a bag of apples, chuck them in a pot, cover with boiling water, place the lid on and simmer for ten minutes. *Voilá*, you'll have a stash of stewed apple to last you the week. Delicious accompanied with those frozen berries or heated up in the microwave and finished off with a pot of Greek yoghurt, and a brilliant balance of calcium, fat and protein.

Do you manage top nutritional marks for a healthy breakfast, but find it's that post-third-glass-of-wine, rushed supper that's your downfall? Welcome to the club. An easy shortcut? Don't punish yourself about your wind-down glass of wine, but attempt to savour it *with* the meal as opposed to before it – this way, you won't get the drastic sugar imbalance that makes us overeat and feel rough the next morning. Accompany that well-deserved glass of red with a quick-fix supper of easy-to-heat soup and a chunk of dark rye, seeded bread. If you've time, cook any vegetables you have lying around in veggie stock and then blitz with a hand-held blender (the best investment you'll ever make, and it means you'll never have to look at a scary, family-size blender again). If you've no time to make your own, soups are so easy to buy – just avoid chilled soups, which are often high in salt and fat, and bulk-buy tinned ones instead. You can't beat a tin of Heinz tomato soup, and I'm a fan of non-creamy lentil and Tuscan bean too. Keep sliced rye or wholemeal bread in small bags in the freezer and you'll be less likely to dash into the supermarket for a last-minute ready-meal or speed-dial that pizza. Finish off with a few cubes of 80 per cent chocolate and a long bath.

Easy-peasy supper skills when you've got a few good friends popping by for Friday night eats

1 Starters are so last season. Serve vegetable crisps, posh nuts, olives and a hummus dip instead.

2 Any time in the twenty-four-hour lead-up, boil some sweet and new potatoes. Let them cool, dollop with Hellmann's mayo and some chopped chives, and you've got a perfect potato salad that can be kept in the fridge until supper.

3 Pretty napkins, coloured glasses and a scented candle are all a table needs to look inviting. Just remember, don't go OTT; it's off-putting to see napkins arranged like origami fans in glasses or ribbon woven through the centre of a table strewn with petals. They both scream 'get a life'!

4   When friends arrive, mix together some soy sauce (a few glugs), an equal quantity of teriyaki sauce, a few tablespoons of runny honey, a handful of sesame seeds and a handful of roughly chopped fresh coriander. Pour over some salmon steaks and heat until tender and pink in the middle. I'd say fifteen minutes should do it.

5   While sipping a glass of white, toss a ready-prepared bag of rocket, sliced soft pears, parmesan shavings and walnuts with olive oil and balsamic vinegar.

6   I'd suggest a Patisserie Valerie tart for dessert, but you can do a shortcut cheap-as-chips pud while also showing a little culinary pizzazz with my abridged Jamie Oliver Banoffee Pie. Log on to Tesco/Sainsbury's/Ocado and order the following (or pop into your local M&S on your way home from work): 1 x ready-made pastry base; 1 x squeezy toffee sauce; 1 x tub of extra-thick double cream; 1 x pack of honey-roasted nuts; five ripe bananas. Layer the sauce, cream and bananas (chopped) inside the pastry case and sprinkle the nuts on top. It looks like a work of art and you don't even need to know the difference between pastry and pasties to make it.

7   Keep the wine flowing. A manageable hangover the next day is a good sign.

Sussing modern dinner-party etiquette when you hate fan-display napkins

I love supper parties. I expect this shows my age. For years, I'd favour propping myself up in a pub or bar or a basement flat, smoking a Marlboro Light and drinking out of a Becks bottle. Dry-roasted peanuts and Japanese rice crackers made a great quick-fix supper and didn't interfere too much with the main aim – to get nicely drunk and talk passionately about inane rubbish until the wee hours. Now, however, I follow my stomach far more than I'd like to admit and seek a nice home-cooked meal and a good bottle of red instead. Propping up a bar in three-inch stilettos hurts my feet and by midnight I'm

Life's too short not to surrender to Pringles and pudding, more booze than the government-recommended units and a boogie to naff tuuuuunes with friends you love. Sometimes, anyway.

counting down the hours until my children run into my bedroom looking for 'fun'. The latest this has ever occurred was 8.13 a.m., and this was only because they all had chicken pox and were dosed up on Calpol to keep their fevers down. It hasn't happened since, and that was four years ago.

Many of my thirty-something, single-girl friends confess to becoming dinner-party divas too. Even the fact that they're sometimes excluded from cliquey 'couples only' affairs hasn't seemed to put them off. Fabulous singleton Zoe professes to favouring fish pie and pink wine around a kitchen table to Martinis at Dean Street Townhouse, even if their waiters are far hotter than any of the hosts in her Smythson address book. My gang of girlies and I call this general consensus the 'private-members backlash'. What we mean by this is that, as successful girls-about-town, we're sick of paying over the odds for a watered-down Mojito and having to join a large waiting list of other medya moguls just to get a good table at the new hot-to-trot spot in the city. All we really want is to get tipsy and catch up over tinned olives and a shop-bought pasta sauce. Not that difficult really.

So, if we're in agreement that what we *really* want is warm garlic bread and a G&T starter, as opposed to poncy rosemary nuts and a £12 glass of house Champagne, why are so many of us driven potty when friends arrive an hour late or fail to bring a bottle of plonk? And don't get me started on the failure to say post-dinner thanks . . . Either I need to chill out or I should ask myself and my gang of trusty gal pals, 'What is the essential know-how to successful supper-party etiquette?'

- Just turn up on time and, if you're hosting, be ready when your friends arrive. I actually have the opposite problem and am so eager to be on time I have to force myself not to be early. This can be even ruder; I have been known to turn up while the host is still in the bath and the food still on its way in the Tesco delivery van. Very bad form. Just get it right.

- Are we old-fashioned to expect guests to turn up with a bottle of plonk or box of chocs? Correct us if we're wrong, but if your host is making the effort to tidy up the kitchen, toss a few rocket leaves with walnut oil and plate the spag bol, surely you can nip to the off-licence and pick up a bottle of Sauv Blanc en route? Too busy? Then click on Majestic (www.majestic.co.uk) or Naked Wines (www.nakedwines.com) and ask them to deliver to your desk. I'm not talking vintage Bollinger or Belgian truffles here; just a £5.99 bottle of something cold.

- I always think it's nice to turn up somewhere and find the host still in food-prep mode. It's far more relaxing than finding a house flood-lit, scattered with candles and rose petals, and your best friend teetering around in fishnets and a cocktail dress waiting ominously at the door for you to arrive. Love the idea of candles, not so sure about the OTT dress code and feeling you'll be served ten courses and be expected to decant a lobster tail. Serve olives and nibbles, pour the wine and let guests chat while you chop an obligatory stem of basil. Far more relaxing.

- My girlies and I are torn as to whether you should tell friends where to sit or wave your hand and ask them to 'sit anywhere'. I always do the latter because I hate too much formality, but I suppose if you want to direct buzzy conversation and seat interesting friends with people you know they'll have a good rapport with, then do the former.

- What is it with fussy eaters these days? If you don't like what you're served, eat what you can and don't make a bloody song and dance about it. Obviously call ahead if you're vegetarian or have a serious allergy to red peppers, but for goodness' sake play down all this wheat intolerance/dairy-wary business and push it around your plate if you have to. Enough said.

- Zoe stresses that guests shouldn't get so drunk they make a fool of themselves. She probably says this because at her last raucous supper soirée I danced on the coffee table with her brother. And then demanded tequila. And then spilt it on her new carpet. Not a great look.

- Always leave before the hosts have washed up and gone to bed and follow up with a thanks. This doesn't have to be a full bouquet of lilies, but a text or card is a nice touch.

The bottom line on booze

by **Hannah Lanfear**, booze journo, mixologist at GloGlo's, the Great Eastern Dining Room, and genius cocktail-mixer

Martini advice

Making the perfect Martini is a tricky business that even seasoned professionals sometimes stumble at. The trick is to keep all your utensils (mixing glass, stirring spoon, cocktail glasses and strainer) in the freezer for at least half an hour prior to beginning.

Your vermouth must be fresh (not opened for longer than a week) and refrigerated; think of it like a wine. Likewise, keep your olives in the fridge so they don't warm up your Martini. Your gin (or vodka, if you must) should be ambient – neither cold nor warm. All of these items being present and correct, you are ready to begin.

Before plunging in with a Dry Martini (seven parts gin to one part vermouth), first try this Martini. At 5:1, it's altogether more approachable, and from this ratio you can decide whether you prefer wetter or drier. Add 50ml of your preferred gin (Tanqueray is our choice for a more pungent Martini, or Plymouth for a smoother sup) and 20ml of vermouth (Noilly Prat has a more robust flavour; Martini Extra has a milder style) to your frozen mixing glass. Now fill your mixing glass to the brim with fresh, very cold ice. Take your chilled spoon from the freezer and stir. You are looking to stir to a point where the Martini is almost viscous and syrupy, as the alcohol is so cold, yet you want to remove some of the burn of the gin with the dilution from the ice. The time this takes may differ, but try not to over-dilute. You can always pop a Martini back over ice if it's too strong.

Once the Martini is properly diluted, pour into the frozen glasses. We like to put ours back in the freezer for up to fifteen minutes to get the ultimate Martini, but it's likely you're impatient to taste the fruits of your labour, so skip this step if you like.

When it comes to garnish, you can choose between olives, cocktail onions (in which case your Martini is now a Gibson), or a citrus twist. Olives should be kept chilled before being added to the Martini. One should always use an odd number and pitted queen green olives kept in brine rather than oil are best. For a Dirty Martini, you should add a spoonful of the brine to the mixing glass as you add the gin, which gives the Martini a wonderful, lightly salty seasoning.

If you like a twist, you could choose between lemon, orange or grapefruit. Grapefruit is wonderful with many gins and orange matches Beefeater especially well, but lemon is, of course, more traditional. Always wash and rub-dry the fruit before use to remove any wax (if you can find organic, unwaxed fruit, all the better). Now cut away a strip of the skin, taking care to get none of the flesh. Pinch the strip of peel over the glass to expel the oils in a spray. The lovely smell of the citrus oil will linger around the Martini. Discard the skin; its role is complete.

Finally, while you're enjoying your perfect creation, ponder these words of Dorothy Parker: 'I like to have a Martini. Two at the very most. After three, I'm under the table. After four, I'm under my host.'

Margaritas

Unrivalled on a hot summer's day, the Margarita is one of America's finest exports. For an excellent Margarita, the key is balance, so for this you will need to carefully measure your ingredients.

Choose the very best tequila you can afford. Look for bottles marked '100 per cent agave' as a mark of quality. Aged tequilas are not necessarily better than blanco; in fact, often the best expression of the agave plant comes from unaged (blanco) tequilas.

Before you begin, you should decide whether you like your Margs straight up or on the rocks. This will dictate to you the glassware you want to use. Blended Margaritas are deeply unsophisticated and all that ice drowns the delicate balance of the drink, so put that thought right out your mind this minute!

Your next move is to squeeze some fresh lime juice. Limes with a smooth skin will usually be juicier, so pick carefully. Roll them on a work surface with pressure from the heel of your hand to break up the flesh cells and increase the yield of juice. One lime will make between one and two Margaritas.

Ensure your glasses are kept in the freezer for at least thirty minutes prior to making. If you like salt on the rim, prepare a saucer of salt. You can use an artisan salt, such as the pink Fleur de Sel, if you want to spoil yourself, but make sure it is of a fine consistency or it won't stick to the glass. Press the outside of the frozen glass into the saucer and then wipe away the excess with a clean, dry cloth or paper towel. You can salt just half the rim if you prefer, so you can choose between salted and unsalted sips, but be sure to get none on the inside of the glass, as the cocktail will be spoilt if any falls in.

Exact measurements are key here: pour 40ml of tequila, 20ml of Cointreau (or a quality triple sec) and 20ml of freshly squeezed lime juice into a cocktail shaker with some ice. Firmly seal the shaker and shake it up, HARD! You want to be jostling the ice cubes so they are breaking up, so give it all the energy you can muster. Ten seconds should suffice. Now carefully strain into your cocktail glasses, taking care not to wash off the salt rim, and garnish with a lime wedge. All you need now is a patch of sunshine and a deckchair.

Cool canapés *(stilettos obligatory)*

Ever since I can remember, at least once a year I like to pretend I live a life of canapés and cocktails. I like to reject the idea of scrambled-egg-on-toast suppers and work deadlines running into the evening and act out my fantasy of serving delectable mouthfuls of modern art while wearing very high shoes. This is also known as 'let's pretend I live in a *Vogue* food shoot and wear desirable, fabulous frocks every day of the week'. My girlfriends and I widely appreciate that this makes the humdrum of our real lives more manageable and allows us to fantasise, for an evening at least, that we live a life of smoked salmon blinis and Martinis.

It serves a few great purposes:

1 It gives us an excuse to kick out the boys, put the kids to bed early and have the living room all to ourselves.

2 It allows us to make our haven the epitome of girlie loveliness. Sweet peas in jam jars, Diptyque candles burning, the coffee table showing off a stylish new Mario Testino book (shove all nasty Arsenal annuals under the sofa).

3 It facilitates a foray into ridiculously decadent food fetishes.

4 It means we can get very drunk wearing high heels and not be required to stumble through the streets of London looking for a cab.

LIFE'S TOO SHORT

The rules are simple:

- Invite a bunch of your best girlfriends.

- Insist they dress up for themselves (this includes indulging in clothes men just don't get, like high-waisted jeans and maxi skirts).

- Serve delicious, one-mouthful canapés.

- Make sure all your pretty glasses are out and remain full at all times.

- Gossip insatiably until you begin to slur your words.

Here are my five favourite canapés to offer on such an occasion. They are easier than they sound and can be made blindfolded (well, almost).

Smoked salmon bites

Make some large croutons from ciabatta bread (or use Ritz crackers if you're short on time), slather with Philadelphia, put a slice of smoked salmon on top and sprinkle with fresh dill.

Fig, Roquefort and Parma ham rolls

Cut fresh figs open into a flower shape, add a blob of Roquefort cheese and wrap in a strip of Parma ham.

Pesto and asparagus puffs

Open a packet of ready-rolled puff pastry and cut into squares just the right size to wrap around an asparagus spear. Spread with pesto, add a steamed asparagus stem, wrap into a roll, brush with egg and bake for fifteen minutes.

Good old-fashioned sausages

Mix some runny honey with sesame seeds and spread over cocktail sausages. Cook and serve on sticks.

Dips and raw veg

Mix a packet of powdered French onion soup with a tub of sour cream and leave it in the fridge. Serve as a dip with raw carrot sticks, baby plum tomatoes, celery and baby corn. No one will ever know it's not from M&S.

Now I've got three kids, this canapé crush is harder to indulge, but I try, I really do. I don't think life would be worth living if it was scrambled eggs and oversized 501s forever more.

Cooking a delicious Sunday lunch without burning the roast potatoes

by **Gaby Roslin**, TV and radio presenter and mistress of roasts

Every Sunday I hear the familiar cry: 'Mummy, are we having Sunday lunch this week?' I then let the girls know that lunch will be served and, as it's a Sunday, of course that makes it 'Sunday lunch'. That's not at all what they mean, of course. It's the roast they want.

It's definitely the favourite meal of the week for my girls and I've now got it down to a T. The nine-year-old loves to peel the carrots and the parsnips (hence the packets and packets I have to buy each week, which proceed to clog up the fridge trays). The free-range, organic chicken gets popped in the oven for two hours, sitting magnificently on its base of onions, carrots, celery, garlic and lots of rosemary and black pepper. His bottom is heaving with the amount of onions, garlic and lemons I've unceremoniously shoved inside. The little trick of putting butter on top and plenty of water in the roasting dish always seems to work at keeping it moist; a fear of mine is that it ends up very dry and tastes like my mum's. My fear is justified, as my late mother was, without doubt, one of the worst cooks on the planet. Everything burnt and chicken always got stuck in your throat. Her roast potatoes were like black rocks, containing no soft insides at all. Trust me, they were harder than golf balls and didn't taste as good!

The trick with the potatoes is the 'boil and shake' – they need a good throwing around in the pan with the lid on once they're soft around the outsides. I then roast them in the oven in extra-virgin olive oil. Forget the cookbook mantra that it's no good for roasting. Pah! It does the trick each time for me. Before you bung it all in the oven, add more rosemary. Great, now the fun really begins. Oh yes, the good old Sunday rows about who's going to lay the table and where Grampy-pie (my daughter's name for their grandfather) is going to sit. The nine-year-old wants him next to her, as does the three-year-old, and it's the same conversation each week. But where are the friends going to sit? They never argue about that!

Kettle crisps and olives in bowls, Ugg slippers on my feet and a hasty application of lip gloss before the bell rings and the guests arrive. Rosé wine in glass and mouth full of crisps (well, it is Sunday after all, and the no-carbs thing has to drop for one day at least), the oven is opened and the glorious smell emerges and envelops the kitchen and our home. By the second bowl of ice cream, I remind myself that it's Monday tomorrow and it'll be back to a day of juicing. Bring on more ice cream for now though. You only live once.

Icing a cupcake when you don't own a mixing bowl

The only way to shortcut cupcakes is to get someone else to do it for you. Enter Betty Crocker, domestic saviour for multitasking women. Make a batch of her ready-made-mix chocolate muffins (but use cupcake cases instead of muffin cases, you'll get more cakes for your money). Once cooled, add the Betty Crocker ready-made butter icing. It tastes as close to Hummingbird icing as you're likely to get (failing that, Nutella is a great quick-fix icing cheat). Add your own pink sprinkles/smarties/icing stars/hundreds and thousands. It takes half an hour max and no one will ever know you haven't spent the afternoon knee-deep in flour, eggs and a hand-held whisk.

Getting unstuck from that culinary straitjacket

While sitting in the dentist's waiting room a few months back, I read in a broadsheet that the majority of women cook the same five meals in close rotation. Many even do the same meal on the same day every single week. That'd be a roast dinner on a Sunday, pasta on a Monday, soup and bread on a Tuesday and by Friday it would be the only thing left in the freezer – fish fingers. 'What the hell?' I thought to myself. 'Who are these women? How unbelievably sad and predict-able.' Then, much to my alarm, I began to realise that *I am one of these women*. For as long as I can remember, Mr S and I have tucked into bagels and cream cheese on a Sunday morning; without fail, Monday is healthy detox salad 'n' veggies night; Tuesday is lamb and feta; by Friday it's my bung-in-the-oven roast chicken; Saturday it's eat out or take-away; and then we're back to Sunday. Oh. My. God.

I asked a few of my girlfriends about their Stepford-wife eating habits and, to our group shame, we all confessed to similar boring meal cycles. Even the most adventurous chefs in the gang were floored when I asked them to impart their wisdom on culinary diversity for the greater good of woman-kind. 'Ummmm . . . sesame chicken stir-fry on a Friday, instead of a roast with frozen Yorkshire puds, and supermarket-bought apple crumble for dessert?' The sad thing is, we all felt so guilty about it. A little like the feeling you get when you've finished reading a fabulous food article in a women's glossy or beautifully shot, glamorous girl cookbook. You feel inspired and uplifted, then slowly it seeps into your subconscious and starts to make you feel totally inadequate for repeating the pasta and mascarpone cycle every Wednesday night without fail. You feel like such a food failure.

The truth is, life is just too unbelievably busy to expect anything less than food monotony most of the time. However, it's also true that, in general, we'd like to be slightly more daring when it comes to cooking those rushed mid-week meals. Surely there's a balance? So, instead of beating our-selves up with the wooden kitchen spoons and self-harming with the cheese grater, I suggest a few of the following:

- Set aside one night per week to cook something totally different (more, if you can). This can be as simple as switching the pasta sauce from mascarpone to carbonara and the accompanying veg from broccoli to baby carrots. Look at www.deliciousdays.com for inspiration.

- Walk into the supermarket and stop in one aisle you never properly look at. For me, this is the meats. I'm so busy stuffing the same lamb escalopes, from the same spot on aisle 6, at the same time, on the same day each week that I realise I've totally bypassed the scrumptious organic steaks on aisle 7. I reckon that if I ask Mr S very, very nicely he may well offer to cook them alongside his famous fried onion, red wine and cream sauce and totally indulgent mash (that actually contains more butter than potatoes). Now this *would* make a change on a Monday night.

- My culinary-rut friend Carla vows that, from now on in, she'll pop into her local fishmonger once a month while out shopping on a Saturday afternoon. Instead of cursing the rain and wishing she'd stayed at home, closed the curtains and run a hot bath, she's going to Kipling's while waiting for her dry-cleaning. Her new method is to go armed with a notebook, ask the fishmonger what the fresh fish of the day is and how he'd cook it, and instead of calling for chow mein at 8.30 p.m. after *X Factor*, she'll experiment with the sea bass. So far, so flash-fried fillets of bream good. For busy girls who don't know their local fishmonger from their local barber, investigate care of Local Food Advisor (www.localfoodadvisor.com) or fork2fork (www.fork2fork.org.uk). Now you really have no excuse. Except, that is, the predictable British rain.

- You could consider buying yourself a new heavy-duty pan, casserole dish or tagine (Different by Design at Sainsbury's do a great selection for around £30 – www.sainsburys.co.uk). If a piece of fresh cod and DVD of *Babette's Feast* don't arouse your culinary senses, maybe retail kitchen therapy will.

- If this all sounds rather too *Ready Steady Cook* for your liking, then do one simple thing, like change your salad dressing. I always make vinaigrette using olive oil, balsamic vinegar, Dijon mustard and a little sugar. By using a nut oil (groundnut, walnut or hazelnut) or a different vinegar (tarragon, berry, anyone?), you'll instantly change the flavour of your salad. If you're feeling *really* brave, you could throw on a few seeds or roasted pine nuts (cheat and use pre-roasted seeds by Munchy Seeds – www.munchyseeds.co.uk). This may well mean we can continue guilt-free with the same roast chicken/pasta and pesto combo without dying of boredom.

- If you're serious about kick-starting your culinary prowess, you could think about going to cookery school. Rick Stein's Seafood School in Padstow (www.rickstein.com) and Divertimenti (www.divertimenti.co.uk) will both have you whisking and marinating in no time. Better still, get the super-chefs at Cookery Coach to come to your home and teach you to make sushi, pasta or chocolate truffles with a simple bish, bash, bosh (www.cookerycoach.co.uk). I still suspect I'll opt for that girlie break in Ibiza, thanks very much, but I'm glad to know where to head for Thai fish curry know-how should I get sick of paella and chilled rosé.

I won't profess that these ideas have turned me into a fly-by-the-seat-of-my-pants chef extraordinaire, serving up beef stroganoff on a whim, but I haven't reached for the fish fingers just yet. The dried pasta: yes. Bird's Eye: no.

Eating whatever you like and not getting fat

I try to avoid jealousy, I really do. It's such an ugly emotion. It's just that when I see girls who are as skinny as Giselle tucking into plates piled high with pasta followed by a triple fudge brownie without gaining a pound, I just can't help it. I want to cry, 'Why isn't that meeeee!' We all have friends who have the skinny gene; I can think of at least five. They eat whatever they like and seem to burn it off just by being them. No cellulite, no spare tyres, no muffin tops, no thunder thighs. I confess, when I was a stick-thin twenty-something fashion journo, I convinced myself I had the SG. I trotted around in size zero Sass & Bide jeans, long, lean arms dangling from a white GAP vest, with a flat tummy that gave the impression I was dedicated to sit-ups. I convinced myself that I could eat whatever I liked, but in reality it was the fact that I skipped breakfast in order to maximise my lie-in possibilities, took two bites from my lunchtime sandwich (while talking on the phone, typing and viewing a rail of clothes hanging beside my desk) and opted for a midnight bowl of Alpen before falling into bed. Not so much 'eat whatever you like' as 'eat whatever you can grab, whenever you remember'.

Frighteningly, now I'm a thirty-something mum of three, eating breakfast, lunch, supper and snacks in between constitutes some of the highlights of my day. I actually wake up excited about breakfast and, once it's finished, start thinking about how early is too early for that mid-morning cuppa and biscuit – 9.12 a.m.? Rather like in an old person's home, I have been known to serve lunch before midday and am the first to jump at the chance of joining the kids for an after-school snack. A Magnum from the ice-cream van is my favourite. Cooking supper, while a chore, marks the moment I can viably open a bottle of white and sip it while stirring the rice. Quickly and with relish.

Sadly, all this focus on food means I have had to face the fact that I'm definitely not the type of girl who can eat whatever she wants and stay thin. I *could* eat whatever I like, but I would be a size eighteen, with a vast jeans overhang. I have come to realise that, while I'll never be a size zero again, shopping exclusively at Evans would make me rather depressed. The middle ground for me is to eat whatever I like in moderation. This way, I can still enjoy mouth-watering delicacies without resigning myself to being as big as a house.

- I've got a hearty appetite, so instead of skipping meals, I'll attempt to pile up the fresh goodies alongside a moderate portion of pasta/fish/meat/risotto. Life wouldn't be worth living without a slab of lasagne or good old-fashioned steak, but if I bulk up the portion with salad and vegetables, I feel full without the guilt.

- My friend Anna looks like a supermodel. She has a whole list of forbidden foods she won't touch and obviously has the willpower of an ox. I tried it for a day and by the evening was licking a Galaxy, just to be close to it without consuming all the calories. I'd suggest binning the idea of forbidden foods. I never go a day without chocolate, but instead of a family-size bar, I'll eat a few cubes or opt for dark chocolate, as it's much better for you (check out Green & Black's selection and you'll never look back – www.greenandblacks.com).

- I'm a snacker. I'd happily keep a packet of HobNobs in my handbag and nibble on them throughout the day, but I try not to. I'll attempt to snack on fresh fruit and nuts instead. My friend Anna reminds me that fruit is still very high in sugar, but to be honest it's either that or a multi-pack of McVitie's, so I'll stuff the consequences and opt for the natural fruit sugar instead.

- My friend Susie is a self-confessed carb queen. We even went on a bread-making course for her hen weekend. Since having kids, though, she says she limits her carb fetish to breakfast and lunch and opts for protein and fresh vegetables for supper. This way, she's got longer to work off the three-croissant breakfast and pasta Bolognese lunch before going to bed. She confesses that if she can't face skipping that mashed potato in the evening, she'll just cut her evening meal in half. Half the fun, but only half the calories.

- Introducing foods that boost metabolism and help burn calories must surely be one of the best easy cheats around. Certainly sounds perfectly lax to me. Drinking a few cups of green tea every day is well known to speed up your metabolism but did you also know that chillies (especially jalapeño and cayenne peppers) and moderate amounts of milk and cheese also have the same effect? Please note that three full-fat grand lattes for elevenses is pushing the 'moderate' rule somewhat. However, a good slab of mature cheddar on a Jacob's cracker followed by chicken marinated in cayenne peppers and a slow slurp of Merlot (just for good measure) sounds like the most delicious way to speed up your metabolism.

- You could be really cunning and use smaller plates and cutlery to fool yourself you're eating more. It works for my pal Dotty. I just can't get my head around eating supper from the only small plates in the house. Plastic. Primary colours. Elmer the Elephant. Enough said.

- Try to stop eating when you're full, not so over-stuffed you feel like a hot-air balloon. This won't be your last meal ever, so stop – you don't always need to scrape the plate clean.

- If you notice that you feel like eating not when you're hungry but when you're tired/cross/bored/sad/watching American sitcoms, try to fill that void with something other than a Twix. I'm the first to dive for popcorn as soon as the box sets appear, but eating because of emotion as opposed to hunger can lead you straight towards the plus-size drawstring trousers. I'm still trying hard to engage with this philosophy; it's just that Celebrations and TV go hand in hand in so many ways.

- The more exercise you do, the more calories you'll burn off. Boring but true. If you can't stand the gym, try walking more. Just a bit.

I love food too much to be a skinny minny. So, begrudgingly, I'll do some of the above. This way I can enjoy munching my way through life, happily fluctuating at around a size twelve, with a few extra rolls here and there and some delightful cellulite around my bottom. A small price to pay when you can still eat cake.

Food shopping on a tight budget

Only recently, I was so overdrawn I presumed there must be major fraud being undertaken on my account. I spent a sleepless night tossing and turning with rage as I imagined a thieving Grace replica going to St Barts using my Visa card and stocking up on Heidi Klein bikinis before she hit the first-class lounge. First thing in the morning, I marched into my branch of NatWest, demanding to see the most senior manager so he could explain what the hell was going on with my account. Even my standing order for my toddler's Tumble Tots class had bounced. The shame of it.

More shameful, however, was the rapid realisation that no thieving sun goddess had been topping up her tan in St B care of my super-saver account, but, in actual fact, I had maxed it up myself, thanks to my trusty obsession with Ocado deliveries and M&S peppered tuna steaks. I kid you not – £694.32

overdrawn, and mostly down to damn sundried tomatoes, Pinot Noir and Gü chocolate brownies (the soft kind, that also go straight to the thighs, but when eaten with Ben & Jerry's double-chunk cookie dough from the tub taste out of this world). This must stop.

Life's too short to count calories.

I met my good friend Willow for a coffee (I drank tap water) and confessed my shameful habit. 'It could be worse,' she said. 'It could be class-As or Net-a-Porter shoes you never wear.' She had a point. However, we both agreed that budget shopping deserved a good stab. Willow gallantly agreed to work at it with me. You see, she too confessed to a little 'habit' of her own. On her second latte, she fessed up to indulging in six-nights-out-of-seven take-away deliveries, and on her third latte, she laid it all bare with the real truth. She's on speed-dial terms with almost all the fast-food joints in her neighbourhood – the Chinese now add Peking duck pancakes in with her order *free of charge* and the pizzeria chuck in a bottle of plonk for being their 'golden customer'. She's on first-name, small-talk terms with the Indian delivery man and he has been known to join her for the peshwari naan before nipping off to his next job. She tells me, in all honesty, that her oven still has the polystyrene filling that it came with when it was delivered from Comet six months ago. No wonder she can't afford the girlie holiday we promised each other this year. She'll be far too busy paying off the poppadom debt.

If we don't get this economical shopping sussed, I can imagine we'll have the bailiffs round in no time, and you can forget our long-weekend in Formentera; it'll be a night at the Holiday Inn on the A406 and home-packed egg sandwiches all the way. Now where's the fun in that?

The revelations of two thrift-food virgins

- When you're in the supermarket or shopping online, do your very own price-check; often, buying supermarket own-brands can save you a lot. Shortcut price-checking via the internet at www.mysupermarket.co.uk.

- I confess, I'd gone a little mad with the trend for buying organic. It was costing an absolute fortune. I now opt for regular fruit and vegetables and free-range or outdoor-reared chickens. I make an exception for organic red meats, but unless you're loaded, eating only organic food will often incur finding a second job, probably at nights. Just don't bother.

- I'm such a sucker for packaged fruit, especially those M&S strawberries that look like works of art, even though you only actually get about twelve in the box. However, on closer comparison, you'll save a good few pounds buying loose fruit and veg. Make the task even easier by getting a local company to deliver loose fruit and veg as part of a 'box scheme'. Riverford (www.riverford.co.uk) and Abel & Cole (www.abelandcole.co.uk) are both great for the laborious task of recycling and saving the planet too. Look for seasonal items to save on cash.

- I know delis exude a sense of middle-class culinary calm, but if you forget the beautifully presented deli cuts and head to Tesco for your cured and smoked meats instead, you'll save a small fortune.

- Willow is now a champion spotter of three-for-two and buy-one-get-one-free deals, which she reckons save her a small fortune every month – though she does have a slightly worrying stash of tortilla crisps. Even though it does feel rather 'all mum's go to Iceland', I have found family staples like pasta, ketchup and biscuits are worth the deals.

- Although I'm pretty rubbish at making puddings, I'm afraid my Gü habit has to stop. I'd been happily slinging boxes of brownies and carrot cake into my trolley until, on closer inspection, I realised I could buy a new winter coat for my youngest for the same price. Shame, because life won't be the same without them, but it's getting cold and my youngest can't survive in his denim jacket right through until January.

- Willow has devised a rather cunning plan of buying up reduced food that is close to its sell-by date and, as long as she eats it the same day, it's harmless. Like the budget-shopping pro she's now becoming, she also aims to go to the supermarket on a Sunday night, half an hour before it closes. Fresh fruit, vegetables and meat that they can't sell the next day is invariably 50 per cent cheaper.

- Unfortunately for me, the busy working mum, and Willow, the girl-about-town-with-no-time-to-cook, ready-meals crank up the shopping cost immensely. Sadly, the more I read about them, the more I realise they're not nearly as good for you as cooking from scratch anyway. Damn you, chicken nuggets, for you are so convenient for us working mums. Even if you can vary cooking from scratch with the odd processed microwave meal, you'll save a bit. As a quick-fix kids meal, I'll now opt for cheese on toast instead of shop-bought pizza, and chicken breast marinated in soy and honey instead of those nuggets. Failing that, they can all have a bowl of Shreddies and a banana.

- Planning ahead is good advice to dish out (I'm famous for it), but not always viable in practice. Having said that, making a quick list of weekly meals before you hit the supermarket will save you from over-buying and incurring costly waste. Sometimes when I sit down for ten minutes to think of the week ahead, I realise the kids may not be at home as much as I thought/we have food left over from the weekend barbeque/I can buy fresh on the day and see what fish or meat is on offer in my local shops. I won't pretend I get round to this every week, but if you just plan the first few week-night meals, you'll be ahead of the game.

Thankfully, it seems Willow and I are now a step closer to reducing that overdraft facility, and that means we're a step closer to cancelling the Holiday Inn on the A406 and booking an EasyJet flight to the sun instead.

Using up those leftovers without feeling like you're restricted to Second World War rations

I don't know about you, but I've always got the odd plate of leftovers sitting under cling-film in my fridge. Day one: it seems half-appetising to reuse it in a salad or eat it straight from the fridge dunked in mayonnaise when you're hitting that almost-supper, snack-attack mode. Day two: it starts to look wistful and you bypass it for the Laughing Cow and honey-roast ham. Day three: it's over; it just looks well and truly sad. Day four: it goes in the bin. Wasteful and expensive, but nevertheless true.

In another life, I'd be conjuring up imaginative cordon bleu meals from the stray pieces of roast chicken. Instead, after a few days of neglect, they gather slimy jelly and head straight for the trash.

There is someone, however, who always seems to conjure up imaginative cordon bleu meals from her leftovers, and that's my sister-in-law Jo. I'm not sure if it's because she's naturally resourceful or just because each and every night she cooks up such a lavish storm for her family that armfuls of leftover food is just another day in the life of her kitchen cycle. Either way, I'm in awe.

I meet Jo for a cuppa and ask what her secrets are. As we discuss soups made from broccoli end-cuts and the possibility of stir-fried this, that and the other, I actually get quite excited by the idea. Stop the press, I even manage to throw some half-decent ideas into the magi-mix. After discarding a whole host of our pooled wisdom for being 'too complicated', 'too much like hard work', 'too unrealistic after a ten-hour working day and two-hour tube-journey delay', these are the top two we come up with:

Chicken and rice stir-fry

Lovingly remove the forlorn leftover chicken from the fridge and add to a wok sizzling with olive oil. Chuck in some boiled rice, a cube of chicken stock, a fried onion (chopped) and some peas. Cook up a treat and serve hot.

Vegetable soup

Gather up all the leftover cooked vegetables from your mid-week supper (this can even include salad). Mix it all up in the food processor with a little chicken or vegetable stock. *Voilá*, soup for Saturday lunch.

Shortcut to a soggy-sandwich-free picnic

Picnics and British summertime don't mix. It's like drinking and empty stomachs or childbirth and glamour – they just don't meet and marry as they should. Which is a shame really because when we have a freak sunny Sunday I always think to myself, 'Wouldn't it be nice if we were sitting beside a river somewhere eating strawberries and drinking Pimm's, the children paddling blissfully in the shallow water.' Instead, we are generally stuck in a sweaty car on the way home from the cinema or sharing the local swings and queuing for Mr Whippys along with 560 other families.

I vowed this summer would be different. We would risk all the soggy sandwiches, warm rosé, squashed raspberries and dry grass in the mouth while biting into a sausage and plan at least one picnic with friends. Check out Enjoy England (www.enjoyengland.com) and the National Trust (www. nationaltrust.org.uk) to minimise the risk of a dog-poo-and-rubbish-infested picnic spot. Seeing as you can never predict the weather either, just hope and pray for sun (and log on to www.bbc.co.uk/weather). Take as many large umbrellas as you can find along for the ride too.

- A Sunday in early August is a good time to choose because a) you've got a better chance that the weather may hold, and b) many people are away somewhere with guaranteed sun and delicious paella, leaving city parks and woods relatively less overcrowded and dog-poo-infested than normal.

- Don't bother with a lovely-looking picnic hamper. You view them in the Cath Kidston catalogue and think, 'Oh yes, this is the life I want,' but in reality you're likely to use them once a year. If that. And even then, they'll get drenched and squashed by the dog. Instead, choose pretty paper plates, cups and napkins from your local supermarket or Nettle Green (www.nettlegreen.co.uk) and bung them in a wicker basket.

- Take bug spray, bin bags, matches, a penknife, blankets, rugs, kitchen roll, salt and pepper, sun block and don't forget the frozen wine sleeves and corkscrew. For a one-stop picnic shop try www.picnicshop.co.uk. A picnic is manageable with soggy sandwiches but a *disaster* with warm vino.

- Forget the fancy-schmancy food delicacies; it's all for show. You'll spend hours preparing them only to leave them in the car boot/sit on them by mistake/be offended when someone asks, 'Where are the crisps?'

- Picking at finger food is the best thing about picnics, so I love lots of tubs of hummus, taramasalata and guacamole, loose breads, plum tomatoes on the vine, radishes, chunks of feta, strips of salami and Parma ham, raspberries and strawberries, crunchy Granny Smiths and, of course, those much-in-demand Salt & Vinegar Walkers.

- If you're going for hot food, save yourself some hassle by avoiding complicated marinated lamb shanks and go for cooked chipolata sausages, grilled halloumi and marinated chicken wings. Wrap them in foil, chuck them in the basket and you're away.

- Don't forget balls, bats and frisbees (www.otherlandtoys.co.uk or www.cotswoldoutdoor.com). Even without kids, it will keep haven't-grown-up-yet adults happy.

- Once you've arrived under grey skies at Highgate Woods/ Clapham Common/Cherwell River/the Cornish coastline,

lay out the rugs and food and let the weather be damned.
If you leave the deckchairs and complicated picnic
baskets at home, you can easily gather up the gubbins
and dart under trees if the rain pours down. Or head to
Pizza Express.

Needless to say, the sun did shine. My daughter got bitten by
mozzies, her best friend got chased by a Dalmatian, my
nephew spat out the labour-of-love chicken wings and my
girlfriend got sunburnt and teary-eyed-confessional after her
fourth glass of rosé. However, it was a thoroughly British
picnic that went on well past when the hummus had dried up
and strawberries stained the rug. The main thing was, it
involved no washing-up and definitely no hot, sweaty, post-
cinema road rage, and for this I'm truly thankful.

CHAPTER FIVE

BEAUTICIAN

Overcoming your can't-be-bothered attitude towards a bit of slap

Considering I've devoted one third of my life so far to working for fashion and beauty magazines, it's remarkable that doing my own make-up fills me with dread. The idea of starting the day with an intensive regime of foundation, powder, mascara, eyeshadow and lip liner is about as appealing to me as setting my alarm clock for 3 a.m. just for the fun of it.

I went through a short-lived goth-come-Madonna stage at the age of sixteen. I straightened my hair and dyed it black, used eyeliner to draw a beauty spot above my right lip, slicked on that extra-thick mascara and applied Rimmel's red lipstick with vigour. Teamed with skin-tight black jeans, sky-high patent stilettos, a rusty crucifix earring bought in Camden Market and a ripped, fingerless fishnet glove, it was quite a look. Although it made me look far older than sweet sixteen and gained me a lot of attention on the night bus home from Kinky Gerlinky, it didn't last long. Red lippy is such a pain to take off after you've been dancing all night, and when that beauty spot smudges with sweat, the effect is more Charlie Chaplin than Madge in 'Like a Virgin'.

Since my KG days, I'm far more likely to be seen with a little aloe vera Vaseline on my lips and the black hair dye has for many years been replaced by the odd blonde highlight. It's boho au naturale rather than sexy siren that ticks all the boxes for me these days. The irony is, I'm still fascinated by women who are slaves to the slap. I watch with intrigue as my girlfriends indulge in intricate make-up regimes before a night out on the town, and I'm like a kid in a candy shop when I pass the MAC counter in Selfridges. I'd lap up the beauty missions I was sent on care of the glossy mags, taking notes like a swotty undergraduate at press launches and listening intently as beauty PRs elaborated on the latest must-have blusher and how it would 'change my life'. However, without fail, I'd always return to my no-fuss, no-frills, out-the-door-in-a-nano-second rituals. Bare-faced beauty by default.

Now, I really wish I could tell you the reason for this was a) my skin is so beautiful it needs no de-shining or cover-up at all, or b) I'm such a youthful, fresh-faced beauty that make-up would only detract from my inner radiance. Alas, both would be bull. The truth is, I'm lazy. I want that extra ten minutes in bed in the morning. Even if I attempt a basic make-up regime before my muesli, it looks great for the commute to work/ school run, but by lunchtime it seems to have been blown off by a passing number 19 bus and I look, yet again, like I've just got out of bed. Even in my most bridezilla moment, I still decided to walk down the aisle with nothing more than waterproof mascara and some 'investment' Elizabeth Arden Eight Hour Cream on my lips.

Sadly, to my niggling discontent, I'm starting to realise that my faithful Lizzie A and some three-year-old Body Shop bronzing balls I use for special occasions may no longer be enough. I used to tell people I had three kids and often, without force or bribery, their unprompted response would be

'WOW, really? You don't look old enough!' Now the standard line is 'Yes, I can tell, children are exhausting, aren't they? You should treat yourself to a facial.' Really and truly, I think the world is telling me my time has come to actually give a shit. To start with, I'll endeavour to obey these eight commandments in the hope of a morsel of beauty salvation.

1 Cleanse. Essential if you want to get rid of spot-making blocked pores. After several recommendations from friends, I tried Sisley's Foaming Cleanser. You'll need to take a deep breath for the price, but it never seems to leave the skin feeling dry like many other cleansers. If you need speed-cleansing, opt for cleansing wipes.

2 Serum. Optional, but for many of my beauty-savvy friends it's become essential to their skin-care mantras. Amazing for deep moisturising of the skin, reducing wrinkles and preparing skin for make-up (it's fast replacing primers in this league). You can use as well as or instead of moisturiser, or even blend it with your tinted moisturiser or foundation. Top brands are Chanel's Sublimage Essential Revitalising Concentrate, Olay Regenerist 3 Point Super Serum and No7 Protect and Perfect Intense Beauty Serum. I must confess that after a month of using No7 P&P, I'm starting to think serum might just be my favourite youth-boosting shortcut. The fact that it retails at around £20 – as opposed to £150 like some serum competitors – is a huge bonus.

3 Moisturise. Studies have finally proved that if you moisturise your skin, even with the most basic of products, you will have fewer lines than if you don't. Every expression causes creasing, but using a moisturiser daily means those creases are less likely to become the dreaded wrinkles. I'm no slave to expensive creams that promise the world; I just want

something that smells nice and works. Even though my skin often needs extra hydration, I tend to choose light moisturisers (a brand like Boots Botanics Day Shift Moisture Cream is cheap and seems to do the trick). You can either reapply if your skin needs the hydration or blot it if you feel like an overdressed house salad. Serums are now fast rivalling moisturisers in the beauty world.

4 SPF. Many new UV protectors are super-sheer and actually impart a glowy sheen to the skin. Try Keraskin Dermalogica and L'Oreal's pocket-sized offerings.

5 Foundation. Cheat and go for Clinique Moisture Surge Tinted Moisturiser (which also comes with SPF, so you can skip step 2) or Sheer Moisture Foundation by No17. If you fancy a foundation that also acts as an 'eraser' (yessssssss!), look no further than Maybelline's Instant Age Rewind, a super-light foundation which will only set you back one crisp ten-pound note. Test the colour on your jaw line; it's the best way of finding a perfect skin tone match. Once you've found the perfect tone, apply by starting around the nose and working out towards the hairline.

6 Cheeks. Smile in the mirror to find the apple of your cheek. Brush a tiny bit of blusher in wide swoops to give knackered-looking, lustreless skin a little fresh-faced oomph. For power blushers, Chanel hits the spot. While you're at it, brush a little bronzer at the top of your cleavage, giving the illusion of va va voom in one fell swoop.

7 Eyes. A quick eyelash curl and a slick of lash-accelerating mascara will give your lashes oomph while boosting their natural length in a matter of weeks. Add a quick comb and tint of the brows using Speed Brow by Benefit (www.benefitcosmetics.co.uk) and your eyes will look

groomed in no time. If you have an extra twenty seconds to spare and want a quick fix to make eyes really 'pop', go for a versatile eyeshadow like Smoky Eye Effect Eyeshadow by Max Factor. It's small, compact and has a crayon at one end for your lids and a defined nib at the other to fine-tune the look. Fast to put on and, unlike some shadows, doesn't make you look like you're ready for the D-I-S-C-O.

8 Lips. Sheer gloss is quick and easy and can even be applied while running down the stairs towards the front door. If you want to save mid-morning hassle, use L'Oreal's Glam Shine Lip Gloss, which gives six hours of shine after just one application.

If you're still stuck for perfect products to suit your sometimes oily, sometimes dry, sometimes puffy, sometimes in need of oomph skin, then sign up for free membership at www.latestinbeauty.com. You enter your age, skin type and hair and eye colour and they'll update you on the latest products to suit you. Even better, pay £1 for a week's worth of samples. Surely even a lazy make-up virgin like me can stick to this?

The essential beauty bag kit

My friend Zoe recently moved from a single-girl basement flat in W8 to a not dissimilar basement flat in W10. She could actually walk the removal boxes from the 'old' end of the street to the 'new' one. She swears she saved her back by editing her make-up collection prior to the move. It's no exaggeration that when I turned up to 'help', I discovered no fewer than three black dustbin liners stuffed full of discarded beauty products waiting for the Westbourne Grove garbage collectors.

Not even my old beauty team colleagues collected that many unwanted mascara wands in a season. Close, but not quite.

Post third mug of PG and fifth chocolate Leibniz, I returned home to rummage guiltily through my own stash of unwanted and unloved make-up booty. Eight mascaras, seven lip glosses, six foundations, five blushers, four eyeshadows, three lipsticks and I don't even like wearing make-up! The first step to saving you time and energy in the pursuit of beauty bliss must surely be to edit your make-up selection. Get out the dustbin liners and check-list the following:

1. The maximum lifespan of most products is two years, but I'd suggest being ruthless and binning anything that you can't remember buying in the last year. Mascara should be discarded after four months to avoid eye infections. To my shame, I realised I'd had some of mine for years, and most of them had been used only once. And that's a generous estimate.

2. Zoe is the ultimate disco queen, but even she suggests keeping a maximum of three disco diva make-up essentials for glam nights out (yes, the Claire's Accessories glitter eyeshadow and coral lipstick that came free with last month's *Elle* must go). The aim is to keep your make-up kit minimal. Identify an essential beauty box of everyday goodies and don't be sidetracked by the 'maybe one day' turquoise eyeshadow. Ask yourself, 'When was the last time I wore this?' Chances are, the turquoise shimmer shadow you're saving for that big night out is one of many culprits clogging up your beauty box and going sticky as the years roll by.

3. Collate a minimalist make-up kit that will give you speed and ease in the morning and leave you looking fresh-faced as opposed to shimmer-eyed-mistake. A suggested hit list would be:

- 1 x foundation

- 1 x powder

- 1 x mascara

- 1 x blusher

- A selection of eye-shadow

- A small selection of lip glosses

- The perfect lipstick

- The perfect lip pencil

- 1 large fluffy bronzing brush

- A small collection of alternative brushes if you need them. A good way to find out is to book a make-up session with Space NK and ask them for a hit list of several brushes to suit your needs. Depending on your attitude to make-up, you may need a brush for applying eyeshadow, blending bases and lipstick application. Remember to wash them every two months to keep them fresh. Clinique's Make-up Brush Cleanser works a treat but to be honest a light shampoo is just as good and well save you a tenner. Just beware of the handle and joins, the last thing you want is loose glue and cracks.

My high-maintenance alter-ego isn't convinced I'll never need that Max Factor Vibrant Curve Effect Lip Gloss in Dominant or that Dior Tailleur Bar Eyeshadow Palette, but you know how I hate clutter, so sticking to the basics has got to be worth a go.

Dealing with mascara angst

To compound the realisation that generally I'm a lazy make-up pariah, I've found that even with fleeting beauty commandments, mascara and I just don't marry. I love the idea of a quick slick of the black mascara wand and the 'come-to-bed' curly-lash look, but alas, it never ends up as I'd imagined. I either a) get caught in the rain and find that even 'waterproof' mascara runs down my cheeks, leaving me looking like a French clown from Cirque de Soleil, or b) get too drunk to take off the mascara before bed and wake up with panda eyes (added to red-wine-stained lips and 'OK, just the one' fag breath), and it makes for one horrendous morning look. My shortcut to 24/7 groomed lashes is therefore simple:

- Step one: find a twenty-minute grooming window.

- Step two: get eyelashes tinted blue-black.

- Step three: repeat every eight to ten weeks.

No clowns or pandas left in sight. Fabulous.

If you still can't face giving up on the mascara wand, opt for lash-enhancing products instead. Lash-pimping is big business and many of my friends vow they really work. Can you imagine a product that helps you grow your lashes darker and thicker without involving any tinting or extensions? Result! In price order go for RevitaLash, Givenchy's Mister Lash Booster or Rimmel's Lash Accelerator Mascara. All work wonders on lashes.

Wearing lipstick without looking like a dodgy 1970s Mills & Boon cover

Bar my fleeting episode of bulk-buying Rimmel red in my teens, my general view of lipstick has been 'go stick it'. I'm pretty sure I represent a whole generation of women who've grown up on lip glosses and Lancôme's Juicy Tubes, the general consensus being that they're quick, easy and don't need reapplying every five minutes, which is perfect when you'd much rather be getting stuck into the rosemary cashews and another glass of red. My friend Emma (who has a collection of thirty-five glossies in her make-up bag) calls us the 'backlash lipstick ladies'. We're the ones who think it's far easier to buy a selection of nude-shade Juicy Tubes while killing time in duty-free than invest in a fuchsia-pink lipstick that inevitably involves a matchy-matchy lip liner, blotting tissues and the need for teeth-checking in the toilet mirror. We've said goodbye to lipstick stains and hello to ease and speed.

The only problem with all this gloss-worship is that you bypass all the fabulous connotations of old-school glamour that come with a good old-fashioned lipstick. Would Marilyn Monroe ever have been seen in a frosted-pink Juicy Tube bought at Gatwick en route to Majorca? I think not. I was struck yet again by the feeling that there must be more to lips when my daughter began applying my beige lip gloss before leaving for her friend's tenth birthday party. *Hello?* If my daughter's pinching my half-used gloss, surely it's time my lips grew up and I invested in a style-statement lipstick for my own use?

I confess, it's not easy to go from quick-slick gloss to the full Monroe monty in one fell swoop, but thanks to several visits to my local Space NK, an evening of white wine and brainstorming with a collection of my beauty industry friends and a flick through the latest Tom Ford lippy collection, I've cobbled together a comprehensive list of shortcuts guaranteed to instantly transform your lipstick know-how.

- Start by looking after your lips. Lipstick use can be drying, so when you're not channelling that A-list pout, use lip balms to avoid dryness and resist the temptation to lick them when they're dry or cracked; slap on the balm instead.

- Pick your lipstick well. Look to Chanel for density of pigment, Laura Mercier for creamy textures and wearability and MAC for hip colours. Want to achieve all this in one genius stick? Pure Colour Lipstick by Estée Lauder comes pretty damn close. If you can't find the shade you're lusting after, try mixing shades you already have in your make-up bag. Just blend them on your palm using a lip brush.

- Use a lip brush to layer your lipstick. Apply by starting at the centre of your lips and working outwards, blotting on tissue between each application. This modern 'stain' effect will last longer and minimises the risk of OTT lips.

- I know it's labour intensive, but if you want to achieve a good pout, outline the lips as a final touch. To save time and gain an equally good pout, just pencil in the cupid's bow and the corners of the mouth with a shade that matches your lip colour (never go darker than your lip colour or the shade of lippy). Instantly fuller lips without collagen: love it!

- Utilise those beloved clear glossies by adding a small stroke in the middle of your mouth once you've applied the lipstick.

- I'm learning fast that the trick to modern lips is to dress them down, not up. You want to aspire to the carefree, don't-give-a-damn attitude of Georgia May Jagger, as opposed to the polished look of an old-school Jackie Collins bonkbuster cover. Team those luscious red lips with skinny jeans and a Breton-striped T as opposed to an LBD with big shoulders. Play it cool, girls.

I'm still not convinced I'll ditch the easy-route Vaseline before the school run, but when getting glammed up for a girl's night out, I must confess I'm tempted!

Cover-star make-up

by **Jemma Kidd**, make-up artist to the stars and queen of the quick flick of the mascara wand

I don't know a girl who doesn't crave make-up shortcuts that will strike that balance between natural and fabulous. Simple. Make highlighter your new best friend. Step one: dab a touch underneath the arch of your brow. It will lift the brow and make your eyes look wider. Step two: dab above the cupid's bow to make lips appear fuller. Step three: mix a little with your foundation to give skin an all-over luminosity and healthy glow. Don't you just love a three-in-one promise?

I'll share a few extra secrets I've used on the catwalk and for magazine shoots but which work equally as well for everyday life. A-list make-up for real girls? We love.

> Apply a touch of light-coloured, neutral eyeshadow at the inner corners of your eyes to draw light into the eyes and make them look bigger and brighter.

2 Before curling your lashes, blast your eyelash curler for a few seconds with a hairdryer on a low setting. The heat will give your lashes a longer-lasting curl. Note: be sure to test the heated curler with your fingertip first, to ensure it's not too hot. Burnt eyelids are guaranteed to dampen your evening.

3 Ensure brows are tidy and defined. Well-shaped brows really shape the face and make your final look polished and sophisticated. A quick way to define brows is with a brow pencil, working from the arch outwards and then on the inner part if needed. Go over them with a brow powder, which will soften the shape and make it last longer.

4 Apply a light dusting of translucent powder over your foundation before applying powder blush or bronzer. It gives the skin a lovely flawless finish and keeps powder-based products from looking patchy on the skin.

5 As scary as it sounds, clue yourself up on a technique known as 'contouring'. Many of my celebrity clients use this to emphasise certain features. Simply apply a matte bronzer or shimmer-free eyeshadow two shades darker than your skin tone to areas such as the hollows of the cheekbones, temples, jaw line and sides of the nose. Trust me, it adds astonishing definition to the face and subtly alters its shape.

6 Dark eyeliner worked in between the roots of the lashes will help make them look fuller and thicker. This is especially useful for more mature faces, as lashes tend to get sparser with age. Definition can also be added to the eyes using half a set of false lashes or individual false lashes at the outer corners of the eyes. This is a great way to create instant glamour and open up the eyes.

Few women have tons of spare cash to splash on make-up, so it's good to know what products are worth investing in and which you can scrimp on. Firstly, prioritise good skin-care creams and foundations. Both will keep your skin looking and feeling its best. A good set of make-up brushes is also worth the investment – it doesn't matter how good your products are, if the tools you're applying them with are poor quality, you may as well be throwing cash down the drain. Spend a smaller percentage of your budget on colour products like eyeshadows and lipsticks. You can often find less expensive products that are just as effective as those by the premium brands and, honestly, changing colours as make-up trends come and go is much easier if you're spending a fiver instead of ten times that.

We all need failsafe methods to nail that from-the-office-straight-out-to-a-glam-supper make-up regime. If your skin's looking tired after hours of staring at that computer, cleanse with wipes and reapply moisturiser, foundation and concealer until it looks dewy and fresh. Smooth out any creases on your eyeshadow with a cotton bud, then add extra eyeliner in a dark colour and smudge it up onto the lid. Dress up natural eyes with a shimmering powder eyeshadow which can be easily applied over existing eyeshadow. Curl your lashes and add another coat of mascara for definition. If you really want to intensify the colour on your cheeks, use pink crème blush, then add a touch of highlighter to your cheekbones, brow bones, bridge of your nose and cupid's bow to bring light to your face. Finish with a creamy lipstick in a deeper colour than your usual daytime look. Perfect for adding drama.

If you're got a little more time than that post-work, communal-toilet window and want a wow party look, grown-up glitter never fails. Just beware of going D-I-S-C-O OTT! Less is more, so use glitter in moderation. Try layering glitter gel eyeliner over dark eyeliner pencil for just a hint of subtle shimmer. For more dramatic sparkle, apply loose glitter on top of crème eyeshadow, so that it has something to adhere to. Apply glitter before making up the rest of your face and dust away any particles before applying foundation. Just don't overdo it – if you have shine on your eyes, keep lips nude or matte and avoid too much shimmer on your face. Failing that, you'll channel that drag queen instead of dancing queen and live to regret it.

I always want to embrace lazy weekends while still looking half-decent. I call this subtle type of make-up 'stealth make-up', as it ensures you look fabulous but not at all 'made up'. Instead of applying foundation, even out skin tone with a tinted moisturiser. Sweep a delicate wash of taupe or beige eyeshadow across eyelids, then curl lashes and define them with a slick of lengthening mascara. Add a flush to lips and cheeks with a rosy stain for long-lasting, low-maintenance colour. Now all you need is a roaring fire and a roast lunch. Failing that, the Sunday papers and a cuppa will do just fine.

Shortcuts for any girl with little cash *and even less time to fanny around in the morning*

Lash extensions may take an hour or so to apply, but they mean you can go make-up free for a month. Just make sure you ask for half a set, not a full one. You want to look naturally pretty, not drag-queen scary.

Dotting a teeny bit of gold shimmer powder on the inner corners of your eyes, just under your eyebrows and on the top of your cheekbones takes seconds but makes you look a whole lot prettier.

3 Feeling hot and bothered? Don't get red-faced; just go to the loo and hold your wrists under the cold tap. Your body temperature will drop by a few degrees and you will regain your icy Grace Kelly poise.

Getting your glow back when you look like Ronnie Wood *after a three-day bender*

Somewhere between the birth of my first child, turning thirty and a trio of domestic appliance malfunctions, my glow went AWOL. This was about the time olive oil looked like a cheap, easy, viable option for skin-care. Weird thing is, I didn't know I had it till it was gone. I spent my twenties so obsessed with spots that I didn't appreciate my plump, per-fectly even-toned skin. Now my glow has gone – upped and left – and my skin is looking dull, lack-lustre and generally sorry for itself. I hate this, but I figure that

Life's too short to spend longer on your make-up than you would on re-writing your CV/ calling your mum/ booking your summer hols.

after spending almost a decade working on a fashion and beauty magazine, I am in a pretty good position to mount a rescue mission. After some serious beauty-expert pestering and a good deal of trial and error, I found it was actually quite easy to get the Austen-heroine-post-moor-walk look back. So here are the shortcuts:

LIFE'S TOO SHORT

1   Exfoliate. Obvious, but every dermatologist I know says you cannot underestimate the power of a good (but gentle) scrub. Choose the level of grittiness that suits your skin and get buffing thrice weekly. It boosts circulation, banishes dead skin cells and generally makes your face look perkier.

2   Invest in a facial oil. Sniff around to find the one you like (Clarins, Darphin and Decléor do great ones) and take a couple of minutes to massage it into your skin nightly. This will trigger lymph nodes into detoxifying, boost blood supply to the skin and ward off dryness.

3   Buy a radiance-boosting primer. I'd always seen these products as an unnecessary expense, but I am not afraid to admit I was wrong. They are genius. They smooth out skin tone, add luminescence, blur lines and wrinkles and generally make you look five years younger.

4   Buy a face cream with retinol in it. One of the only ingredients proven to have a real anti-aging effect, this comes in its most powerful form in a cream prescribed by a dermatologist. The downside can be red, flaky skin with increased sun sensitivity plus the hassle of a visit to a dermatologist. If you want an over-the-counter retinol alternative, try Vichy LiftActiv Retinol HA Night or Philosophy Help Me Retinol Night Treatment.

Having a face as fresh as a daisy when you're juggling motherhood and a career

by **Louise Redknapp**, TV presenter and the epitome of glowing gorgeousness

My attitude to beauty basics is short and sweet: skin is key. Looking after your skin really is the most important thing you can do to achieve a fresh-faced appearance. I swear by wearing SPF, even in the depths of winter. You'd be surprised how much sun damage occurs in day-to-day life (and miles from a white sandy beach!). Once I've factored up, I'll apply moisturiser – Liz Earle, Angelique and Vichy are my top brands. I'll finish off with a light foundation and not too much powder, so my skin looks glowing and glossy. Who can be bothered with an intricate morning skin-care routine? Not me; that's why I've perfected this quick-as-a-flash morning ritual. Just how busy girls like it!

Nailing nails

My friend Kitty is the perfect example of a groomed nail goddess. You can meet her anytime, anywhere and her nails will be perfectly shaped, perfectly manicured examples of Fairy Liquid lusciousness. I once bumped into her at a summer festival mosh pit. It had rained relentlessly for two full days, my hair was matted, my gilet smelt like a soggy goat, my Hunters no longer looked cool now they were covered with noodles from the discarded Thai food stall and my nails were simply a disaster. I might have been having a ball, but my nails had died a slow death. Kitty, on the other hand, looked the epitome of shabby chic in her oversized parka, manicured cuticles poking out from the army-green sleeves. Where is the bloody justice?

The next time I saw her, I really had no excuse for nail neglect. A hot summer evening in July, a girls' night out we'd all been looking forward to for months, and a new much lusted-after Isabel Marant dress purchased at a snip on eBay to show off. However, my nails let me down yet again. Somehow, in between a frenzied array of work deadlines and the arduous task of getting three end-of-the-week-tired and ratty children fed, watered and bathed in order for me to clip clop down the path at 8 p.m. when Mr S arrived home to take over parenting duties, my nails were lucky to get a wash, let alone a paint of on-trend gloss. Not so for Kitty. Deadlines met, child in bed, hands slathered in Clarins hand cream, nails beautifully shaped and double-coated in Chanel's new deep-purple matte lacquer, she rocked.

My nail envy can't even be put down to mourning the loss of my once fabulous cuticles. I've never managed to do more than bite off an uneven, jagged nail while waiting for a green light in the car, and I can honestly say I've never owned cuticle oil in my life. I enjoyed my fair share of freebie manicures when I worked on a glossy, but the best bit was always the hand massage, and it generally went downhill from there. Even when the most willing manicurist tried to twist my arm and encourage experimentation with a deep-coral mist, I'd almost always retreat to the comfort of au naturale clear gloss. After some serious PR spin, I once left the hip new opening of a West End salon with deep-fuscia-pink finger- and toenails, but by the time I'd reached the tube station, I felt like a cross between Pat Butcher and a Stringfellow's stripper and had to duck into the nearest Boots and remove immediately. Really bad form for a style journo.

The truth is, many of us feel life is just too short to indulge in fortnightly manicure and pedicure sessions (and I could write a whole new chapter in the time it takes for all that triple-coat business to dry). Not only is time a luxury, but not many of us have a monthly budget that extends past the phone bill to a 'nail fund' either. Having said that, I think many of us would like better nails; we just need a few quick, easy shortcuts to achieve and maintain them. I vow to give these a try.

- Invest in a cuticle oil pen (Marian Newman's Right Here Cuticle Oil Pen is great) and apply it to the base of your nails twice a day. This pen is a genius idea and means no messy spills or fiddly cotton buds are required. It's the perfect choice to use on your commute to work in the morning.

- If, like me, your nails break easily, think about increasing your intake of protein and calcium, which will help strengthen them. You could also pop a daily capsule of Phytonutrients with MSM (www.theorganicpharmacy.com) or folic acid to help the strength of your nails and slap on some hand and nail cream after you've used the cuticle oil. Kitty also swears by Sally Hansen's Hard as Nails Strengthener, a snip at under a fiver and, by the look of her luscious nails, brilliant at fortifying them too.

- To have a successful DIY manicure at home, remember the four-step rules:

  1 File your nails working in one direction from the outside edge towards the centre.

  2 Apply base coat.

  3 Apply two coats of colour.

4 Add a clear, glossy coat at the end to protect against chips.

- Forget the fifth 'rule', which is to match your finger- and toenail colours. If you're going to paint both, go for different colours that work well together. Kitty's a fan of hot-pink fingernails and pale-mint toenails. Worn with that festival parka, it works.

- If you're going for a professional mani and haven't got the luxury of a full spa day, head to a quick nail bar for a 'file & coat'. You'll still get a good nourishing treatment, reshape and polish and will be out in under half an hour.

- If you're bored with the standard reds and plums, seek out nail colours that will excite you. I must confess, even I'm tempted to work a whole new look with Rococo Nail Apparel's polishes in Stone Cold Karma and Jaded Luxe. I know they sound like Ibiza club nights, but on nails they look seriously chic.

- Keep your New Romantics range by Rococo (or faithful Black Pearl by Chanel) in the fridge; polish lasts longer when kept cold. If you're going out after work, grab it from beside the semi-skimmed milk and carry it in your handbag, so you can touch up chipped nails if you need to.

Inspired by Stone Cold Karma, I lacquered up and prided myself on my new-found boldness. I took a tip from Kitty and ran my hands under ice-cold water for eight minutes to speed up drying before heading out for a loaf of bread and to collect my youngest child from nursery. I was so busy admiring my new Karma that I almost drove into the back of a white van and, honestly, channelling Alexa Chung was wasted on the mums at nursery (too busy looking for their toddlers' macs), leaving me to ponder on the possibility that, now that I have a new-found nail life, I just need a day-to-day life that meets the high standards they set. Could someone please ask me out for a raspberry Martini at a trendy beach bar in Ibiza? My nails await you.

Smell good enough to eat

by **Nicky Kinnaird**, MBE, founder of Space NK
and unstoppable business and beauty guru

When you're searching for that perfect scent, test a few of your possible favourites on a scent strip to narrow down your choices, then spritz the fragrance on the inside of your wrist to see how it reacts with the chemistry of your skin. If you want to find something that really works for you, I'm afraid a quick sniff and snap decision just won't cut it. Take the time to smell the initial top notes and how it smells on first contact with your skin, then, after about ten minutes, smell it again as the heart notes of the fragrance start to reveal themselves. If you've got a little extra time to spare, wait before you buy and make your final decision an hour later, when the skin has fully warmed up the scent and you can experience the fully developed fragrance with its base notes coming through. Vowing to test and buy using this method will save you so much time and money collecting endless scents that smell wrong on you.

I like to wear fragrance on the warmest parts of my skin: my inner wrists, just below my hairline and behind my knees. Just remember, a light touch is always best. Your fragrance should only be smelled by those who get up close; it is not a substitute for room fragrance, with you as the carrier!

I often wonder why many women have an array of shoes to choose from depending on their mood, but want only one signature scent for every day – this doesn't make any sense! There's nothing more pampering than having a capsule wardrobe of fragrances tailored to match or even uplift your mood or the day's activities. Before bulk-buying in haste, bear in mind the following to cut through the immense quantity of choice out there:

- Floral scents make you feel feminine and flirty. In fact, we have been culturally conditioned to associate flowers with femininity. The Aztecs made their own fragrances by steaming flower petals, and Chinese women spritzed on rose water during the Tang Dynasty. Ideal for a summer wedding.

- Meditation and yoga impart that Zen feeling, but so can woody notes such as oak and cedar. These masculine notes mixed with florals help ground you and make you feel calm. Zen in a bottle; what's not to like?

- Warm Oriental notes such as vanilla, sandalwood, musk and amber often make you feel romantic and sexy. Perfect for a seductive date or those winter festivities.

- Fresh citrus notes and mint make you feel upbeat and happy, but these bright smells do evaporate quickly, which is why you will often find them mixed with florals or longer-lasting notes such as sandalwood and vanilla.

- If you really do just want *one* all-round pleaser I'd suggest Laughter Eau de Toilette by Space NK. Indulge me in some beauty speak, and I'll tell you why. With top notes of bergamot, lime, grapefruit and neroli, a herbal heart of rosemary and coriander and a sensual dry base of amber, musk and a twist of ginger, it's an all-round subtle scent. This combination of ingredients make it appeal to both women and men alike; useful when you're nabbing the first fragrance you can reach first thing in the morning!

Remember, too, that if you want to further extend a fragrance's staying power, smooth on an unscented body lotion before applying your perfume – the oils help trap the scent, so it will last longer. To further intensify the perfume, layer the scent over the same brand's scented body cream, lotion or oil.

My final tip? Just beware of overdosing on one tried-and-tested scent. Too much of a good thing can be polarising and no matter how much you love something, you can go off it very quickly if it becomes too popular and you start smelling it everywhere – Giorgio Beverly Hills was a great example of this in the early 80s. Be warned!

Plucking that perfect brow

The obvious shortcut to plucking that cover-star brow is to perfect the art yourself and religiously tweak away daily to keep it looking pristine. Sadly, brow-plucking is yet another area I've never quite mastered and, more often than not, my brows look like I've had a bad accident with a lawnmower in the dark. I once plucked my brow so thin it was almost invisible. Eye pencil as a substitute is almost as scary as your other half wearing full drag for supper.

My answer was to take the lazy-girl route and get an initial consultation with a professional to shape my brow. If you can find a local salon that offers threading, I'd opt for this, as it uses a small thread twisted around the root to shape the brow and leaves none of the soreness and red patches associated with waxing. A good friend of mine says her local high street in Tooting is full of beauty salons offering threading for £2.50, but failing that, try Selfridges or Harvey Nichols – www.blinkbrowbar.com. Once you've been given the perfect eyebrow shape, all you then need to do is follow the line daily to keep them tidy.

Invest in some precision tweezers such as those made by Tweezerman (www.tweezerman.co.uk) and if you're *really* serious about brows, get the pointed ones for nabbing super-short hairs and the slanted version for shaping. Use an old toothbrush to comb them through before plucking and it will help you keep the shape. Just aim to do it before bed, not before work. Red, angry eyebrows never work with a power suit. As long as you don't run into a lawnmower late at night, all these top tips should keep your brows in half-decent nick.

Shaping that bush

After all this preoccupation with easy gloss or old-school Jerry Jagger red lippy and the quest to give your not-enough-sleep, too-many-cappuccinos dull skin a lift, you'd think we could leave the question of bush shape alone. Quite frankly, with life running at a million miles per hour, we need another beauty 'issue' like a hole in the head. Ah, but here's the thing: the shape of your beloved bikini line has never been more topical. Just think about the media frenzy that was whipped up after Rachel Johnson's waxing story in a recent issue of *Vogue*. Anyone would think she was the first woman to fess up to having a Brazilian. Not only is waxing (or not) a hot debate, but the low-maintenance, lazy-girl's triangle (basically, anything goes as long as no stragglers are poking out of your bikini bottom on the sun lounger) is being rivalled by five bush camps.

- The Brazilian. The thin rectangular strip favoured by many a maintenance Ms. A little porn star, but clean and simple.

- The Boho Brazilian. Dreamt up by the sisters who set up London's fashionable Strip waxing bar, this style is more natural on top and all clean underneath.

- The Hollywood. Every single hair in sight off, leaving you with a prepubescent naked muff.

- The Sicilian. A neat triangle that is hairy yet groomed.

- The Rainforest (phrase coined here and now). No maintenance, and just as nature intended.

My friend Rose confides that bush shape has never been more debated than on a recent girlie holiday to the Greek islands. Six girls, six different bikini lines. Forget the issue of who was gracing the cover of *Harper's Bazaar* that month, the real question on everyone's lips was 'What shape are you?' The usual holiday intrigue about which shape of swimwear looked hottest by the pool (bandeau, halter-neck, string, tankini, cut-away, all-in-one) had been swiftly overtaken by a longing to know who'd opted for that August Brazilian, who'd dared to wax it all off and, hush!, who'd bathe loud and proud with the Rainforest sprouting from beneath their new turquoise Top Shop bikini bottoms?

No sooner had the six luscious ladies hit the pool bar and ordered a round of Daiquiris, the subject of bush beauty was broached. Would anyone own up to the Hollywood and be really honest about the fact that they actually felt like a teenager waiting to hit puberty? Would anyone dare to bare the Brazilian but sheepishly reveal the fact that it encourages friction burn when wearing skinny jeans? And who would be the girl to claim that 'the bush is back', because, let's face it, she'd really rather spend her well-earned time and cash browsing in Habitat than hoiking her legs behind her ears in an attempt to be waxed to perfection?

Four Daiquiris and a multi-pack of Ready-salted Walkers later, it seemed that, while the Brazilian is still a hot favourite amongst some, the majority were leaning towards a more natural Sicilian-type bikini line. One blonde proudly proclaimed home-waxing the cheap and easy way forward; others admitted that having a landing strip made them feel more cheap stripper than thirty-something mum of two. Thankfully, no one fessed up to a full Garden of Eden down there in her new Heidi Klein's.

What everyone agreed on was the following:

- Exfoliate before any type of waxing. Making the skin softer and removing dead skin cells will help you avoid ingrown hairs.

- Wear loose cotton undies. Nothing like a tight, scratchy G-string to fill you with de-fuzz remorse.

- Half an hour before the big ouch, apply No-Scream Cream, which will take some of the sting out of waxing (www.stripwaxbar.com).

- No time for applying fancy-schmancy creams? Fifteen minutes before waxing, take a paracetamol or ibuprofen to nip pain in the bud.

- Waxing from home is cheap and fast, but you have to be brave. Before applying the wax, use talcum powder, as it helps the strip to rip effectively, then go for DIY with Bliss Poetic Waxing (www.blissworld.co.uk). If you can't bear the idea of wax, try epilation using the Veet Ultimate Bikini 5-in-1 Rechargeable Bikini Trimmer. It comes with a cooling spray, which is a big bonus.

- If you're going to opt for a waxing salon, find a haunt that offers a diversity of shapes, so you're not forced into anything. Enquire about the use of chamomile wax; it can ease the pain and redness. In a good salon, you should be in and out in half an hour, max. I'd recommend www.fernskinclinic.com.

- Getting a beautician to come to your home saves a lot of hassle. Waxing while watching *EastEnders* is the best way to take your mind off the job in hand.

- If you're sure of your shape and have a bit of dosh to spare, you could consider laser therapy, which aims to permanently remove hair after a series of six sessions (www.skinclinics.co.uk). For a good DIY alternative, invest in a Philips Lumea, which permanently removes hair, but will set you back £400 for the privilege. Just remember, however much these shortcut a lifetime of waxing, once trimmed, there's no going back. You may well change your mind about a tiny page-three strip when you qualify for your free bus pass, so be generous with your choice of triangle.

- If you have a problem with ingrown hairs, hold a hot compress against them. It helps ease the sting and encourages the hairs to come out. Then gently remove the hairs with a pair of pointed tweezers.

- If you're looking to give your bikini line some seriously VIP treatment, it's time to embrace the facial for your lady bits. Oh yes, it's the 'Brazilian facial', the new treatment straight from the US of A and available at www.ministryofwaxing.com. Perfect for removing dead cells, treating ingrown hairs, rehydrating skin and, wait for it, acquiring 'lady-garden accessories', making it possible to dye your hair pink or customise it with diamante gems. Totally bonkers, but totally 'now'.

Just because your bush is hidden beneath M&S briefs, don't use that as an excuse to neglect it until a week before you hit the beach. At least offer it a *little* TLC two weeks before the white sands. OK, ten days? Nine? Eight?

Making mad hair manageable

Trawling make-up counters with relish and indulging in an in-depth beauty routine that would rival any *Vogue* cover shoot may not be my thing. Hair, however – well, that's something entirely different. Don't get me wrong. I don't style my locks with tongs, I don't whip up elaborate up-dos in front of the mirror, I don't even wash it more than once a week. I do, however, *love* hair. Maybe it's because I don't have great legs, my stomach isn't as flat as it used to be and I can't apply lippy to save my life, but whatever the reason, my mane is honestly my best asset. Glorious, blow-dried Jennifer Aniston-esque locks they may not be, but I do have a long, pre-Raphaelite mess of curls. And that's a good thing because, in my mind, my hair covers a multitude of other sins – bad skin days, for one; big Dumbo ears, for two.

Life's too short for a bad-hair day every bloody day.

In truth, my long mass of hair isn't really about making a big style statement. I haven't grown it out over the years to keep in with that occasional on-trend big-hair moment, or even to capture my inner Botticelli. If I'm honest, I've probably let it grow wild and free out of fear. As a child, I had bowl cut until the age of ten, when I persuaded my mother to take me to a 'proper salon'. I returned home with the worst cut you've ever seen – a cross between Aled Jones and Horrid Henry. Every year I'd go along full of hope, clutching tear-sheets from *Mizz*, and every year I'd return home with the same tomboy cut. I looked on with envy as the girls at school who sported long, blonde locks had the cool gang dropping at their feet. I, on the other hand, was left to play football with the boys or, worse, spend time in the loos trying to slick down the wispy bits to hide my sticky-out ears. Forget a boyfriend, I'd have been lucky if even the dorkiest of boys knew I existed, let alone asked me out bowling.

You can see why, once I'd managed to grow out that awful short-back-and-sides cut to a bob, and then eventually a shoulder-length mane, I just kept on going. My poor children have fallen victim to my hair issues too. Both my sons resembled Rapunzel until, at the age of four, Mr S whisked my eldest off for the chop. I still can't think about it without welling up. Needless to say, in recent years, I have forced myself to re-train my attitude to healthy hair and visit my trusty hairdresser every couple of months, *for a trim*. I almost forced her to sign a contact stipulating a one-inch maximum before I let her scissors anywhere near me. Fortunately, I've managed to let my hair demons go and generally make it through my forty-minute cut without a stiff drink.

On a good day, my long, curly hair is a blessing; on a bad, it's worse than a 'before' picture plugging Frizz Ease. So as to enjoy more good days than bad, I'm always looking for top tips to achieving healthy-looking hair. I won't profess to have attempted all of the tricks I've gathered up along the way, but between myself and an array of girlfriends – with a tomboy crop, sleek bob, blow-dried perfection, laid-back loose wave, afro and come-to-bed curls between us – we've covered most bases.

- Once you've washed and conditioned, rinse more thoroughly than you think is needed. You'd be surprised how much hair damage is due to product build-up, so easily avoided by one extra rinse under the shower head.

- For afro hair, opt for products rich in essential fatty acids, which are perfect for nourishing hair and scalp.

- If dandruff is a problem, use tea tree oil on the scalp. My friend Abi swears by it and hasn't been bogged down by the white snowflakes for months.

- Pat dry your hair instead of roughly towel drying, and avoid brushing it when wet; this only makes split ends worse. Use your fingers as a brush instead. If, like me, you're prone to tangles, try to avoid getting rid of them from the root; I always end up tearing chunks of hair out this way. Instead, work from the bottom up. I hear patience helps too; I just don't have an awful lot of this where tangles are concerned.

- For frizzy or damaged hair, use a drop of serum while the hair is damp. It will help you achieve nice bouncy curls as opposed to an overall wild, frizztastic disaster.

- Invest in a good dry shampoo (two of my best blow-dry divas swear by Batiste Dry Shampoo and Klorane Gentle Dry Shampoo) or a styling spray with PolyfluoroEster (such as Living Proof: No Frizz Hair Care System Styling Spray). Both give hair great volume without encouraging that thick, gunky feeling of product over-use. Massage it into your hair from the roots down.

- If you're a fan of hair straightening, consider thermal reconditioning, which will permanently smooth and straighten hair. It adds moisture to achieve this, so it's actually good for hair's shine factor.

- I find that the best time to play around with my hair is when it's dirty. Putting it up in a ballerina bun or half up-do, leaving a few stray stands over the face, is the perfect way to try a different look while avoiding washing it for a few more days.

While friends experiment with the new straightening methods direct from LA salons and others console themselves over heartbreak with a new pixie crop, I will probably continue to have the same long, curly hairdo at the age of eighty. As long as the old people's home has a little bit of serum and a diffuser, I'll happily curl my way to the next game of Scrabble, knees safely tucked under my patchwork blanket.

Salon-styled hair every day

by **Lisa Eastwood**, celebrity hairdresser and proud owner of shiny, groomed tresses

I confess, I have the craziest, frizziest hair in the business – so, believe me, I know about taming and treating wild locks! I also cut and style the hair of many A-list women, so it's in my interest to keep on top of easy, failsafe styling know-how. No one has the time for laborious hair-care regimes, especially after you've hit that snooze button in the morning. These shortcuts should help.

- Eating your greens is the first easy tip to great, glossy hair, as boring as it sounds when all you fancy is a Big Mac. Broccoli and the dreaded buzz word 'exercise' both help. Seriously, you want gorgeous hair? Get moving. Anything that stimulates blood flow to the head will boost those roots and give hair shine.

- Wash your hair regularly. In an ideal world, you should wash hair every other day, but twice a week is a realistic goal for good maintenance. For maximum results, it's that crucial 'blood circulation' again, so massage shampoo into the roots for as long as you can (five minutes, if you're not running late). Condition, then comb through when wet.

- Look for shampoo and conditioners loaded with protein. I love Shu Uemura, but if you're strapped for cash, go for Pantene.

- Vow to undertake an intensive hair-care treatment once a week. Kérastase do brilliant nourishing products that will boost your hair's condition if you leave them in for half an hour.

- Every girl needs a good hairdryer. My motto is that a dryer must be light, fast and hot. Parlux is a good name to know. Before you dry, spritz your hair with Heat Protector Spray by Oribe, which coats the follicles and stops the dryer burning your hair. The last thing you want is long-term crispy, singed locks. Bad, bad, bad.

- If you need a quick fix to take your hair from the office to the dance floor, turn your head upside down and massage the roots with your fingertips. Add a little serum and hairspray, and you can leave that air of drab, dull hair at your desk.

- When you're looking for the perfect hairdresser, always go on recommendation. Make sure you have a consultation first and always, always start with a trim. If your stylist can't get this right, you've no hope.

- Once you've sourced a faithful hairdresser, remember that they might double up as a therapist, but they're unlikely to be mind-readers too. Always take a reference of your preferred style from an online source or glossy mag.

- Even if you're rising up your thirties, don't be afraid to grow hair long. It's a myth that the older you get, the shorter your hair should be. My client Demi Moore is a great example of this. Her long locks have never looked more fabulous and just get better with age. Forget the pixie crop; long hair is where it's at!

Bronzing without morphing into a vintage croc clutch bag

I may as well come straight out with it: PC or not, I love having a suntan. While many of my girlfriends work the English Rose look, I still lust after the beach-bronzed, tousled, sea-swept-hair vibe channelled by the Elles, Claudias and Siennas of this world. In my eyes, I look a million times better when sun-kissed. Or, after a fortnight in Ibiza, sun-snogged.

While I'm in this confessional mood, I may as well go the full monty and own up to a few more sun sins:

- Sin 1 – In my early twenties, at my tanning peak, I indulged in sun beds once a fortnight. Even in December.

- Sin 2 – At around the same time, I remember going on a Greek island-hopping adventure with Mr S. By day ten, I was applying baby oil and doing a good impersonation of a lizard schvitzing in the midday sun.

- Sin 3 – I've burnt my skin more times than I've burnt toast and, although I favour muesli in the morning, a toaster is a firm fixture in my life.

So you see, my attitude to tanning is about as cool as being seen in a little black dress and Choos at Glastonbury. Not. Very. At. All.

Many of you Nicole Kidman lookalikes will delight in hearing that now is payback time. Since hitting my thirties, the sun damage has begun to rear its ugly head and bite back with a vengeance. Sun lines have popped up all over my face and, to my horror, I recently noticed a prominent mole on my bikini line had almost tripled in size. After a night of hot sweats, imagining my three kids growing up without a mother, I got it checked out at the Mole Clinic (www.themoleclinic.co.uk). Being the sun-lover that I am, my first thought on getting the mole all-clear was 'How far am I to the nearest sun-bed salon?' Not too dissimilar to the George Best rehab/nearest pub scenario.

Thankfully, as the years roll by and the squint lines stare out and gloat at me from the bathroom mirror, I'm learning to embrace a much healthier attitude to tanning. While I still long for the sting of sunburnt cheeks and the feel-good factor of that pre-weekend sun bed, I tot up the crow's feet and opt for a Friday-feeling Crunchie instead. I'm still partial to that summer sun-kissed look, but a few of these shortcuts have helped me embrace my inner beach babe without resorting to baby oil and direct sunlight at 90°F. I'll leave that crispy, dark-chocolate look to my vintage croc clutch, thanks very much.

- Head to your nearest tanning salon for a full-body spray of St Tropez or Fantasy Tan. No streaks, no too-orange ankles, no flight to the Maldives needed. Time-consuming and expensive to do on a regular basis, but worth it in the lead-up to your best friend's birthday, where you're dying to wear that new Whistles body-contour dress accessorised with bare, bronzed legs.

- DIY fake tans. I'm not a huge fan of fake tan, but it's growing on me. Top tips to success are to prime the skin first by taking a hot shower and shaving your legs, underarms and bikini-line (shaving the day after will take a layer of the self-tan off). Exfoliate thoroughly and dollop some Vaseline on your nails and cuticles to prevent staining (the ultimate giveaway). Evenly apply your fake tan. Wash your hands well afterwards. I once forgot and looked tangoed for at least a week. After experimenting with tons of cheap brands and ending up with orange-stained undies, I gave in and speed-dialled my friend and fake-tan mistress Ellie, who works the natural bronze look like an expert. She suggested four hot favourites: Clarins Delicious Self Tanning Cream, Rodial Brazilian Tan Light, Garnier Ambre Solaire No Streaks Bronzer and the new, hot-to-trot St Tropez Naturals range. I've never looked back.

- Save time by just faking the legs. Another fake-tan-fanatic friend of mine advises to start faux-tanning legs in May, so you're ready for that Top Shop floral sundress that demands bare legs in mid-June. Her tip is to keep legs a shade browner than the rest of you by opting for a darker self-tan, like Sienna X.

- Tint the face instead. Fake-tan your face, and you run the risk of looking more Orangina than Bahamas bronze. Opt for tinted moisturisers instead: Guerlain's Terracotta range is fab. You could always bronze up the cheekbones using bronzer too. Keep some Body Shop bronzing balls or Bobbi Brown Shimmer Brick in your handbag and use them on your cheeks and brow after work and before Happy Hour.

- Sun it, but go easy. Admittedly, if you're ever in the Balearics in August, you're likely to see me on the beach attempting to simultaneously make sandcastles with three children and turn the pages of the latest chick-lit read. I do, however, regularly slather SPF 20 on my face (with total block in the corners of my eyes), a slightly lower SPF on my body and SPF 50 lip-block on my lips. In recent years, I've even been known to sport a wide-brimmed hat between 11 a.m. and 2 p.m., when the sun's at its hottest. Don't make my cash-saving mistake of hoarding leftover Sisley SPF 20 year upon year. Sunscreen loses its power after twelve months, and I learnt the hard way. Blending lobster-stylie with the bright-pink sunset at cocktail hour is such a bad look.

Sussing all the anti-aging jargon *(and deciding whether Botox and fillers should remain the exclusive domain of footballers' wives and MILFs)*

The game 'has she or hasn't she' is a brilliant one to play when passing time in any swanky bar on a night out. It's also a good pastime when watching presenters on prime-time television and isn't a bad way to kill time when flicking through the cheap weeklies on the way home from work. I must confess, though, this pastime was much more fun when boob jobs were more D-cup than double FF and Botox was subtle as opposed to the frozen-robot effect. In recent years, women's obsession with surgery has turned beautiful faces into freak shows and spoils all the fun of 'has she or hasn't she'. It's now more likely to be 'We know she has, but what *was* she thinking?!'

I'm actually not anti cosmetic surgery at all; it just saddens me when women take it too far and transform themselves into scary science-fiction figures. I'm certainly not going to go all coy and pretend I've never indulged in a little

Life's too short to max up that Visa in an attempt to look like a sixteen-year-old cover star (especially when you're a mother of three in your thirties).

bit of artificial youth-boosting myself. After a particularly knackering period of toddler-induced broken sleep, I had supper with one of my uber-groomed and gorgeous girlfriends. After a large array of tapas and an even larger glass of Pinot Noir, she slipped me the number of her Botox guru. The business card spent two weeks burning a hole in my jeans pocket until, after yet another 5 a.m. start and shock-horror chance glimpse of myself in the rear-view mirror, I punched the number into my phone and took the plunge.

When I arrived at the clinic, I felt like the new girl on her first day at school. All the big-kid pros mulling around the waiting room looked like they knew exactly what they were doing; coiffed blow-dries and Manolos at the ready, these women meant Botox business. I, on the other hand, clutched my satchel bag nervously and wondered if I could crawl out from behind the sofa and nip into Starbucks for a comforting hot chocolate instead.

Just under an hour later, I'd had a syringe containing Botox inserted into various 'problem' areas on my brow, and my forehead felt like it'd been hit by a cricket bat. I walked to the nearest tube, convinced everyone knew my secret. My eyes watered as I dabbed the little cotton wool pad to the needle-prick on my crow's feet. Relaxing? Pampering? Nourishing? No. Worth it? I wasn't so sure.

A week later, however, I saw what all the fuss was about. I looked refreshed, revived and ten years younger. People asked if I'd been away on a spa mini-break and words I hadn't heard for years, like 'radiant', 'glowing' and 'healthy', were bandied about when engaging in day-to-day pleasantries with colleagues and mums at the school gate. I felt bloody amazing. Never mind that no one could tell the difference between my cross, sad or happy expressions, and that Mr S fessed up to preferring my face much more 'before I started all this nonsense'. I was wrinkle-free and loving it.

Really and truly, you want to know the low-down? Life's busy; I'm time poor and, more often than not, can't justify spending £250 on my wrinkles when the gas bill's just come in. If I'm *really* honest, I also quite like the fact that when I laugh my face laughs with me. It's also useful that when I'm cross with my toddler for throwing his fish fingers across the kitchen floor, he knows I'm fuming without me having to raise my voice. The lack of frown lines is seriously confusing when trying to discipline your children.

Luckily, I'm not a footballer's wife with a pillow face, and I don't qualify as a MILF with a surgery habit either. However, I am a thirty-something working mum who views cosmetic advancement with intrigue. For those of you who are a little like me, here's the beauty low-down you need to know now, plus the ways to get it all fast, with or without a syringe in sight (or a two-hundred-quid bill burning in your pocket).

Invasive

Botox

So, we've heard it bandied about a million times in our favourite magazines, but what is Botox? OK, short and sweet: a doctor will administer several injections into your facial muscles. You may feel a little frozen afterwards and side effects can include headaches and minor bruising, but you'll notice an improvement in lines within three to seven days. Depending on your skin type, the effects can last up to four months, sometimes longer. If you're going to opt for the syringe, what you should ask for to avoid the 'I can't raise my forehead or smile properly' effect is a gentle approach to lines using light Botox (or 'baby Botox'). Most savvy, modern women want prevention from aging not a cure (say hello to subtle radiance and goodbye to the deep-freeze look). Costing from £200, these reputable doctors will work with you to avoid 'android syndrome':

- Dr Sebagh – www.drsebagh.com
- Dr Prager – www.drmichaelprager.com
- Dr Nasbet – www.julesnabet.com
- Dr Eccleston – www.medizen.co.uk

Xeomin

Touted as 'the new Botox' by my girlfriends in the know, this neurotoxin injection works like Botox in freezing facial muscles to stop lines and wrinkles. Costs from £200. Try Dr Dancey – www.bijoux-medispa.co.uk.

Combination cosmetics and dermatology

If you've got a fortune to spare and are hell bent on going down the tox route, then consider going for a combo of light Botox with great dermatology and non-invasive skin-care maintenance. A slow, considered approach to the signs of aging seems a far more gentle option to me. Dr Lowe is great for this (www.drnicklowe.com), as is Dr Prager (www.drmichaelprager.com), if you can get an appointment after he's seen almost every top-tier A-lister on the planet.

P.S. Always check a doctor's qualifications and ask to view case studies of previous clients. A practice may be cheap, but will you end up looking like a war victim with wonky eyebrows?

P.P.S If you're opting for invasive procedures, don't make the mistake of doing it right before big events or holidays. Botox can cause bruising and peels can leave skin red and scaly. Such a bad look in snaps. Instead, make your appointment a few weeks before and take anti-inflammatory medication and arnica to help calm down the reaction.

Non-Invasive

OK, I'll be honest with you; I tussled with the previous section on syringes for months. You don't really want to hear about the late nights debating with my conscience and endless conversations with my sister where she tried to talk me out of even mentioning the 'B' word. My overall thinking was simple: 'Can I really write an up-to-date, honest guide for modern women and not give the low-down on Botox and fillers?' Eventually I concluded that I could not. Choice is surely one of the best outcomes of being a modern woman in a modern world? But, seeing as you're asking, my gut instinct is: don't go there if you can avoid it. Shouldn't we try our best not to perpetuate the fight-all signs-of-aging beauty myth if we can help it? So, what can we do to pamper a face that needs more sleep and less stress without succumbing to the A-list, quick-fix option?

Facials and DIY treatments

More and more women are opting for a gentle, non-invasive route to great skin, and if you ask me, an hour-long facial massage or DIY exfoliation beats painful injections on the relaxation scale hands down. The idea of combining massage and enriching skin-care products to hide the signs of 'my life is bloody knackering' must surely be high on any thinking woman's agenda? On the high street, Clarins, Decléor and Darphin are great for a truly relaxing facial experience that also plumps and hydrates the skin.

If you want a real treat, my beauty guru pal Shazza swears by Eve Lom. When I ask why, she says simply, 'They use gentle wax to open the pores for extraction and a lymphatic drainage to help remove impurities under the skin. You won't find a woman whose skin doesn't radiate the moment she walks out.' Sold. Check www.spacenk.com or www.evelom. co.uk. You could also try the diamond microdermabrasion, acoustic wave therapy and laser no-needles face lift at the Derm Clinic (www.dermclinic.co.uk).

You could also try a DIY facial peel or exfoliation to help smooth wrinkles and give you a quick-fix flawless skin tone. Alpha hydroxyl acids might sound scary but if your skin's not too sensitive, products that use AHAs are a great way to smooth fine lines – fast. Good buys include Dr Dennis Gross Alpha Beta Daily Face Peel and Sarah Chapman Overnight Exfoliating Booster. No salon, no syringe, no worries.

Another more natural option is to defy gravity and the dreaded needle by opting for a facial massage that works from the inside of your mouth. Yes, really. Facialist to the stars Nichola Joss has pioneered the treatment of massaging skin 'internally' and, although it can hurt, her technique visibly raises your cheekbones (www.nicholajoss.com).

DIY creams

Surely applying a face cream guaranteed to reduce wrinkles and plump up and nourish skin is by far the easiest/quickest/cheapest shortcut to beautiful skin, with the added bonus of keeping our morals intact. OK, so here's my low-down of the best anti-aging lotions and positions on the market.

1. Lancôme Genifique Youth Activating Concentrate and Estée Lauder Re-Nutriv Ultimate Lift Age-Correcting Creme Extra Rich. Both promise to re-boost gene activity to prevent anti-aging. Wow, I feel like I've stepped onto the set of *Star Trek*. A sure-fire way to give skin a flawless glow, but beware – neither are cheap.

2. Dr Sebagh Serum Repair. Get a touch of Sebagh's miracle work without the surgery by putting this on your Christmas list. With a mix of hydrating and collagen-boosting ingredients, it will make you look visibly prettier and younger within days.

3. Dr Nick Lowe's The Secret is Out range contains peptides that fade expression lines and instantly lift skin.

4. L'Oreal Youth Code Serum. Fans of the highly regarded Youth Code range will love the fact that this product contains ten times more Pro-Gen gene technology than the day cream. Luminous skin in one nifty, sleek bottle.

5 Trilogy Certified Organic Rosehip Oil. Massage this into
skin before bed and you'll have noticeably plumper, fresher
skin by the time you're eating your morning muesli. Smells
delicious too.

6 Nivea Visage Q10 Plus Anti-Wrinkle Day Cream. Slather this
on before work and within four weeks fine lines will look
smoother. A snip at around a tenner.

Pop a pill

Believe it or not, you can actually pop a pill after brekkie and
achieve facial plumping and uplift in a matter of weeks. Face
Up-Lift Capsules by Dr Nirdosh state their main ingredient as
silicon dioxide, which reverses signs of aging. Surely this is the
stuff of beauty miracles? Check out www.drnirdosh.com.

There is no doubt that these cosmetic shortcuts can make you
look younger and save you bags of time undertaking DIY facial
exercises in front of the mirror. Having said that, many *do* cost
the earth and the invasive methods really and truly make you
question the whole arena of growing old gracefully. My late
grandmother, who had the most beautiful laugh-lined, life-
lived face in the world, would turn in her grave if she knew I'd
been anywhere near a needle in pursuit of a frown-free brow.

The point is, if you have the dosh, you're lucky to have a
multitude of ever-evolving choices at your fingertips. Just
consider carefully what approach you want to take to aging.
Many great doctors now fully embrace 'aging maintenance',
which incorporates dermatology and cosmetic procedures, but
still, is this manufactured approach to slowing the natural
process of aging a beauty ritual we really want to hand on to
our daughters? I'm certainly hoping to teach mine to laugh
more in life, not how to get rid of the signs of it. However, I'm

not going to preach, for I too have lines, wrinkles and tired skin that bug the hell out of me, and I too have experimented with the needle. However, what I will say is this: whatever you decide, just attempt to stay savvy and aware. If you've got the money and inclination to indulge in a multitude of 'beautifying' methods, use modern science and skin-care hand in hand to avoid that irreversible wind-tunnel look. This will only shortcut your way to freak-face, with a huge credit card debt to boot. Oh yes, and a daughter who eventually thinks it's normal to have a mother who looks younger than her. Oh dear.

CHAPTER SIX

FASHIONISTA

Decluttering your wardrobe without breaking out in hives

The thought of decluttering my wardrobe used to have me hot under my Whistles Peter Pan blouse collar. Surely this sort of fashion organisation was only necessary if you were a stylist for French *Vogue* or an uber-rich, ultra-groomed slave to trends who overhauled each Chloe/Balenciaga/Burberry garment in their closet to make room for the new season 'must-haves'? I stress the past tense here because, in recent years, I've realised that decluttering my wardrobe is almost the only failsafe shortcut to saving time and money in the fashion stakes.

I came to this realisation after my first child was born and the much anticipated 'moving house mayhem' was upon me. Once I'd labelled the boxes for 'chick flick DVDs – no chucking', 'wedding snaps – handle with care' and 'Grey Goose vodka – pack for easy access', it was time to sort out the goods for 'Grace's wardrobe – *do not touch*'. Working in 'fash-on', I was under the illusion this would be swift and easy. How wrong could a girl be? Take note: this took a full day of hard graft. How was it possible that one style-savvy girl-about-town could have such an array of fashion faux pas in one small space? Stone-washed skinny jeans with *ankle zips*, fuchsia-pink prom skirt with tulle underlay, fitted blouse in shimmery cream satin with waist darts? Bad, bad, bad. It wasn't until I'd shifted through the shameful Bros stone-wash and 'I am obviously a repressed six-year-old' tulle that I realised I had a few forgotten gems hidden in the depths of the fashion void.

Ever since rediscovering a Vanessa Bruno hip-skimming LBD beneath piles of jeans and a long-lost Kate Moss for Top Shop floral blouse down the back of the GAP sweatshirts, I've vowed to attempt a wardrobe overhaul at least once a year. Here is my tried-and-tested, failsafe route to closet nirvana – and it won't cost you a penny.

1. Pick a free afternoon when the in-laws aren't popping over and Selfridges doesn't start its sale. Empty the contents of your wardrobe. If you're lucky enough to know someone with a clothes rail, borrow it and hang garments on it for easy viewing. Pile your jeans/jumpers/tracksuits/Ts close by.

2. Be ruthless and edit out anything that comes under the following heading:

- Too small (and even if you lost a few pounds on that pre-summer Special K diet, it would still be on the wrong side of snug).

- Too big. Boyfriend baggy jeans work; oversized men's shirts do not.

- Too battered and worn to pass as anything other than bag lady. Love a vintage sundress with the odd tear here and there; however, a tweed skirt with a missing panel, no zip and a frayed hem is best binned.

- Too passé. Yes, those stone-wash, zipped skinnies must go.

- Haven't worn it in the last year. It sounds harsh, but I usually find that if I haven't worn something in the past year (eighteen months at a push), it will remain unworn for the next five. After my first few wardrobe declutter sessions, the same few items popped up, unworn and unloved. I'd delude myself that maybe, just maybe, I'd have the chance to wear my beaded bolero with faux-fur edging, a snip at £12 in the summer 2002 Top Shop sale, for the school run, but yet another year would pass and it would still be gathering dust.

3 Repeat this cycle with your undies, hosiery, shoes, bags and coats.

4 If you really want to fine-tune your closet à la glossy-mag fashion stylist, this would be a good time to put outfits together. By teaming looks (and, if you're feeling brave, accessories that work with them), you'll have a much better idea of what you're using and what's going to waste. My fashion editor friend Gayle goes as far as to Polaroid these outfits, complete with slouchy maxi bag, Ray-Ban shades, ballet pumps and chunky men's watch, miraculously taking all the stress out of 'What the hell do I wear today and I'm already half an hour late for work?!' Now that's devotion for you.

5 Once you've sorted through all those piles of old-season jeans and T-shirts you never knew you had, put your 'keep' items back into your wardrobe and chest of drawers. Again stealing wisdom from style guru Gayle, you could use this as an opportunity to morph into a fashion fanatic and replace hanging clothes in colour order, stack jeans in similar styles,

take out any clothes that need mending, altering, washing or dry-cleaning and replace all wire hangers with wooden ones. I've never been this organised, but that doesn't mean I wouldn't like to be.

6   Whether you colour co-ordinate your frocks (fabulous fashionista) or just bung them back into your wardrobe on mismatched hangers (me), you'll still be left with a heap of discarded wardrobe booty piled high on your bed. Now's the time to get rid. You know me and my clutter phobia, so I love this part. Bin, charity, eBay or swap are my usual hot four options. If you're time poor, there are companies/individuals popping up who'll eBay clothes for you for a cut of the cash. Try Nikki Bull (nikkibull2000@yahoo.co.uk). Failing this, clothes-swapping parties are now a rite of passage for women in their late twenties and early thirties, but thankfully come minus the group humiliation of hen nights. Text those girlies with a known stash of unworn Reiss goodies now.

At this stage, I'd advise giving in to the strong impulse to open a bottle of Pinot Noir. Seeing as you've discarded that size ten LBD, there's no point in denying yourself a reward. If you can be bothered to nail the process properly, take your vino glass in hand and jot down a few of the clothes you need to fill the gaps left in your wardrobe. On my last closet clearout, for example, I realised I had about 75 per cent boho, summery, wafty clothes – perfect for my alter-life living beside the ocean in Ibiza – and only 25 per cent items for my actual life living in wet, windy, congested, stressful London. After I'd edited out a few floaty skirts that no longer did up around my three-kids middle and ditched a handful of halter-necks that had long lost their original white zing, I could see that what I really needed was a functional stay-dry trench coat and a wear-everyday grey cardigan. Once I'd eBayed those maxi skirts, I went straight to GAP before you'd time to say, 'I want to look like Claudia Schiffer on the school run, not an incense-burning old hippie.'

If you're anything like me, you'd *like* to have time for this type of military closet overhaul twice a year – just as the weather changes and those white broderie anglaise sundresses are clogging up your wardrobe instead of snug, black roll-necks. Alas, in practice, I only ever manage this once a year, and even that's probably an exaggeration. But for the sake of style shortcuts, I *do* try.

I should add one final note here: if you have the cash to spare, you can bypass the obligatory chaos of a DIY wardrobe clearout and go straight to the preferred choice of most wedged-up celebrities. Pay a top stylist to do it for you. I won't beat around the bush: this really is the ultimate busy woman's shortcut to wardrobe salvation. Gayle Rinkoff, celebrity and TV stylist (www.gaylerinkoff.com), offers this service, and you can also check out www.practicalprincess.com.

Selling your prize gems on eBay, enabling you to splurge the proceeds on the new Marc Jacobs clutch

Before prepping that Reiss velvet jacket for sale, make sure you're absolutely committed to letting it go. There's no guarantee it will sell for more than a fiver and you'll get tarnished as a bad seller if you remove an item because you didn't get the price you wanted. Decision made to say farewell (even if you only earn enough for pick 'n' mix), then proceed with these easy steps:

Step 1: Photograph your items on a digital camera. Don't spend ages trying to create an enticing scene; simplicity is best, so go for a white background. Snap at least four shots from different angles (front, back, details and label).

Step 2: Upload the images.

Step 3: Log on to www.ebay.com and create an account.

Step 4: Write a description of what you're selling. You need as much detail as you can – measurements, colour, fabric, age and any imperfections. This doesn't require Shakespearean prose; however, adopting descriptive words will entice buyers: 'Stunning, hand-embroidered, authentic, limited edition Liberty shawl' and so on . . .

Step 5: Select a selling price. If you start low, you'll encourage people to bid. I know it sounds laughable, but pricing a designer gem at as little as £10 will be sure to generate interest.

Step 6: Choose a postage method, postage price and payment method. Don't worry if the specifics of this sound daunting; all the options are listed on the site. Just bear in mind when deciding on payment method that PayPal is the most efficient way to receive money. Who wants to wait around for a cheque that runs the risk of getting lost in the post?

Step 7: Download the eBay app for your iPhone, so you can 'watch' your item whenever you choose.

Step 8: Respond to all the random questions fired your way, e.g. 'How many inches is the cuff?' and 'What shade of lilac is the lily embroidery on the hem?'

Step 9: Wait for the bidding to start.

Step 10: Once your loot is sold, send it off to Finland/ Glasgow/San Francisco and reward yourself with a surf on www.net-a-porter.com. Just try not to spend all your newly earned cash at once.

Choosing underwear that gives oomph as opposed to a VPL and four breasts

I confess, I'm an undies hoarder. Maybe it's because I'm sentimental about the memories they evoke, or maybe it's just because I'm running scared from the fact that I no longer live the life of matching Agent Ps. M&S comfy hipster pants would be more apt. Whatever the reason for my hoarding, my underwear drawer is dated and downtrodden. I may well own a Myla silk camisole in black, but I can't reach it behind the piles of disorganised white cotton, low-slung briefs, inside-out black opaque tights and ancient bras with the underwire poking through. That lovely Myla number may as well stay scrunched up in a ball forever more; I just haven't the time to find it in the morning beneath the depths of tangled Marks & Spencer lace.

My friend May's attitude to undies is no different from mine. She has a whole *three* drawers devoted to bustiers, thongs, hipsters and suspender belts, most of which haven't been given an airing since the millennium. After a straw poll of other girlies, it seems we're all hoarding lingerie in the hope of capturing our inner Victoria's Secret cover girl, when in actual fact we live 99 per cent of the time in grey-from-overuse, three-for-two panties. Not only this, but most of our kit is badly fitting, digs in at the back and distorts our otherwise OK busts into hoiked-up, over-inflated, page-three 'stunners' or, worse still, makes us look like we have four breasts.

A few years back, after breastfeeding my third child for six months and basically handing over any pert loveliness to my footloose and fancy-free single friends, I decided to embark on an underwear mission. My pre-kids bras no longer fitted, my all-in-one suspender corset number was gathering dust, my bust was crying out for some retail TLC and my boob self-esteem needed lifting (in more ways than one).

First stop was to get myself measured professionally – Rigby and Peller every time (www.rigbyandpeller.co.uk). Failing that, M&S will do the trick (www.marksandspencer.com). Once you've sussed your size (34B, seeing as you asked), you can work out what styles suit you and what you're actually going to wear day to day and for that occasional come-to-bed seduction session. To shortcut the underwear maze, remember a few of these tried and tested facts:

- Boy-cut hipster knickers are brilliant for hiding VPLs and are comfy for almost every occasion you can imagine.

- Low-rise thongs are unflattering and uncomfortable for just about anyone who isn't a flat-stomached, no-bottom, size-eight waif.

- Big, high-cut knickers are perfect for that end-of-the-day, trackie-bottoms comfort factor. Cotton, white, generously sized and ideal when accompanied by a large supper of lasagne. Sorted.

- Although most of my girlfriends agree that padded bras offer good support and a little much-needed oomph, try to avoid over-padded numbers, as you'll end up more Dolly Parton than 'hello, boys' Eva Herzigova.

- No-wire, seamless bras are great for everyday ease and if, like me, you don't want a big OTT cleavage they tick all the boxes for understated style. I love my lace triangle bras by Calvin Klein and nylon spandex micro-mesh cross-back bra by American Apparel. The latter is a snip at around a tenner, so you could even justify nabbing one in white and one in hot-pink or purple – fab worn with a racer-back vest (www.americanapparel.co.uk). They are comfortable, have clean lines and are easy to wear under almost all the tops I own, including the faithful white T.

- Balconette bras are your best option for a lifted bust and because the straps are skinny and further apart than on alternative bras, they're the perfect choice for low-cut tops and frocks.

- For a minimising bra, sports bra or how-the-hell-do-I-keep-my-bust-pert-in-a-backless-dress bra, then head to Marks & Spencer. Trusted undies and value for money. See, your mother was right about some things.

- Red undies only make you look like a hooker. Turquoise, hot-pink or even grey are good experimental choices, just not red. Never ever.

After ransacking the high street, I came to the conclusion that, whatever your size, shape and style, the following are essential:

- Extra control M&S magic knickers or the TK Maxx version of Spanx (a snip at around a fiver per pair). They'll hold it all in for that fitted-contour Reiss dress occasion.

- A few pairs of flesh-coloured knickers. Essential for when you dig out that sundress and fake tan those legs to wear bare.

- A good sports bra.

- A couple of blow-you-away, sexy-siren sets. You can't beat Agent Provocateur (www.agentprovocateur.com), Myla (www.myla.com) or Cos (www.cosstores.com) for this.

- For your everyday, bog-standard, matching-if-possible, comfort-is-key sets, try M&S, Calvin Klein (www.calvinkleininc.com), Elle Macpherson (www.ellemacpherson.com) or Top Shop. One-stop shop at www.figleaves.com and you'll bag everything you need. The free returns policy means that if that lacy plunge bra rides up your back or cuts in under the armpit, it'll be refunded or changed in a flash.

Jordan I may not be, but at least my new, improved, less hoarding, more what-I-need-for-my-life attitude to undies means I can make the most of the body I have. Now I just need to dismiss those *Curb Your Enthusiasm* box sets and make time for that black silk Myla number and Mr S will be happy too.

Nailing the ultimate wardrobe essentials

Believe me, I want to have a chic capsule wardrobe, I really do. I just get sidetracked by tie-dyed silk caftans at the beach boutique on holiday and by lace blouses in River Island that look great in the campaign shots, but maybe not so great on me. This does lead me to ponder on the enviable classic chic of women I admire. I just want to know the answer to one simple question: how do they cut through the crap to find fabulous staples they wear over and over again, defining their style and avoiding big fashion boo-boos along the way? Take my friends Jacky and Missy. Admittedly they work in the 'style industry' so have trend know-how at their fingertips, but I don't think

I've ever seen them in anything as shock-horror as stone-wash jeans or a satin pussy-bow blouse in the five years I've known them. Not even a bad bag or an 'oh, she really shouldn't have' heel. My friend Ros has the same effect. She might update her Breton-striped GAP knit with a parka or

Life's too short to wear a bra that gives you four boobs.

trench to suit the occasion, or accessorise her various jeans and Ts with a trusty Louis Vuitton scarf, but she never looks dated, overdone or try-hard. Somehow, these girls just know how it works.

Even in the height of my heady fashion days, I never quite pinned down that grown-up classic air of sophistication. I was still the boho girl-about-town who embraced wacky new designers and one-off, risk-taking odds and sods. While the rest of the fashion pack played it safe in black Lanvin, oversized Tom Ford shades and the obligatory Chanel chain bag, I'd never be scared to rock up in a colourful maxi skirt, bashed-up old 501 jackets and a Portobello Market leather tassel bag. I remember some years ago attending a swanky party in New York. While all the skinny minnies around me donned little black dresses by Balenciaga, I went to the other extreme in a wafty, floor-length chiffon dress. By the fourth Sunrise Margarita, the skin-mins teetered off the dance floor with blisters inflicted by their sky-high heels; I just went barefoot. Worked well with the frock, and my feet were eternally grateful.

Still, my closet clearout is testament to the fact that 'experimental' can also equate to 'disorganised chaos of fashion mistakes', so I think it's about time I looked into nailing a few classic must-haves to fuse with my medley of boho gems. My eternal hope is that this may shortcut some fashion angst.

Gaining inspiration from Missy, Jacky and Ros, with a nod to our role model Emmanuelle Alt, as well as designers who pride themselves on beautifully cut staple masterpieces (cue Stella McCartney, Margaret Howell, Phoebe Philo, Burberry), here is a quick hit list of grown-up trusties:

- The classic trench coat. Burberry if you're loaded; H&M if you're not; Isabella Oliver 365 if you're somewhere in between (www.burberry.co.uk; www.hm.com, www.isabellaoliver.com).

- A blazer, tux or tweed jacket. Any sort, as long as it's fitted and works equally well with jeans and a dress. Try Zara (www.zara.com) or Cos (www.cosstores.com).

- A pea-coat. Head for Joseph (www.joseph.co.uk) or Warehouse (www.warehouse.co.uk) and team with a roll-neck or crisp white shirt.

- The perfect little black dress. Even as queen of boho, I cling to my Roland Mouret like a life raft from October through to May, when it's far too cold to air those wafty maxis. My Reiss belted, big-shoulder number skids in a close second (www.reissonline.com), but if you're looking for a simple black frock for under £40, check out Forever21 (www.forever21.com).

- Roll-necks in black and camel. Cashmere or a wool mix fit the bill. Look no further than Marks & Spencer, Primark (www.primark.co.uk) or Johnstons (www.johnstonscashmere.com).

- The Breton-striped long-sleeve T-shirt. GAP usually has all you need when it comes to well-made, soon-to-be-well-loved cotton Ts (www.gap.eu).

- The perfect white T-shirt. Harder than it sounds to find. American Apparel (www.americanapparel.com) and GAP are worth a look.

- Jeans that make you look a size smaller with an extra two inches on your legs. Cigarette or bootleg win hands down every time. Head for the jeans floor in Selfridges (www.selfridges.com) to blow your mind and your budget, or Uniqlo for less explosive but equally wearable alternatives (www.uniqlo.com).

- A lazy-day, off-duty sweatshirt and trackie bottoms or harem pants. Any faithful high-street brand will do. Just avoid chav sports logos and go for plain grey marl if possible.

- Something with an animal print. French Sole's leopard-print ballet pumps go with just about everything (www.frenchsole.com).

- An f-off fabulous bag. If you can afford anything by Katie Hillier/Mulberry/Chanel/Prada, I still think it's worth the spend. If not Sara Berman does great leather bags which are just as much of a statement (www.saraberman.co.uk) or nab a soft leather maxi-bag from Whistles (www.whistles.co.uk).

- Ray-Ban aviator shades, or similar rip-offs. All you need to know about looking cool with a hangover.

To make sure you save bucks on any new essential purchases, log on to Daily Candy (www.dailycandy.com), who give daily updates on all the best sample sales and shopping discounts. I love a good bargain, especially when it starts with 'Miu Miu' and ends with 'bag'.

Life's too short for cheap, itchy viscose.

One last tip, though: don't attempt to buy them all at once. Firstly, you'll have your bank manager leaving you nasty answerphone messages by dawn. Secondly, you run the risk of losing your individual oomph and flair while channelling that sophisticated air of glamour. Instead, invest in a few classics if and when you can. Use the cheap and cheerful high street for basics like T-shirts and knitwear, and build up a capsule collection of staples to mix 'n' match with other much-loved items in your existing wardrobe. Now we have really no excuse for sporting badly fitting chinos and our other half's lumberjack shirt in the hope of capturing our inner fashionista.

Standing out from the crowd without looking like a dodgy extra from *The Rocky Horror Show*

The only teeny-tiny glitch with the Breton stripe, trench coat, leopard-print ballet pump combo is that we all run the risk of wearing it on the same day. Any semi-stylish girl knows that clone wars are even worse than viscose fashion faux pas. For day-to-day, no-brainer throw-ons, the basic wardrobe essentials tick all the boxes. Ease, speed, effortless chic, we like. Too much ridged conformity, we don't. If you're anything like me, this may well have the same effect as forbidding an errant teenager to smoke. See that twenty-a-day Marlboro-Light habit coming atcha fast? In short, too much safe dressing can tip you over the fashion cliff straight into a sea of deviant risks, testing boundaries and pushing new limits. Oh dear, I see distressed leather jeggings, a one-shouldered, puff-sleeved origami blouse and a chiffon cape with a sequinned appliqué tiger head emerging from the waves. *Do not go there!* Take it from me, I've made a few fashion mistakes in my time, and it's just not worth it (a Mr Byrite scratchy, neon-pink roll-neck with dungarees and clogs says all one needs to about bad clothes choices).

So how do you mix up that GAP white T and Cos tux combo with something statement and not end up looking ridiculous or pleading bankruptcy to fund it? Invest in a gem by a niche new designer, of course. To avoid appliquéd-sequinned-tiger-head syndrome, here are a few places to start.

- Top Shop Unique (www.topshop.com). Great innovative clothes that look like they've walked off the Milanese catwalk, but don't involve the same excessive zeros on the price tag.

- Check out your local high street for designer link-ups. Valentino for GAP, Lanvin for Hennes, Julien MacDonald, Jonathan Saunders and Preen for Debenhams, Louise Gray for Asos, Jil Sander for Uniqlo, Roksanda Ilincic for Whistles, David Koma for Top Shop and Missoni for Converse. So goddamn good it does make you wonder why you'd ever want to pay silly prices for full-price designer booty again. Just a bit, anyway.

- Browns Focus (www.brownsfashion.com), Liberty (www.liberty.co.uk) and www.farfetch.com are all hot beds for showcasing cutting-edge new design talent. My money's on Jean Pierre Braganza. Anyone who has worked for Roland Mouret is likely to have the power to instantly transform you from sluggish to sensational. It's amazing what uber-talent and a few metres of draped black silk can do for a woman.

- Click on to www.start-london.com and find your favourite cutting-edge designers even if you're hundreds of miles from east London (and don't have a trendy mullet haircut). Press 'buy' on anything designed by Acne and you can safely presume you'll look seriously edgy without a hint of ridiculous.

- Mix with some Office pointed courts, your favourite maxi bag and Ray-Ban aviators and tell me you haven't totally nailed a look. Don't be shy now, work it.

Making the most of the high-street jungle

by **Eliza Doolittle**, pop starlet and owner of the best legs in London

The best way to cut through rails and rails of high-street viscose blouses and faux leather jackets is to keep your eyes peeled for a cult item. I'd go for anything kooky or a little bit weird (in the good sense!) and avoid the trend-driven pieces that will make you look like everybody else. I bought two great cropped tops from River Island that had such interesting frilly shoulder details, I knew they'd stand out a mile from other slave-to-trend items that would be past their sell-by date within months. Just think Chloe Sevigny fused with Lady Gaga – risk-takers who have their own sense of innovative style. 'Trendy' I hate; individuality is what gives me a fashion buzz.

I'm a big fan of defining items that suit you and buying up lots in different styles and bright colours from high-street locals like Top Shop, H&M, River Island, Urban Outfitters and Box Fresh. I've got a massive collection of shorts (denim, tie-dyed, wool, 70s stretch cotton – all in different colours and cuts), which I'll team with funky tights, costume jewellery (my thing is gold statement rings – pile them up and load them on!) and trainers (Vans are my new crush). I'll buy up items I trust and know suit me, then mix with vintage finds, basics from American Apparel, leggings and Ts from Primark or designer specials.

My motto is, never plan too far ahead. If you book a Saturday shopping day in and build up to it, chances are you'll be stuck for inspiration and end up with something you'll never wear. I much prefer to buy on impulse. I find I stumble across the perfect pair of dark-denim 70s Charlie's Angels shorts when I least expect to! One last motto for the road: go for designer link-ups. I know you have to queue round the block, but getting a designer dress for a fraction of the price is the best shortcut I know for looking creative at really affordable prices.

Being your very own in-house stylist

Only celebrities can employ a stylist to dress them before they step out the front door. For the rest of us, simple styling tools are useful for all those last-moment fashion hazards. Keep the following in a little box in your top drawer:

- Tit tape.

- Large and small safety pins.

- A needle and thread.

- Bra clips (to turn a normal bra into a muscle-back bra).

- A lint roller (to de-fluff clothes).

- Gel pads (to ease the pain of killer heels).

- Nail varnish or liquid glue. Kills tight ladders dead in their tracks.

- Clear furniture polish. Sounds crazy, but ideal for polishing bashed-up leather handbags.

- Pampers Aloe Vera Baby Wipes. Watermarks and stains on all your leather goodies (bags, boots, trousers, bomber jackets) and those faithful flip-flops gone in a swipe.

Also remember:

- Put shoe trees in your favourite blow-the-budget shoes and boots.

- Keep anti-moth sachets or lavender bags in your wardrobe.

- Look after 'best' dresses by hanging in clear garment bags.

Suss uber-style without spending more than a few quid

by **Natalie Hartley**, senior fashion editor, style blogger and one of the few girls who can carry off a contour dress

Forget maxing out the Visa on designer booty you can't afford; your best bet is to update, raid and style it up. My top tips:

Update

- The best way to breathe new life into your scuffed winter coat or creased-up-and-shoved-to-the-back-of-the-wardrobe military jacket is to customise. Change the buttons from cheap plastic to faux gold or vintage-style. If you're a fan of antique markets, you'll find tons to choose from. If you prefer a lie-in on a Sunday morning, check out John Lewis, VV Rouleaux or Barnett Lawson. If you're not totally freaked out by the idea of a needle and thread, you could embrace the cyclical military trend and go for epaulettes sewn onto the shoulder, easy to buy from any department store haberdashery.

- If you failed to get the Brownies' sewing badge and hate needles with a passion, you could always try updating an old coat by investing in a belt to style it up. Go for a wider belt if the coat has more structure and a skinny belt if the coat's loose. I always lose the classic belt on any trench and replace with a length of leather or ribbon to add colour and texture. Almost every girl on the street has a trench coat, but hardly any will fasten it with thick cream ribbon. The same applies to your favourite empire-line dress. Attach a loose strip of leather under the bust. If you choose a contrasting colour, it'll breathe new life into the dress. Great for cleavage action too.

- Don't lose heart when your favourite jeans give at the knee – endeavour to make the rip a feature. Use scissors to rip holes around the pockets, and you could even stitch on other fabric swatches. I suggest the pocket area and not the front for a reason; the desired look should be subtle not boy-band.

- If the colour of the season is grey and you only own black, turn to Dylon for a cheap cheat's way of introducing new-season colour into your wardrobe. Dye an old, tired top, pair of trousers or jeans.

Raid

- Raiding the wardrobe of your other half, mum or even grandma is free, so it must be worth a go. Wear your skinny-leg trousers, some simple stilettos and add a pair of socks nicked from your boyfriend's top drawer to finish the look. I promise it will save you blending into a mass of clip-clop heels. Ribbed-wool grey socks are the best, so give him some for his stocking filler and you'll both benefit. While you're snooping around his flat, pinch a blazer, which can be belted if it's too big, a work shirt that you can accessorise with his discarded cufflinks and your favourite fitted V-neck jumper.

- Your grandma's kilt safety pin is another good borrow. Use it to close a cardigan or add to an oversized jumper, about a sixth of the way down the front. If you find a vintage brooch she's happy to lend, gather the bottom corner of that boring cast-aside jumper and pin it in; it will add great shape. Check out her scarves and bags too – an old scarf can be used as a head wrap for summer or around the neck in a loose bow to make a plain jumper look more interesting. You could even double it up as a belt for that wet-day mac. If by any chance you stumble across an old broken wristwatch, discard the strap and wear it on a long chain around your neck. Who cares if you can't tell the time? It looks cool.

Style it up

- We all lust after a wardrobe full of Lanvin when really we should be paying the BT bill. Do not fear! You can easily change the look of a simple shirt by buttoning it up to the top; it will instantly give a more masculine edge. Wear loose over jeans or leggings with some great shoes, and suddenly that boring almost-ready-for-Oxfam shirt becomes sexy androgynous. Whenever I'm in a Lanvin-lust rut, I turn to a blazer and sling it over any outfit; it has the same sexy, masculine effect.

- Use up that leftover trench-coat ribbon to tie round the neck of a collared top in a loose bow – it looks a bit kooky without trying too hard.

- Change the look of your floral T-dress just a tad by wearing a lace body underneath. You can undo the front of the dress as far as the bottoms go, revealing the simple lace body underneath. You could even wear a coloured bra under that. A sure way to vamp things up a bit.

- I never leave clothes alone. I always roll up the hems on my jeans and trousers, layer a shirt underneath jumpers, wear a gilet over a leather biker jacket, rip the shoulder of my shirts to reveal a little bit of flesh on the arm, switch the colour of my shoelaces to match my mood (add red to brown leather or purple to black lace-up boots), layer coloured tights underneath fishnets, rip the hem of an old jumper so it dips down at each end to create a flattering shape. Bonkers, maybe. A no-brainer way to change the conventional style of clothes, absolutely.

Looking a size twelve, when you're really a size sixteen *(plus)*

Alas, my friend Cassie tells me that many shortcuts to wardrobe essentials and skinny jeans know-how are lost on her. She's a size sixteen, and says it straight. Breton stripes make her tummy look more Vanessa Feltz than post-baby Zoe Ball and tit tape is utterly useless on her F-cup bust. She says, in no uncertain terms, that she'd need masking tape to even consider wearing a backless dress. 'Don't go all exclusive and write this book for food-hating women,' she says. 'Just tell us size-sixteen-plus girls how we can enjoy pasta, love our curves and still look a size twelve in our clothes.' Seeing as I'm a size ten to twelve and fast approaching the next size up, I think it's worth a try.

- I lent Cassie a beautiful Miu Miu chiffon top printed with Deco flowers for a job interview. It's fluid enough to fit us both in different ways, but the low plunge makes her cleavage knock spots off mine. It reminds me that bold prints on a dark backdrop work wonders for slenderness.

- Avoid high-neck and sleeveless tops like the plague; they always highlight big boobs and tums. Instead, go for a wide and open neck that will break up your top half.

- Empire-line little black dresses are a godsend for highlighting the décolletage, and a high waist with a fluted skirt will show off your top half, skimming over areas such as hips and bum.

- Cassie has a selection of cardigans that she'll opt for every time chunky knits come back in trend. Big knits equal big hips (and torso); thin cardies equal an opportunity to show off your great boobs and chunky statement jewels.

- Look out for three-quarter-length or floaty sleeves or a puff shoulder seam on tops and dresses. A billion times more flattering than spaghetti or thick straps on anyone other than Kate Moss.

- When choosing that wear-everyday winter coat, go for a knee-length, tailored coat as opposed to short jackets that end above the bum and make it look huge.

- Make sure your tops don't leave a gap between them and the top of the trousers. Midriff exposure is only OK if you're sixteen and have a pre-kids, flat-as-a-pancake tummy. If your tops rise up, layer them up or wear a contrasting-coloured longer vest underneath.

- Cassie was given a gorgeous embroidered, balloon-shaped smock top as a Christmas pressie from her mum. I've never seen her wear it. 'Do you think I'm mad? Loose smocked tops add bulk and make me look huge. Size sixteen suicide' was her simple explanation. She swiftly swapped it for a wrap top with fluted sleeves in dark-grey and cream that highlights her great waist and boobs.

- When going for skirts, always opt for A-line as opposed to mini or bias-cut. The latter are style sins for almost anyone with a 'real' body.

- If your office environment demands smart gear, opt for a block-coloured trouser suit or jacket with a fluted knee-length skirt and as-high-as-you-can-bear shoes. This long, lean line trick works every time for making you look taller and slimmer. Just avoid pleated or too-tight pencil skirts and boxy, short or double-breasted jackets, as they always make women look bigger.

- Any woman knows a good heel takes off pounds; why else do you think Manolo Blahnik and Christian Louboutin are thought of as saints in fashion circles? When Cassie turns up for supper in fabulous high courts under long black jeans, at least two people ask if she's lost weight, when in fact she's put on 5lbs over Christmas.

- Utilise accessories. A great Louis Vuitton or Alexander McQueen-style scarf or good talking-point costume jewellery worn with sleek black lines work every time.

- Avoid lycra, pleats, too-tight belts, leggings, spray-on jeans, see-through blouses and shoes with ankle straps unless you really don't give a stuff what anyone else thinks of you.

Cassie thanks me for these and tells me she'll slip me a fiver for the high courts and jeans comment. She says, too, that, in all honesty, when she's having a 'fat day' (which, let's face it, we can all relate too), it's her faithful Jigsaw black low-plunge dress with a fitted grey cardigan over the top and chunky Solange Azagury-Partridge necklace that wins hands down. Thank God black and bling never fail us.

Finding jeans that make your legs look longer *and don't give you a huge overhang at the waistband*

Learning the lingo on jeans is like learning a foreign language. For starters there's the cut – skinny, boot-cut, boyfriend, high-rise, cigarette, and that's just the tip of the iceberg. Then, of course, there's the wash – faded, vintage, dark-wash, sand-blasted. And let's not forget the customising – rips, diamante, turn-ups, zips. You almost need a PhD in denim just to suss the basics.

I may not have that denim PhD but, believe me, I am devoted to my favourite jeans. I rotate a faithful pair of baggy Levi 501s (with skinny roll-ups at the bottom) with a pair of dark-denim, mid-rise, wide-legged Made in Heavens almost every day of the week. If it's a special occasion, I might switch to a pair of skinny Sass & Bides, but it would have to be something seriously momentous, like visiting the queen, to consider anything other than my faithful denims. My friend Lulu swears she hasn't worn anything other than jeans for the last two years. However, unlike me (who chucks my 501s to the back of my wardrobe in a discarded heap before bed), she keeps hers in neat piles on her 'denim shelf' and organises them into styles and cuts. We once attempted a self-imposed denim detox, the aim being to wear anything other than jeans for a full fortnight. We lasted three days and decided it would be easier to give up booze and chocolate instead. Amazing, considering we both mark 7 p.m. each evening with a large tipple.

Detox or no detox (of the Citizens of Humanity kind, not the 7 p.m. G&T), I'll cut to the chase here: how many of us really care whether our jeans are tapered or slouchy, distressed or indigo, True Religion or Top Shop? What we *really* care about is that they are half-decent, don't give us a huge overhang that wobbles out when we reach over the table for some extra olives and can be worn for a full day without being so tight they give us thrush. A tall order when we probably don't want to spend a fortune either. A few shortcuts to ensure your jeans do just that:

- Log on to www.ilovejeans.com or go on a mission to Selfridges and use their Bodymetric jeans-fitting system. Both will help you find out which style and shape suits you best. Once you've got tips on whether to go for medium-

rise, flared or skinny, you'll avoid extra hours in the
fitting room.

- If you want impartial best-friend advice on those mid-rise
flares (when said BFs are in fact on a work conference in
Milton Keynes/on holiday in Santorini), head to Westfield
London and use their 'tweet mirror'. Once snapped in your
mid-rises you can post your picture on Twitter or
Facebook and have your closest friend's honest opinion in
moments. This sounds impossibly scary to me (I'm not
even on Facebook to chat, let alone to ask people's
opinion on my denim-clad arse), but fashion friends in the
know ensure me it's the future of shopping solo. Go forth
and tweet, it seems you'll never again need buy a pair of
bad builder-bum jeans (www.westfield.com/london).

If you want a one-stop shop for fabulous, investment jeans
and think you can buy before you try, log on to www.
donnaida.com. Every designer from Acne to J Brand is here
and, as any fashion-savvy girl will tell you, Donna Ida is the
last word in denim. Mine will be a brand-spanking-new pair
of J Brands, please.

Donna Ida or Primark, save yourself time by bearing in
mind the following:

- The darker the jeans, the more flattering the look. It's a
fact. If you're worried about adding inches, stay away from
white and stone-wash.

- If you haven't got Naomi Campbell legs, it's best to avoid
cropped jeans, big turn-ups or very baggy jeans – they'll
only make legs look shorter.

- Whatever your height, if you wear floor-skimming slim
jeans with a high heel you'll add inches to your legs and

take pounds off your bottom. Just don't make the
mistake I always make of choosing these same long
jeans to wear with flats. I guarantee you'll end up with
shredded hems and when it rains you'll be soaked right
up to the knee.

- Generally, I'd steer clear of low-rise. Much better to leave
exposure of major bum crease to the builders.

- My jury's still out on mega high-rise flared jeans. Sure they
are great for channelling 70s chic, but they seem to leave
me with tummy-track marks and make me feel like I'm
wearing a pair of thick, flapping, blue-denim curtains. Nice
for a window, not so nice for me.

- Go for big pockets every time. So much more flattering
on the bum than no pockets, or trying-to-be-trendy
wonky pockets.

- If you're petite, curved seams on your favourite jeans will
help to elongate your legs.

- Super-skinnies are perfect for tucking into high stiletto
boots, high ankle boots or Uggs. Dark washes will
lengthen legs so opt for black/dark denim over a faded
shade. Be careful of wearing with flats if you've got a
'normal' figure (i.e. 99 per cent of the population). This look
was surely designed by sick men to make the average
woman look ridiculous.

- Avoid OTT customising such as diamante overload, tattoo
detailing on the thighs or major rips accompanied by
stone-wash and paint-splattering. You'll just resemble a
try-too-hard WAG who hasn't learnt anything from VB's
metamorphosis into style icon.

- I'm still convinced the boot-cut is forever faithful, while other fad styles come and go. It's the cut you'll return to after major-flare or spray-on jeans taunt you when you check your reflection in the public-toilet mirror.

- Remember that jeans give, so you can take a chance on a slightly-too-snug fit. Just ensure that you can do them up without lying down and going blue while holding your breath. Alas, the length may shrink when you wash them, so opt for the longer rather than shorter option unless you want to end up looking like Norman Wisdom.

- However fab the jeans, it's actually offensive to mankind to spend more than £250 tops, tops, tops.

- I know it's better to wash jeans inside out and on a cold cycle, but to be honest I usually turn the washing machine on when I'm delirious from tiredness and am lucky to remember to add the Fairy tabs. Mental note to self: try not to do this. If you really want to preserve those much-loved Hudsons, wash less, wash cold and dry naturally.

- If you've accidently shrunk your favourite boot-cuts to fit a toddler or the knees have given way and you don't want to impersonate the 1980s Matt Goss from Bros, do not fear. Use your kitchen scissors and snip them as high-as-you-dare between the knee and thigh – *voilá* you've transformed them into summer cut-offs. Roll the bottom half-an-inch and no one will know they're not brand-new-season Paige shorts.

It would seem a crime to embark on a denim detox now I've invested so much effort in becoming a shortcut jeans genius. Someone else can embrace ladylike chic and stride out in pencil skirts, cream cashmere twinsets and oversized pearls, leaving me to retreat to the comfort of my faithful boyfriend jeans by Current/Elliot. Style and comfort on two blue legs.

Easing that shoe-spending guilt while still getting your fix

Mr S tells me we need to have 'a serious chat'. Oh God, panic sets in. He's having an affair. We set aside an evening, put the kids to bed and sit down solemnly on the sofa. I brace myself for it. He's shagging someone ten years younger. But no, it's worse than this, he's found me out, and there and then exposes my shoe habit. And you know what? He's right. I've hidden from it for too long. Taking my hands, he goes on to tell me exactly how he discovered my guilty secret. It was one night when I was working late. During a game of hide and seek played out by my three children, the 'truth' (that was precariously piled on top of a wardrobe) came tumbling down on their little blonde heads in the form of the following:

- six pairs of ballet pumps

- twenty-eight pairs of stilettos

- four pairs of Converse trainers

- three pairs of Ugg boots

- three pairs of stiletto boots

- two pairs of cowboy boots

- more Havaianas than you'd see on the beach in Brazil

After running upstairs to see what all the commotion was about (heels, laces, boxes, tissue lying everywhere) and applying arnica to the brows inflicted with heel-lash, he decided to confront me with it. I stared at piles and piles of shoes, many only worn once, others that never fitted in the first place and some that, in the fresh light of day, looked frankly ridiculous. Four-inch platform wedges? In *gold*? I'm already five-foot-nine and Mr S the same height; did I want to tower over him as if on a gold-glitter dance podium?!

The thing about shoes is they promise so much. We can all picture the scene. Monthly paycheque arrives in your account. A morning of Saturday shopping beckons and Selfridges' shoe department has your name written all over it. In you walk, and it's not just wall-to-wall shoes that stare out at you; it's the promise of who you'll become and how you'll feel if you wear them.

- The stiletto – sassy, sexy and slinky, you will wear me, drink Martinis and have men falling at your three-inch-heel-clad feet.

- The wedge – a red-hot vixen who oozes confidence and will no doubt be invited on a private yacht to St Tropez the moment you slip me on, having parted with a few hundred quid for the pleasure.

- The funky boot – I am Sienna Miller and will bag my new hot-to-trot man in a flash.

- The ballet pump – oh, French chic and sophistication, come hither. You are now mine.

- The shearling winter boot – a long country walk, an open fire, red wine. Inner peace and calm is now within reach.

- The thong sandal – think Nicole Richie, think Matthew Williamson, think floaty boho, think the smell of Piz Buin sun cream, think carefree summer vibe even though it's hailing outside. Think joy.

After clearing up the mound of dusty strappy sandals, I speed-dialled some fellow foot-fetish friends. I confessed my shoe-hoard sins and shared my 'promise of greater things' theory. We unanimously agreed that there is a conspiracy theory at work here. Failing that, we must all be so miserable in our humdrum lives that even a spanking-new leather court in black patent seems to offer us salvation from overtime/ironing/domestic dysfunction/PMS/mortgage arrears/an empty fridge. My friend Tara even confessed to easing a broken heart with no less than four pairs of Top Shop sale shoes in one fell swoop. Two pairs were a size five; she is a size seven. It was the fix she needed, not the boring practical details.

That momentous habit-exposing day forced me to do two things:

1. Face the fact that 85 per cent of my shoes were impractical, three-inch stilettos. Perfect for a life as a style-whizz fashion journo; a joke when working from home/doing the school run. Keep the best for girls' nights out and weddings, and sell the rest on eBay.

2. Address the fact that unless I enter intensive therapy (not of the retail kind), I'll still need the occasional shoe buzz. However, I need to be realistic about what fits, what suits my lifestyle and how many pairs I can viably justify without starting to hide stashes of Office boxes in the cellar.

If we're really honest, most of us have more shoes than we'll ever need to function in day-to-day life (one winter boot, one summer sandal, one dressy high heel, one work-wear sling-back, one trainer), but will that stop us buying more? I think not. A genius shortcut then came to me at 3 a.m. the following morning. Allow impulse to run riot once every so often. We should all be allowed the indulgence of a cheap trend-buy occasionally. However, in the long term, our aim should be to invest in classic styles that we love and will offer longevity beyond a Saturday night on the dance floor/job interview/come-hither-to-bed first date.

- **Investment**: Vivienne Westwood pirate boots. These boots were my 'reward' for selling on more stilettos than I dare to admit post-shoe fallout. I worship them (literally) and team with skinny jeans in the winter and sundresses or a cut-off denim skirt in the summer. They just get better with age. Buy new if you can afford it or try eBay if you want to hunt for a cheaper used pair (www.viviennewestwood.co.uk).

  Cash-cut: Flat riding boots. Russell and Bromley always have a huge selection (www.russellandbromley.co.uk).

- **Investment**: Christian Louboutin black court shoes. It goes without saying that you can't beat the red-soled, 55mm-heeled court. Even if you've vowed never to buy high heels again, make these your final pair. It took me a year of saving to buy them, but every time I almost impulse-bought heels, I'd slip £20 away, and the fund built up quickly. Well worth the wait.

  Cash-cut: Black courts with a twist. Try Office (www.office.co.uk) or Kurt Geiger (www.kurtgeiger.com) for a selection of close seconds, or Pour La Victoire for a modern take on the classic that will also prove you're in the fashion know (www.asos.com).

- **Investment**: Chanel two-tone ballet pumps in black and cream instantly make a boring pair of jeans or a cut-off denim mini with black opaque tights look wow (www.chanel.co.uk).

  Cash-cut: Ballet pumps. Ideal for almost everything except major A-list events (and how many of us attend these?). Multitasking women's lives in a shoe. For a more realistic price than Chanel's, look no further than French Sole (www.frenchsole.co.uk) and Pretty Ballerina (www.prettyballerina.com).

- **Investment**: Prada thong sandals. So lovely you almost want to wear them and nothing else. Cold but true.

  Cash-cut: Havaiana flip-flops. Almost as nice as those Prada thongs, but because they're a fraction of the price, you can afford to get them in an array of colours to mix and match with your sundresses and bashed-up boyfriend jeans. Look for them at www.office.co.uk.

Once you've splashed the cash (even if it's only £20 on some Primark gold ballet slippers), looking after your shoes will make you less likely to forget about them. In the past, I was the prime suspect for buying, wearing once, shoving to the back of my wardrobe and resorting back to the comfort of my bashed-up high-top Converse. The ultimate shortcuts to keeping your favourite shoes gorgeous for longer are:

- Store them in the boxes they came in or, if you're Mrs Organised, clear shoe-boxes. If you really are on a Carrie Bradshaw shoe mission, invest in a shoe closet at around £400 from www.saveyoursole.co.uk.

- Make sure you have a box of polish nearby for day-to-day scuffs and, if you're adventurous, a monthly polish.

- Deodorise much-loved shoes by leaving them in the freezer while you're out at work. It will kill all known stinks. Just don't forget about them when they fall between the peas and Ben & Jerry's.

- Vow to get them professionally polished and re-heeled twice a year. If you've saved all year for a pair of sexy stems, get the leather soles protected with rubber ones – www.saveyoursole.co.uk even have them in red, perfect for those scarlet Louboutin soles you're terrified of trashing. Guaranteed to keep them as good as new.

Life's too short for shoes that look like prize jewels (and cost the same) but don't actually fit.

I must confess, my answer to any bad news, happy news or just in-between news is to hit a shoe shop. Luckily for me, those beloved pirate boots have so many straps that by the time I've undone them all my local branch of Office will be closed. Now let's just be thankful for the shoes that I've got and the fact that Mr S isn't shagging a busty, blonde twenty-six-year-old.

Picking f-off, fabulous shoes you can actually walk in

by **Beatrix Ong**, shoe designer, business owner
and never seen without masterpieces on her feet

The number one mistake women make when buying new shoes is nabbing a pair that don't fit. Remember, the shoe should fit you; you shouldn't try to fit the shoe. If you're desperately trying to squeeze your feet into sky-high pointed boots just because you love them in the shop window or you've seen them in a trend feature in a glossy magazine, you're likely to be disappointed when you're crippled after wearing them on a night out with the girlies.

You want style and comfort, so walk around the shop in them, imagine you've been wearing them for five hours and ask yourself, 'Will I still be smiling or will I be heading to Boots for a multi-pack of plasters?' The golden rule is that shoes should be snug, not tight – there's a big difference. Leather and suede give a little, patent doesn't, whatever the sales assistant might tell you when encouraging you to part with your cash.

If you've got a shoe collection to rival Imelda Marcos and can only justify buying one pair this season, then I'd say go for a flat pump; you can't beat them for style and comfort. If pumps say 'boring' to you, wait up – try going for a flat with a twist. I always try to incorporate a quirky design feature or interesting fabric on flats to avoid the boring trap – this way, you'll get a talking point with the added bonus of wearability. Just don't go for anything too crazy. You want to walk into a meeting with your shoes making a positive statement, not a style faux pas! If you've got a little extra to spend, indulge in a fabulous, statement heel. Go for a heel under 10cm and you're likely to get away with wearing it all day. Team with a fab LBD and you'll be good to go straight into the evening. Even if your date doesn't get your die-hard devotion to that newly purchased statement stiletto, you'll feel fabulous, and that's what counts.

Striking the balance between a bit of bling and looking like a rusted-up OTT Mr T

Once Mr S had shamed my shoe habit and at least half had ended up on eBay/at Cancer Research, sparkle was elevated to number one accessory fetish. It goes without saying that I'm a girl with a pulse, so bling rapidly became an obsession. Not only did I become fixated on diamonds (faux or real, just give me zing), but also aquamarines, rubies, emeralds, sapphires, white gold, costume jewellery and long, dangly pendants from Accessorise, worn all together over a maxi dress. I'll be honest with you and admit to having an invested interest in jewels of all descriptions. Mr S is in the business, and Christmas wouldn't be Christmas without a new charm for my charm bracelet, at the very least. Lucky for me, because I hate cheap perfume and red Ann Summers undies, and now – boo hoo – stilettos are out of the question too.

I have friends who define their style with their beloved wristwatches and stud earrings, and others who mix and match long drop pendants from Whistles with friendship bracelets from Diva, Benirrás Beach in Ibiza or a random stall at V Festival. Many stylish girlfriends then complete this look with an f-off piece from Solange Azagury-Partridge or Shaun Leane. For the sake of ease, I'll call them 'the two jewel camps': simple and elegant versus experimental and cutting-edge. Often the two camps merge, and then you're left with what I call 'elegant grunge'. Try out the look by fusing a diamond line bracelet with beaded friendship ones. Add a fitted army jacket and over-sized battered-up maxi bag, and you're away.

- If you want to go for simple, elegant pieces, opt for a good independent jeweller. I give the nod to Justice in Bath and Winchester (www.justice.co.uk), Lombards Jewellery in Islington (www.lombardsjewellery.co.uk) and Peter Jackson in the north (www.peterjackson.co.uk). By going to the big Bond Street names, you'll have to pay more just for the fancy box and trimmings.

- Real diamonds out of your league? Cheat with cubic zirconia set in real gold. Failing that, head to Top Shop for the mock crown jewels and tell everyone you bought them in Tiffany.

- If you think diamond line bracelets and single-diamond solitaire pendants look more at home in old snaps of Princess Diana, invest in a statement piece instead. If you've got cash to splash, you won't be disappointed with Solange (www.solangeazagurypartridge.com), Lara Bohinc (www.larabohinc.com), Stephen Webster (www.stephenwebster.com), Alexis Bittar (www.alexisbittar.com) and Wendy Mink (www.wendyminkjewelry.com). All offer designs so goddamn fabulous you can accompany them with a bin liner and still feel amazing. If you want something almost as wow but closer to the price of that bin liner, head to Accessorize (www.accessorize.com) or Diva (www.diva.net.au).

- If you're still harping after the good old days of friendship bracelets, but dread the thought of re-treading the path of

scuzzy, free-with-*J17* plastic ones, go for an upgrade.
Start at Merci Maman (www.mercimaman.co.uk), where
you can get your beloved's name engraved on a silver disc
which is knotted onto a thin, tan leather band. Not ready to
engrave a heart with the name of your on-off boyf? Head
straight to Lombard's Jewellery for a chakra bracelet – so
boho-babe you may have to nab several to dangle
together – or Links of London for their silver and thread
friendship bracelets (www.linksoflondon.com). The skulls
and exclusive range by Cat Deeley are like gold dust.
Good enough for Ms D, Daisy Lowe and Kate Nash,
goddamn good enough for us.

- I must confess to having a slightly childish crush on
  charm bracelets. Just boho and frivolous enough to
  make you feel twenty-one again. Well, almost. Annina
  Vogel makes the best in town (www.anninavogel.co.uk),
  but you'll find a huge selection in Miss Selfridge too
  (www.missselfridge.com).

- Before you head to the pawnbroker with that three-sizes-
  too-big heirloom ruby cocktail ring left to you by Great-
  aunt Maud, try it with ring clips, which you can buy from
  most local jewellers.

- If all else fails, go for an oversized men's watch and be
  done with it. A vintage Rolex, if you can justify a grand
  plus, or nab your boyfriend's oversized sports watch if you
  can't. Works just as well with jeans and a roll-neck as it
  does with a sex-kitten short dress.

- To keep your sparklers just that, sparkling, clean them with
  warm water, a spot of washing-up liquid and an old
  toothbrush.

- If you're reading this thinking, 'I can't even pay that overdue wad of unpaid parking fines, never mind buy a selection of prize gems,' don't lose heart. Raid your jewellery box for naff gold – not forgetting to check behind the sofa cushions for that long-lost broken single earring – and sell it for cash. Online gold-buying companies tend to promise the earth and deliver manure, so head back to your local jeweller for a better deal. Check out member listings at www.jewellers-online.org.

Choosing a handbag you love so much you'll want to sleep with it

by **Katie Hillier**, uber-cool accessories designer, creative consultant to Marc by Marc Accessories and design consultant to the Victoria Beckham bag collection.

The whole idea of an 'it' bag is a completely manufactured phenomenon. It's the perfect example of a very clever branding and PR stunt. Step one: design a blow-the-budget bag. Step two: send said bag to a heap of A-list celebrities. Step three: wait for them to be papped using them. Step four: as soon as the pics appear in a few leading style magazines, overnight the bag will miraculously turn from your average leather maxi to cult must-have.

Instead of charging up my Visa card in order to keep up with these cult creations, I'd much prefer to invest in something I actually love, something that will stand the test of time and something that's functional and versatile. Ask yourself a few of these questions when you're browsing on the bag floor of your favourite department store and it may help save you time and money rather than nabbing something you'll go off within a year:

- Is this bag so gorgeous I'd want to keep it forever and hand it on to my daughter?

- Is this bag stylishly timeless? Beware of anything that screams 'on-trend for one season only' or is covered with logos. Look to the Birkin bag as an example. It's classic and iconic, not because it's covered in bling or OTT logos, but because it's simple and tasteful.

- Does this bag show the hallmarks of being well-made? Looking for a nice edge-paint, lots of useful pockets within and an inside that looks just as lovingly designed and beautifully presented as the outside is a start.

- Will this hurt to carry? Bag-induced backache is a really bad look. Especially if you've just spent your month's wages in one hit on it.

- Is this bag versatile enough to meet all your needs? Think about every step of your average day and ask yourself if the bag works in all scenarios. Most women need a bag that can take them from the office to dinner out, and something that can carry all their essentials (phone, make-up bag, wallet, tube-reading material), as well as random throw-ins (high heels to change into for an impromptu date, a laptop for that last-moment 'I'll tell the boys I mean business' pow-wow meeting).

- Does it have enough room for everything you usually carry around? As controversial as it sounds, I always empty the contents of my existing bag into my possible purchase. If you can't do up the clasp and still haven't found room for your iPad, then forget it.

- Slouchy may be in, but beware: structured bags hold their shape much longer and will stand the test of time.

- Does this bag make me look rich? Always a bonus if you're not.

- Finally, close your eyes and feel the bag. You should think 'yuuuuuuuummm' at just the feel of it. If you think of nothing but the overwhelming odour of leather, then forget it.

The bottom line is, if you buy a bag that offers you all this, you can be sure it'll make you look and feel fabulous, even if you're just wearing your boyfriend's jeans and some scuffed-up Converse. Victoria Beckham gave me her 'Victoria' bag as an extra thank-you for working as technical consultant on her bag range. I confess, I've used little else since and feel a million dollars even if I'm popping to the local shop for a pint of milk and the weekend papers.

True, most women don't have thousands to splurge on a bag, but you can still find designs that tick all the right boxes on the high street. Sure, most Top Shop bags haven't been lovingly hand-made by an ancient Italian leather specialist, but these days a lot of effort and thought has gone into the design, and it shows. You may find that if you're just spending £25 as opposed to two grand, you can be frivolous and spoil yourself with a satin clutch too. It's also worth browsing around for a vintage bag if you want to stand out from the crowd. If you don't like the occasional scratch or weathered strap, then obviously second-hand bags won't cut it, but if you don't mind some lightweight wear and tear, then there are great deals to be made. I always go to Relic in London for mine. Eve, Fiona and Clare have impeccable taste, wise insider's knowledge and willingly help out vintage virgins looking for something a little different. This shortcuts hours of trawling around antique markets in the rain too. Soggy leather and a bad mood to boot? Such a bad start to bagging your new summer satchel.

Embracing click-chic without leaving your desk/sofa

My dear friend Sarah works in the City. She's at her desk by 8 a.m. (latest) and rarely gets home before midnight. Supper is generally a can of Diet Coke, half a Prêt sarnie and a Snickers bar. By the weekend. all she wants to do is flop with a capital F. The last thing she ever wants to do on Saturday morning is set the alarm clock and shop with a capital S. This doesn't mean, however, that she doesn't want to look groomed and fabulous in various cult on-trend delicacies. Oh no, no, no, no. Sarah still needs beautifully cut tailoring for power meetings and figure-hugging contour dresses for Saturday night soirees with her new flame. Oh how I envy her (Earl Grey and a 9.30 p.m. bedtime story, anyone?)

The answer to her shopping dichotomy is simple. Mouse. Browse. Click. Deliver. Go shimmy in Dolce & Gabbana gorgeousness. In short, online shopping is her salvation. Unlike Sarah, I haven't thrown myself into click-chic with quite the same gusto. I confess, I hate changing rooms with a passion (wobbly bits, awkward bra straps, taking things on and off while a toddler strangles himself in the curtain). I also have virtually zero windows for clothes shopping left in my diary. But even with changing-room phobia and Westfield-mooch-day envy, I'm still not 100 per cent convinced about the one-virtual-frock-stop. Call me old-fashioned, but I like to feel the fabric of clothes and hold them up against me (and breathe in) before I even consider parting with a few well-earned pounds. I know that if you shop online you can usually return things as quickly as you can say Temperley-at-my-wardrobe.com, but doesn't queuing at the post office for half an hour after trudging up the road in the rain cancel out any easy-peasy benefits? I think I'd prefer to wait thirty minutes in Top Shop, thanks very much. At least you can look at pretty girls and pretty clothes to pass the time.

Sarah tells me I'm missing the point and to be a modern woman in the modern world, hell-bent on sourcing shortcuts, I need to get with it quick smartish. I set myself the 'arduous' task (yeah, really) of sussing the best online fashion websites for here and now. The mission: to research it and not spend a penny. Almost as hard as spending a full day in a Häagen-Dazs ice-cream parlour without licking a scoop.

Designer

www.net-a-porter.com
www.asos.com
www.matchesfashion.com
www.glassworks-studios.com
www.mytheresa.com

Mid-range

www.mywardrobe.com
www.farfetch.com

High street

www.asos.com
www.topshop.com
www.boohoo.com

www.uniqlo.co.uk
www.ebay.co.uk/outlet
www.zara.com
www.missguided.co.uk
www.hm.com

Members only

www.cocosa.com
www.gilt.com

Discount

www.theoutnet.com

American brands

www.oxygenboutique.com

Accessories

www.benna.co.uk

Ethical brands

www.fashion-conscience.com

Sarah tells me that to avoid buying a 'quick-return job' and become an overnight online connoisseur, I need to remember these shortcuts:

- Many sites give you the option of selecting a 'designer preference', which alerts you as soon as items arrive by your favourite designer. Sarah swears that hot frocks sell faster than hot cupcakes, so you need to get in there fast. She nabbed a beautiful white blouse by Chloe this way, and even I would have been hard pushed not to take out an extra overdraft facility to make it mine.

- Make sure any site you choose has a friendly returns policy and preferably pays for goods to go back should you decide they're not for you. Sizing can vary from label to label, so an easy turnaround of clothes and shoes are essential. If you want to be a serious pro like Sarah and have the wonga to match your enthusiasm, you could order your usual size, plus one size bigger and one size smaller to make sure you get the perfect fit.

- As scary as they sound, 'virtual assistants' are handy for being online savvy.

- If you prefer to go all techno and cruise instead of credit-crunch, try a fashion app on your phone. I'm loving www.my-wardrobe.com's My-TV, which is like a personalised fashion channel, and www.stylebookapp.com, which is a brilliant fusion of stylist and fashion PA in one fingertip touch. I actually drew breath when I heard that you can input images of your wardrobe and get looks sorted or stored in archives on a week-to-week basis. Stylish and time-saving encapsulated within one small screen.

By this stage, I'm frankly gagging to get clicking and am not sure I can resist that pair of Uniqlo skinnies a second longer. I may not be a 'priority customer' and I may not know my Cocoas from my Co-op, but those jeans look bloody fabulous. Whipping my credit card from my wallet, I click the mouse a few times and then head straight for the kitchen to make breakfast. The beauty of this? I'm still in my PJs! I am in disbelief that online shopping has taken me so long to master and love. The next day, my dark-blue jeans arrive and, wait for it, fit. Now I just need the bank balance to fund all this mouse-mania and I'll be one very happy lady.

Vintage shopping without smelling like a musty old pipe

I confess, I have a crush on Kate Moss. This isn't because she's got great, pert boobs. It isn't because she doesn't seem to give a toss what people think of her. It's not even because she spends every summer sailing on a yacht around Formentera. In all honesty, it's because when she wears vintage, she looks like a style goddess sent from the heavens. When I wear vintage, I look like I've rummaged blindfolded through the under-funded, under-stocked charity shops of the British Isles. And I smell of dead people. It's a fact.

I was scarred for life when, aged twenty-one, I bought a coral chiffon sundress from a vintage stall on Portobello Road. I parted with £15.99, trotted off home radiating an aura of 'I'm soooo boho cool, ya know', teamed it with wedges and a faux-croc clutch and convinced myself I looked identical to Twiggy in David Bailey's shoots for *Vogue* in the 70s. Sadly, I did not. The kind lady at the corner shop asked if I had grandchildren, and my flatmate came home and enquired about the smell of 'old damp clothes' in the kitchen. Said smell was me. It seemed a bad idea after that to wear it to a friend's birthday party that weekend. Best stick to Warehouse for the sake of safety and aroma. After working on a fashion magazine for almost all of my twenties, you'd imagine

Life's too short to queue for an hour for a free fitting room in Hennes.

I'd morph into the kind of fashion editor whizz who could team Levi 501s with a vintage camisole I'd 'just stumbled upon on Portobello Road' but, alas, at every attempt I was stumped.

As a gaggle of fash-mag girls desperate to fill our lunch hour with something that included both shopping and a bargain, we'd regularly traipse up the road to the vintage haunt Blackout in Covent Garden to see who could nab the best bargain. Like a pack of eagles descending on their prey, we'd arrive in a flurry, barge through the door and be on a mission to see who could swoop the most fabulous one-off Victorian heirloom for under a fiver (only to then wear it with glee to the office the next day). While the rest of my girl-gang gathered up armfuls of snake-skin clutch bags, 40s kimonos and floral T-dresses, I'd be left trying to jam my elephant feet into size-four shoes or looking at a moth-eaten cardigan wondering if I could jazz it up with a brooch to stop myself looking like a Stepford Wife on a bad day. Alas, it just wasn't meant to be.

Half a decade on from my Blackout, black Friday experience, I have to confess I've finally, *finally*, started to turn a corner and have begun to take steps towards a style identity that embraces more than just a fusion of designer and high street. Ironically, I think the turning point came when I left my full-time job on a magazine to juggle freelance writing with looking after three kids. It was on one of those only-too-familiar days when you feel like screaming, 'It's wet, we're all killing each other at home and if we don't go out we'll stand a good chance of committing grievous bodily harm on one another' that I arrived (by chance, and looking like a drowned rat in need of a double vodka) at the vintage shop Cha-Cha-Cha, hidden away down a local backstreet. Owned by a fellow mum-of-three with a magpie eye for vintage finds, it proved to be the perfect alternative to pissing off fellow customers with my bored brood in Starbucks.

The atmosphere was far less intimidating than that of a gaggle of twenty-something fashion girls all competing for that prize Pucci piece, and while my kids tried on floppy sunhats in front of the mirror, clomped around in 20s heels and ate the Rich Teas I was passing them in quick succession from the fitting room, I braved the elements. Maybe it was the fact that the kids had finally stopped fighting over the remote-control, but after all those years of being a vintage phobic, I started to see what the fashion fuss was all about: adding vintage to your wardrobe means you can give an air of charm and individuality to a look. A vintage Ossie Clark dress worn with your same old stilettos will no doubt knock spots off a Karen Millen frock for a night out, and you surely can't beat the ease of swapping your work-day bag for a clutch to take a look from day to evening. Adding a sequinned bolero to jeans and a vest will have the same effect. Equally, a simple floral T-dress worn with flats is such an easy thing to bung on with a simple grey GAP cardigan, for either a day with the kids or a Monday morning in the office.

I confess, I made a run for it just as my youngest was about to smear his Rich-Tea-encrusted fingers down a prize Galliano evening jacket, but it did offer a window into the benefits of vintage charm: a) the chances of anyone ever looking identical to you are almost zero; b) you'll often find clothes and accessories far cheaper than anywhere on the high street; and c) vintage garments create a talking point if worn well. Having said this, knowing the shortcuts are key if you want to avoid being stuck in a charity shop looking at the mish-mash of clothes and running a mile for fear of the unknown.

1 | Go straight to the vintage boutiques frequented by those in the know: Annie's Antiques, Beyond Retro, Cha-Cha-Cha and Oh La La in London; Pop Boutique in Manchester and Liverpool; Blue Rinse in Leeds; Armstrong's in Edinburgh; and Hobo's in Cardiff. Consider leaving the kids and decoy biccies at home if at all possible.

2 | If you want to bypass trawling the city's vintage shops (getting blisters and sweaty armpits while you're at it) searching for a Moss-esque gem, seek out vintage fashion fairs instead (in London head to SW3, to the Frock Me! Vintage Fashion Fair (www.frockmevintagefashion.com); further north, the Leeds Vintage Fashion Fair is worth a peek (www.leedsvintagefashionfairs.com). This is where all good vintage lovers and collectors set up stalls and sell their wares. It costs a few quid to get in, but you'll find yourself knee-deep in hidden treasures. Just turn up early to nab the best bargains, be prepared to barter (stallholders expect it) and take your own plastic bags (no sleek Harvey Nics holders here). You'll be surprised how even a vintage novice can find a classic masterpiece here.

3 | If you're heading for charity shops, zip past the junk and shortcut the flash booty by heading to a postcode renowned for rich, stylish types. The same applies for jumble sales: try the Wills Moody Rock 'n' Roll Jumble Sale in north London (www.willsmoody.com) or Rumble in the Jumble in Glasgow. Also try car boot sales. I've been tipped off about Hatfield Car Boot Sale in Hertfordshire (01992 468 619) and Hewitts Farm in Kent (www.hewittsfarm.co.uk).

4 | Online vintage shopping may well trump any other shortcuts for ease and speed: www.youlovefashion.com is an online notice board for vintage shoppers; www.devoted2vintage. co.uk offers next-day delivery and full refunds; and even www.

net-a-porter.com has a sleek, chic One Vintage section offering everything from 30s capes to 70s dresses at the click of a button. Just make a note to beware of sizing issues – sizing has changed a lot over the decades – and make sure that whatever site you choose allows you to return goods if they don't fit.

5 If it's investment pieces you want, target items by renowned 70s classic designers such as Ossie Clark, Pucci, YSL or Chloe. They will gain value the longer you keep them.

6 Try things on. You may think you'll look like Laura Bailey at the Serpentine Summer Party, but in reality you may look like your Great-aunt May once she'd lost her sight in both eyes.

7 If you want a vintage classic without the hassle of changing rooms, go for accessories. You can find designer handbags with amazing detailing or oversized 70s shades almost as cheap as chips, and even I can make a snake-skin clutch and Jackie O shades work with pretty much anything (and that includes jeans and a T).

8 Make sure you check that gem of a 70s Givenchy classic for moth holes, sweat marks and damage. A small rip under the collar or cigarette stain on the cuff can be kind of cool; a massive moth hole on the nipple or stinky BO stain, not so cool.

9 If you find something that suits you but is slightly too big/long/ill-fitting, remember that you don't have to abandon the search and start again. A one-stop drop to any good dry-cleaner with an alteration service and they can nip-and-tuck it to fit you. You'll be amazed how raising a hem can transform a look from granny to groomed.

10 If you do buy something, give it a good airing, dry-clean it and spritz it with your favourite fragrance, a sure-fire way to prevent smelly-pipe syndrome.

Shortcuts in mind and spurred on by my new-found vintage confidence (all hail), I left my brood with Mr S, a Disney DVD and a mega bucket of popcorn and headed to my first local vintage fair. Immediately, I gravitated to a stall which was organised by colour, which is far less messy for the head. I instantly know to avoid colours like pea-green, orange and red which, quite frankly, make me look like a pile of puke. I bypassed a black fur jacket (except it wasn't real fur, but crusted-up viscose – definitely more Pat Butcher than Miss Moss) and a pair of camel leather slouchy boots, which I loved but they were a size too small, and finally spotted a pair of original 70s mid-waisted Chloe jeans. Jeans are a safe bet; they either fit or they don't. And styles like mid-waisted, flared, skinny and boyfriend-cut stand the test of time. I reckon that if I team them with a Primark white vest, my favourite wedges and some form of summer tan – fake or real – I may just have passed my initiation into vintage shopping. Just remind me to wash them once to get rid of the stink. Or maybe even twice. I want to look cool, not so OAP that I'm stone-cold dead.

Dressing for festivals minus the garish floral wellies

By **Sophie Ellis-Bextor**, pop princess and 'I just threw it on but look goddamn fabulous' fashion hero

I love festivals and never miss a good opportunity to get in the creative festival spirit and boogie around a bit. What better place to let your hair down and experiment with styles? If you ask me, it's the perfect time to rock a look that's a little more adventurous than your day-to-day wardrobe. Maybe you wouldn't be seen dead in a sundress, cowboy boots, a floppy sun hat and chunky costume jewellery on the school run or in the office, but festivals are a great time to let loose and take risks on the fashion front. A few shortcuts to making festival dressing more cool than catastrophe:

- Be optimistic, but don't rely on warm, dry weather, especially in the UK. Take a satchel bag with opaque tights and a cardigan, in case that sun turns to thick, grey cloud, and pack a mac for those inevitable heavy showers.

- I'm over festival welly overload. I prefer to opt for bashed-up leather boots instead. I've got some great ankle boots with a small block heel which I bought in Urban Outfitters that look fab with dresses. They've already seen a few puddles on the streets of London, so I don't care if they get mud-splattered and trodden on. Obviously, if torrential rain is predicted for that weekend at V, you'll need to take wellingtons, but I'd suggest a simple black pair of Hunters instead of garish designs. Florals and spots look far too try-hard.

- If you're standing in a field all day, you want to feel relaxed and that you have the freedom to run around without ruining a special frock or new leather jacket. Most of the time I'll go for vintage and often my tights will already be laddered before I leave the house – this way I can forget about high-maintenance and keeping clothes pristine and concentrate on the music and having a good time.

- I love to wear playful, girlie clothes at festivals. Play-suits and 50s dresses are a good, quirky option and take away the issue of what tops work with what bottoms. I never wear jeans at festivals; it seems a waste of an opportunity to play around with style.

- One of the nicest festival items I've ever bought was a huge poncho from the Oxfam stall at Goodwood's. It doubles up as a blanket, so it's super-warm, and the fringing and oversized buttons make it stand out in the crowd.

- Apply the same easy, no-fuss rules for festival make-up: the last thing you want is to look heavily made-up. I just apply simple make-up in the morning (some mascara, eyeliner and lip gloss) and then chuck them in my satchel. Half the time I forget about reapplying, but it's there if I need a quick slick of the mascara wand.

- If you want to take a simple outfit from the day to evening at festivals, just buy cheap knick-knack jewellery or hats from stalls to jazz up your outfit. This way, you're not carrying around an extra look for the evening, don't need to navigate your way back to your tent after a few drinks to find your 'night clothes' and can layer up those kooky cheap and cheerful accessories. The beauty is, once you've enjoyed them, you can leave them behind in the mosh pit at the end.

CHAPTER SEVEN

BODY & SOUL BEAUTIFUL

Staying fit without falling into the abyss of shiny black lycra leggings

I joined a flash gym. Once. Ten years ago. I spun, ran and lifted dumbbells for all of three months and then concluded that my pursuit for a body-beautiful was exhausting, expensive and I'd much rather get home from work, slip into a hot bath, don comfy slippers and read the leftover Sunday supplements instead. I suppose you could say that gyms and I, we just don't marry, unlike Mills & Boon, Richard & Judy or Elle & 'The Body'. It's a shame really, because I'd love to have an uber-buff bikini body, I really would. I'm just too lazy.

Now, that's not to say I'm an obese coach potato with huge wobbly thighs, high cholesterol and Domino's Pizza on speed-dial; I'm just no Paula Radcliffe either. Expensive, flash uber-luxe gyms full of Madonna lookalikes make me feel inferior, and the rigidity of an hour-long, 10.45 a.m. Tuesday spinning class is impossible when you throw three kids and a career into the mix. I might make the first week (oldest two children at school – check; toddler on play-date with neighbour – check; feature for glossy magazine filed at 11.12 p.m. the previous night – check; fridge filled with delicious, healthy grub care of Ocado – check), but I can almost guarantee that by the second week of spinning salvation one child would be out of action with a winter cold/I'd still have 1,000 words to write for a feature/there would be nothing in the fridge except some old parmesan and an out-of-date Frube.

I'm too vain to reject the *whole* idea of fitness in pursuit of cashmere bed-socks and *The Sunday Times Style* mag (although what a delicious idea), so you may well ask what replaced my brief foray into gym-bunny dedication and those uber-sleek Nike lycra gym leggings as my quick-fix answer to lazy-girl exercise. After attempting yoga for all of a week, pilates for all of four days and a celeb home-fitness DVD for all of twenty minutes, I came to the conclusion that to stay remotely fit without slipping into a void of paralytic boredom, I'd have to find a form of exercise that a) I could suffer without too much hard work and b) didn't feel like exercise at all.

- Be honest and bin the 'exercise is such a joy' garbage. Unless you're Madge, getting fit will feel like bloody hard work and a chore you'd rather skip. Don't get me wrong, I know that endorphins are a great buzz, but then so is listening to the new Cee Lo Green album while getting ready to go out. Fact. Also true is that, unless you go on some ridiculously strict calorie-controlled diet (the one thing that's more boring than half an hour on a running machine), getting active in some way is the only failsafe option to looking half-decent in a sundress.

- I've always found that swimming is about the only exercise I can call semi-enjoyable. I just lost the habit in my early twenties and would always opt for an after-work glass of red and gossip with the girls instead. As a child, we'd holiday in remote Cornish cottages almost every year – much to my disdain, when friends bragged about the delights of Spain/Disneyland/Center Parcs. One of my only pleasures after a marathon session of Connect 4/ Monopoly with my siblings was to hurl myself into the sea, even when the rain was torrential and my lips had long turned blue from the August freeze. In my late teens, swimming was a cathartic escape from my slightly mad and obsessive thesis-writing at university. I then progressed from the local baths in Manchester to frequenting the free women's ponds on Hampstead Heath, a liberating breath of fresh air when dealing with the day-to-day perils of being an over-worked fashion junior. My history of swimming came back to me after cancelling my direct debit to said flash gym and handing that celeb fitness DVD over to Oxfam. I began to wonder why I didn't dip my toe into the water once again. Swimming ticks all the boxes for busy girls who want exercise shortcuts.

1 It can be done as cheap as chips. Local pools and lidos charge from £1 and you often don't need to take on a hefty membership fee. Check out www.lidos.org. uk or www.outdoorswimmingsociety.com if you feel seriously brave.

2 Because it's a solo, non-structured sport, you can do it if and when it suits you without the pressure of a set time or the risk of letting down a group.

3 It uses almost all your muscles, so you're doing a whole-body workout in a non-strenuous, non-sweaty way.

4 Just being in the pool for half an hour to forty minutes a few times per week is enough to count as your weekly exercise quota. Just make sure you actually move in the water and don't treat it like an extended bath.

5 You can use your swimming time to have your one shower of the day.

6 It eliminates having to buy an expensive gym kit. All you need is a half-decent cossie (www.figleaves.com or www.speedo.co.uk), an old towel and some shower gel.

7 If you find doing monotonous laps staring at a ceiling with chipped paint boring, think about waterproof music-players and earphones. Flash, but very good for zoning out and killing time during those laps (www. earphonesolutions.com or www.swimmer.co.uk).

- Even if swimming isn't your thing (too wet, too cold, too much hassle, no pool near work/home), the trick is to find some form of fitness that doesn't feel like slow torture, suits your day-to-day life and doesn't break the bank. An evening run, a long weekend walk, a game of tennis, dance classes, martial arts classes or a cycle round the block might all be worth a thought.

- Get motivated, not jaded. If motivation's your weak point, you could consider a personal trainer or run-buddy who will nag you to get out of bed and into those Nikes and reward you with a latte at the end (soya, natch). Both www.ukpersonaltrainers.com and www.nrpt.co.uk are one-stop personal-trainer shops. If you're London-based, I've heard from my local 'buff brigade' that Giselle Bailey at Results will have you toned and trim and giving Tracey Anderson a run for her money within weeks (www.equalsresults.co.uk). The thought of a personalised, twice-weekly, half-hour session resulting in a beach-bod with attitude is almost good enough to convert a sit-up cynic like me.

- Press-ups sending you into panic mode? You could consider making moderate exercise a fundraising activity instead. If the thought of thighs like Cindy Crawford doesn't push you to run a mini-marathon, maybe raising a few hundred quid for Cancer Research will. Check out www.ideasfundraising.co.uk for innovative ideas.

- Be realistic. More often than not, hitting the snooze button or giving in to the craving for a post-work Martini wins hands down over sweaty aerobics or bending backwards in pursuit of that perfect 'arched cat' pose. Try not to make unrealistic demands on yourself – i.e. a two-hour, burn-baby-burn workout every night of the week – just set yourself small targets. You only need thirty minutes of moderate exercise every day, which could even include brisk walking for fifteen minutes to buy that lunchtime sandwich and then back to your desk. Failing that, the Pilates Magic Circle is a lightweight tool that you can squeeze while watching *Grand Designs*. Gym-level toning for under £50, and you can do it in the comfort of your living room. I like this. A lot. (www.amazon.co.uk.)

- Reward yourself with retail heaven. My friend Kate swears by an 'exercise equals reward' system. In short, a session of pilates equals a post-class skinny muffin, and a month of pilates plus an end-of-the-month paycheque equals Myla knickers/a Top Shop frock/an Accessorise straw stetson.

- Slot it into your life. Find a time of the week that suits you best. If you hate early mornings, then don't schedule a 6.30 a.m. run, but opt instead for a lunchtime one or a midday Saturday romp. If you have an allergic reaction to any form of structured exercise, just try to be more active in your everyday life. Get off the bus a stop early en route to work, take the stairs instead of the lift when you're at Bluewater and cycle with the kids to that movie matinee. Even a little Mr Muscle-friendly housework and ironing have been touted as good calorie-burning forms of fitness. They may not be intense martial arts, but they're better than nothing and come with the added bonus of a dust-free living room and pristine clothes.

- Don't use the age-old 'I have no time' excuse. We're all busy. Fact. Many companies have cottoned on to this and have designed workouts that won't take much longer than queuing for that take-out salad and bag of Snack a Jacks in Tesco Metro. Virgin Active run fast classes that can skid in at just twenty minutes (www.virginactive.co.uk). Or, if money's no object, enlist Absolute Fitness to collect you at lunchtime from your office. They'll customise a workout just for you and get you back to your desk within the hour (www.absolutefitness.co.uk).

- Try not to expect miracles. A super-buff bod won't be instant (or, if you're me, achievable), but you *will* feel more energised immediately.

I'm probably one of the least fitness-motivated people on the planet. You're unlikely to see me on the school run in skin-tight workout leggings and a scraped-back 'I mean business' hairdo – I'm lucky to screech the kids in at 8.45 in anything other than my PJs. However, since my 'how much?!' swish West End gym membership was binned in favour of my local, rather more OAP pool, I haven't looked back. My four-times-per-week-at-random-times-of-the-day swim may not give me the body of Elle, but it helps me fight the flab and makes me feel immeasurably better about myself than if I sat on the sofa gobbling up a Galaxy instead. I will gobble that Galaxy, just after I've swum a few slow, lazy laps first.

Achieving that flatter tum (not washboard, just more abs than huge fleshy folds)

You should have gathered by now that I'm no big fan of strenuous exercise. The only minor snag here is that there are times when I'd like a flatter tummy. I don't dwell on it that much, but occasionally, when I slip on a snug LBD and see my pot-belly bulging out or my toddler asks me, 'When baby come?', I think to myself that it would be nice to have a navel that is taut and stretched, not hidden in folds or, worse still, protruding from excess lasagne. True, a firmer set of abs will not change my life. Also true, it won't give me the key to eternal happiness. What it will give me is great pleasure when I don a skimming white vest or itsy-bitsy bikini, and this would be a lovely feeling once in a while.

Life's too short to do an exercise you loathe.

I invited my friend Natali over for a cuppa. She's a fitness freak and an immaculate example of the disciplined body beaut. I poured the tea: PG for me, boiled water with lemon for her. We pooled our tummy knowledge and came up with the following shortcuts:

- Oh delight! It seems the gods are on our side. The first step towards that flat(ter) tum we all dream of is not, in actual fact, one hundred sit-ups per night, but correct posture. When walking, sitting at work staring at your computer screen or on the bus/tube commute home, remember: *shoulders back, head high and suck your tummy in*. Natali stresses that it's this simple. Just imagine you are wearing a very tight corset! Pull your belly button in towards the back of your spine. I tried it, and yes, it does feel awkward, as I prefer the slump method, but I reckon re-training my posture must beat gym squats any day of the week.

- If, like me, you're likely to re-slump within sixty seconds, try swapping your uncomfortable office chair for a Swiss ball. If your boss isn't loving your new-found tummy cheat, then get one for your living room. Think of it as an adult version of the space hopper, although you don't even need to move around the room. Just sitting on it engages your core muscles and promotes better posture. Not great for channelling that *Elle Decor* vibe, but you can always hide it in the garden shed when friends come for Happy Hour.

- If you can't face sending emails on a glorified Tellytubby ball, try some pelvic-floor exercises while in the car waiting for the green light instead. The pelvic-floor muscles are part of our inner core, and the stronger our inner tummy core, the stronger our outer layer will be. To strengthen your pelvic-floor muscles, sit comfortably and squeeze the muscles ten to fifteen times in a row. Avoid holding your breath, or tightening your stomach, buttock or thigh muscles at the same time. If and when you get used to this, you can try holding each squeeze for a few seconds. Every week you can add more squeezes. I feel like an NCT teacher writing this, but Natali swears the pelvic floor is our gateway to tummy success. Interesting, very interesting.

- Correcting posture and pelvic-floor suction may be neat tricks, but surely sitting as straight as a plank won't rid your of all layers of tummy fat? I'm right, not even sit-ups will do this. The only failsafe way to shift them is through cardio, as this will burn more calories. Gym-phobic? Yup, thought so. The good news is that dancing the night away burns 400 calories an hour, so you don't even need that direct debit to LA Fitness, just a night out boogying with any willing girlfriends. Recapture those *Fame* days – just don't make up for the lost calories by guzzling strange sugary cocktails.

- If you're hell-bent on getting that washboard stomach in time for summer, then the most beneficial tummy exercise is the plank, as it uses your whole core. Just brace yourself.

  1 Lie face down on the ground (or on a towel or exercise mat). Position your elbows and forearms underneath your chest.

  2 Prop yourself up to form a bridge using your toes and forearms.

  3 Maintain a flat back and do not allow your hips to drop towards the ground. The first time you try this, hold for fifteen seconds, then increase to thirty, and then to a whole minute. Don't forget to breathe.

If you feel exhausted just reading this, do not fear. Take comfort in the fact that bloating often compounds the feeling that your flabby tummy is growing by the hour. Taking regular probiotics helps reduce bloating, and there won't be a plastic ball in sight. Prebio 7 is great (www.nutriglow.com) or just add two Activia yoghurts into your daily diet. You could also try drizzling a tablespoon of linseed oil on your evening portion of veg. It's great for calming the gut and will make your tum noticeably less preggers-like.

Achieving thighs and bums that are a bit
more toned and honed *than dimpled, wobbly jelly*

The fact of the matter is, I don't really care if I'm past the age when I can viably get away with wearing itsy-bitsy shorts with wedges on a scorching hot day. I just want legs that look half-decent in a not-too-short sundress and won't cause major embarrassment when flashed on the beach in August. We live in a modern world and, while I can't afford leg lipo and restructuring (is there even such a thing?), there must be a multitude of lotions, potions and exercises I can try that will make my legs firmer and more toned and less like the pale-pink jelly I served at a recent kids' party. I don't expect miracles, just a small improvement on catastrophe.

For all of you who share my cellulite despair and wish to wear anything other than long black palazzo pants this summer, listen up.

- My super-toned and sleek pal Sophie swears by a quick, freezing-cold shower morning and night. If this sounds like torture, have a warm shower and blast those thighs with ice-cold water at the end. Surely the cheapest, easiest place to start zero-tolerance cellulite busting?

- Following her freezing torture (sorry, also known as 'shower'), Sophie pops a Murad Firm and Tone Supplement (www.murad.co.uk), which she vows help her to don denim hot-pants during summer. It's close to a hundred quid, but a shortcut worth trying if you're on an anti-cellulite crusade.

- My friend Tallulah is a big fan of lotions and potions to reduce cellulite and lift skin. Together we split the cost and tried and tested tons. To really see if they work, the trick is to apply them daily for a month to just one leg and then compare. Failing this, take your own before-and-after shots with a close-up zoom lens. Scary but practical. Too much like hard work? Take my word for it; these are the best of the rest: Soap & Glory Sit Tight; Sisley Celluli-Pro Slimming Complex; Biotherm Celluli Laser D.Code Advanced Anti-Cellulite Care; Rodiał Bum Lift (although this gel is so hot it has a waiting list); and, for a quick night-before denim-mini fix, go for Prtty Peaushun Skin Tight Body Lotion, which has added concealer. Fabulous.

- Cellulite-obsessed friends tell me that if you cut down on smoking, drinking, salt, sugar, caffeine and fizzy drinks, this all helps in the long run. Your body automatically stores these in fat cells, so they're bound to show themselves in bottom dimples. A life without lattes and white wine? I'm not sure I can stick to this, even for that beloved pert bottom in a skimpy bikini.

- Squats and long walks (basically get those thighs moving) all help in the quest for a perfect posterior. Not as fun as slathering on nice-smelling cream, but definitely cheaper.

- Maybe instead of giving up Galaxies (impossible) and undertaking daily squats (double impossible) you could invest in the Evita Slimsonic 'Smart Lipo' device. It promises to melt cellulite, with results in fourteen days. OMG. Loving this.

- If you're really serious about cellulite, you could enlist a super-whizz professional to take over the arduous task of thigh-dimple angst:

  - CACI international (www.caci-international.co.uk or call 020 8731 5678). Ask for eight sessions of Faradic technology, a high-powered massage that speeds up fat-cell metabolism. Hurray!

- VelaSmooth (www.velasmooth.com). Ask for ten treatments and see fat cells shrink.

- CoolSculpting by Zeltiq (www.beyondmedispa.co.uk) is shockingly expensive at nearly a grand, but it simply freezes away pockets of fat, leaving you with an instantly flatter tum/perter bum.

- If all else fails, aim to give the appearance of toned, firm legs and bottom, even if underneath all turns to jelly. The best way to achieve this is to wear Solidea Silver Wave shorts (www.victoriahealth.com). Not only do they hold all your bits in a tight, neat package and help with good posture, but they stimulate circulation and water drainage too. An illusion of being slim and sculpted while still being lazy old you. Very clever indeed.

It seems that the quest for a pert, toned posterior is big business. I've started to wonder how many other millions of women have reached desperation after a backside reveal in the mirror and resorted to Spank-type pants and high-powered massages. I must confess though, even with short-cuts, this does sound like an awful lot of hard work. I'm now seriously considering a dimmer switch in my bedroom instead. If I prance around in my undies, lights on very low, I'll never be caught off-guard by my dimpled bottom again. I suppose at a push I might continue with a cold-shower blast to improve things a little. But only if it's baking hot outside. And I have a fluffy hot towel to hand. And I remember. That's a lot of 'ifs'.

Life's too short to let cellulite angst get the better of you.

Work that celeb body without killing yourself trying to achieve it

by **Tess Daly**, TV Presenter and body-beautiful

Before I start, let me dispel a myth: just because you're on the telly, doesn't necessarily mean you've got an army of personal trainers and a fleet of dieticians. Just like most working women, I have to put a lot of effort into staying in shape, hard when you've got a full-on career and two young children. The average woman doesn't have an army of personal trainers and nutritionists at hand to keep you in constant check, so you have to work at it. It's also true what they say about new, surprising 'problem areas' springing up as soon as you cross the thirty-something hill. I mean, who had to think about hiding muffin tops and bat wings in their early twenties! Aging is undeniably indiscriminative and unfair!

I'm a woman who wants to stay fit and healthy; I'd be lying if I said it wasn't important to me. However, I'm certainly no slave to the body-beautiful. Who doesn't want to look good in a pair of skinny jeans or a summer dress and sky-high stilettos, but at what cost? I'm not going to kill myself to achieve it. Life's too short and, to be honest, I prefer to spend my time hanging out with my family and friends rather than slaving away every single morning in a hot Bikram studio and then every single night on the treadmill, throwing in some weight-training before lunch.

Having said this we all realise you can't do absolutely nothing and expect to keep your body in good condition. The trick is to attempt to find a good balance. Some short and sweet core top tips which have helped me to keep my body in a shape I'm pretty happy with since having kids are as follows:

- Find an exercise you enjoy (I daren't say 'love') and attempt it as many times a week as is viable with all your other commitments. I enjoy yoga and find that if I give it my all at several weekly sessions, it keeps my body in pretty good nick. It also comes with the added bonus of offering quiet time away from the hubbub of work and family life.

- Stay active. Even if you can't stand a spinning class or doing fifty laps in a pool, being active in life is a great way to keep your metabolism on high and your desire to reach for the biscuit tin (for the fifth time that day) on low. Walking instead of driving or taking the bus and cycling instead of hopping on a train are both little things you can do to stay on the go.

- Although I'm a sucker for a good home-made pudding, I try to eat well most of the time (and watch my intake of banoffee pie!) Now I'm cooking for two growing girls, it's even more important to set a good example to them about having a healthy, balanced diet and a good understanding of nutritional know-how. Sure, enjoy that pizza or burger, but attempt a diet with an abundance of fresh fish, chicken, hearty soups, veggies, whole grains and fruit most of the time. It may sound boring, but it's worth a try.

- I'm a big fan of exfoliating. I was inspired to start up my own beauty line – Daly Beauty at M&S – because I didn't want to sacrifice looking good, but as a mum of two never had enough time to spend on myself. The idea was to get a little glamour on the go: great-looking skin with minimum fuss or prep time. I exfoliate in the shower, and then apply my Daly Tan fake-tanning cream – it's a really light formulation, so no streaks. A tan is the perfect slimming accessory to any outfit, no matter what the season. Just be clever – fake it, don't bake it.

- I know it's a cliché, but drinking tons of water does it for me. Upping the H2O flushes out toxins and is great for that broken-night's-sleep/work-stress skin. Brilliant.

- I pop a complete B-vitamin complex to give my skin and energy levels a boost. Great for those winter months when you're stressed, knackered and an early night or a holiday seem a million miles away.

- If all else fails, high shoes are great for slimming legs. I couldn't survive a party without my Jimmy Choos. No good on the beach, I hear you cry, in which case ditch the heels for a good halter-neck bikini, guaranteed to enhance your good bits and hide a multitude of sins.

I won't profess to miracles, but a little bit of fitness, a balanced (ish) diet and great shoes are worth their weight in gold.

Minimising the risk of turning into a comatose wreck after a boozy night out

Don't we all aspire to be sophisticated drinkers? Sadly, it's a fine art many of us haven't quite mastered yet. I'm no exception. I always have the best intentions prior to a night out, it's just that sometimes it goes pear-shaped after that first glass of vino. Drinking in my late teens was for getting drunk: no supper before I hit the pub, mixing Cinzano (even the mention of the C drink makes me feel like I need to vomit) with cheap white wine, and then a few pints, just to round things off. In my twenties, I was either drinking cocktails at fashion parties or pregnant and so sticking to Pellegrino.

Now I'm in my thirties, I still attend the obligatory 'mwah, mwah' fashion parties with free, scary-looking cocktails, but they're certainly not an every-night occurrence. While I've gratefully accepted that age has brought with it a more measured approach to drinking, I confess that at times I slip into reckless mode and become the supper-party host who fiddles around with the iPod to find dance tuuuuunes and rallies the menfolk for spirits instead of After Eights. Yes, that's the same reckless streak that rears its ugly head at weddings, as I race friends to the bar and can be found throwing shapes with Grandma next to the dodgy strobe lighting at midnight. In case you're wondering, it's the same minx convincing the girls on our nights out to 'stay for one more'. Great fun for getting a party started, horrendous to live with the morning after. Did someone say 'children'? 6 a.m. Relentless tussles over who plays with the plastic *Toy Story* figures. Jarring headache and inability to see straight. Such a bad combination.

Seeing as I'm not going to start turning down the occasional invite to dinner and endless bottles of Pinot or mums' nights out at the local Thai any time soon (in a word: lifeline), it may be time to look into hangover elimination:

- My friend Zoe swears by taking a regular supplement of milk thistle, especially in the few weeks leading up to the Christmas party season or wedding bonanza. Milk thistle strengthens and detoxifies the liver and, according to Zoe, lessens chronic, post-six-Martinis hangovers. I'll be trying this one – www.solgar.co.uk.

- My equally-as-booze-friendly pal Nelly religiously eats a good-sized snack before she goes out. Nothing new here, but apparently it's what she eats that counts. Fat helps absorb toxins, so she goes for rye toast with full-fat cream cheese and Marmite. Not too bad for bloating (who wants a full-to-bursting stomach when they're slipping into an LBD?), easy to make and great for absorbing the alcohol.

- We all know the 'don't mix' rule. Boring, but sadly it's the key to easing the possibility of comatose syndrome the morning after. If you can't face sticking to one civilised bottle of Merlot and crave that Vodka Cranberry after a shocking week in the office, then drink it first. Spirits at the end of a night (especially after a bottle of that Merlot) is a recipe for disaster. And pink puke.

- Nelly usually manages to drink a glass of water in between every glass of Pinot. Failing this, she'll opt for Spritzers. She's never ended up with wonky lipstick or a doner kebab at 1 a.m., so I reckon it's worth a go.

- As a rule, white wine is safer to drink than red, and more expensive wine safer than cheap (fewer lethal congeners). A good reason not to opt for that £2.99 bottle of red.

- My friend Kara's last words to me on a night out are always: 'Evian and Nurofen'. Taken before you collapse into bed, you'll ease the pain of that mouth-like-a-carpet effect. Repeat once you get up.

- The morning after is likely to be horrendous even if you stuck to Spritzers and ate your body weight in toast before you went out. Death by drinking, no. In need of a liver transplant, yes. If you can face food first thing, opt for fruit sugars (hello, OJ) and something fried. Mr S makes a mean post-raucous-dinner-party scrambled eggs on toasted bagels. One of the many reasons I married him.

- If you're serious about avoiding that nightmare hangover, take a vitamin C and D supplement the day after. They both aid in ridding toxins.

- To de-puff eyes in a hurry, wrap an ice cube in a napkin and press around the eyes. The perfect quick, easy and free 'day after' de-puffer and firmer.

- When all else fails, wear sunglasses, crawl your way through the day eating carbohydrates and swear never, ever to drink again. Works for me every time.

It's true, I may not go out as much as I used to. It's true too that there are plenty of evenings when I'll happily opt for a quiet read and a hot mint infusion instead of my favourite Italian with friends, followed by an aperitif back at ours. Believe it or not, it's also true that I've been known to embrace a detox with gusto, just to find out how 'pure and fabulous' I'd feel after a few months of Evian and mung beans. However, once I've detoxed and glugged fruit infusions for Britain, that boozy night of drinking white wine and seeking out good tuuuuunes inevitably appears on the horizon. This is exactly why it helps to come armed with toxin-reducing tips. Life really is too short for an eternity of mint tea and meditation.

Beating that winter cold when you don't have an at-home Boots counter

Sniff, snivel, cough. Sniff, snivel, cough. Sneeze. Oh God, how I hate the winter cold. And, to top things off, it's guaranteed to be hailing outside. And it's probably only late September. I know you'll be thinking it's the late night at the local Italian that's done it, but you'd be wrong. It's been *X Factor* and trackie bottoms for weeks now. I'm not getting old; I've just discovered a new sushi take-out with free delivery. And a new obsession for guessing if and how much Botox Louis Walsh has had in recent weeks.

Anyway, sniff, snivel, cough. I presume we all know the answers to warding off a cold in the first place: tons of sleep, nutritious meals, multi-vitamins, vigorous exercise and perfect personal hygiene. However, even personal trainers and health gurus must catch colds sometimes, leaving us mere mortals with a phobia of black lycra jogging-pants and fetish for puddings and wine in need of some shortcuts. To overcome the snot-fest before it turns into full-blown man flu, try these:

- Drink tons of liquid. And that doesn't include caffeinated cappuccinos or booze. The idea is to rehydrate not dehydrate. Opt for water or orange juice (great for cold-busting vitamin C). They'll flush out toxins in the body and help the production of mucus – all that snot and phlegm is a real bane, but they are there to trap germs, so the more the merrier. If you've got a sore throat, drink lots of clear soups (chicken soup even has anti-inflammatory properties), hot herbal teas and home-made lemonade with ginger.

- Cut down on dairy, even if your comfort drink of choice is a very milky hot chocolate. It will only compound the 'I can't breathe' syndrome in your sinuses.

- Take an echinacea supplement and max up on vitamin C. If you can manage extra fruit and vegetables rich in vit C, it'll save you that trip to Boots.

- If you feel really blocked up, try eating chillies, a spicy clear soup or adding a little bit of hot sauce to your food; they'll all aid in decongesting your sinuses. If you don't fancy extra-hot HP on your supper, boil a pot of water and place a towel over your head. Breathe in the vapours for as long as you can stand it and before you pass out. It helps break up mucus and unplug your nose and ears.

- Rasping sore throats are best dealt with by gargling with warm, salty water. It will help ease the soreness and kill bacteria.

- If you're waking up the neighbours with your hacking cough and the cupboard is bare of Benylin, try a hot ginger tea to calm it.

- My friend Kat swears that a cold aggravates her eczema no end. She keeps a stash of Ecz-Easy Balm next to her paracetamol and slaps it onto her skin. The natural combo of olive, castor and black cumin seed oils means it's gentle on the skin (www.organic-ideas.co.uk).

- Rest as much as you can. If you're a working mum like me, this is almost as impossible as having an all-expenses-paid Harvey Nics charge-card. If this is the case, take a Nurofen Cold and Flu and attempt an early night. Sorry, no full day of bed-rest and grapes here.

- Vow to buy and pop a daily Get Well, Stay Well capsule the moment you reach a chemist. At under £30, it's a small price to pay for warding off infections and treating them fast if you fall victim to the dreaded lurgy again.

Getting a good night's sleep *(and that doesn't include tossing and turning with worry about work)*

My friend Nelly is stressed. Very stressed. She can't sleep and it's driving her crazy. I sympathise. Really I do. Recently I had a short bout of restless nights myself. It has to be said that at 3.12 a.m., when you've been staring at the ceiling paralysed with worry for over an hour, you couldn't care less about cellulite, bat wings or milk thistle. If you were to ask us then what we really want, a flat tum, honed bum and bat-wing-less upper arms would fall well off the radar and running in at full speed to nab first place would be an uninterrupted, worry-free good night's sleep. Since when did shut-eye become so difficult to achieve?

Take any number of my good friends and they'll tell of similar sleep woes. Zoe takes regular sleeping pills to abate chronic insomnia (in the past I've received emails from her at 3 a.m. – what the hell is she doing pinging mates at this hour?). Nelly averages about five hours of broken sleep a night, and Lara bemoans her toddler, who sleepwalks or cries for cuddles anywhere from two to ten times every night. It's amazing that any of us actually manage to get any work done, we're so knackered, let alone conduct a semblance of a social life. No surprises then that we need that Vodka Cranberry to rev us up on a Friday night. Failing that, we'd be fast asleep on the landing, still in our trench coat and ballet pumps.

The myth of 'growing old gracefully' – and with it reduced worries and increased happy-clappy spiritual calm – generally sounds like wishy-washy bull to me. You grow old, worry more, sleep less and look shattered as a result. In our early twenties, we lay awake for a nanosecond, worrying about what bar to hang out in after work on a Thursday night; now we're rising into our thirties and beyond, we lie awake at night sweating over work promotions, childcare issues, mortgage repayments, missed deadlines and our spouses, children and parents all getting very ill at the same time and dying suddenly. Yes, for some busy women I know, it really has got that bad.

Luckily, I may only experience mild midnight-panic every so often, but insomnia-suffering friends and I all agree on a few things. The first is that, with a good night's sleep, you feel you can tackle the world. A cliché, I know, but indulge us if you will, for we're seriously knackered and in need of a glimmer of hope about the future. The second is that, without one, you feel like a deranged zombie who may well kill using your mobile phone and car keys during an incident of road rage over a parking spot outside M&S. The third is that the more you stress about not sleeping, the more you don't sleep. The fourth is that the more you attempt to dull your overactive brain into slumber mode by drinking a glass (or three) of red wine, the higher the chances you'll fall asleep but then wake a few hours later, mouth like dry sandpaper. The fifth is that *you just can't bloody win*.

OK, so Nelly is now seconds away from ringing her doctor and begging for some sleeping pills. My friend Lara confides that if she has yet another week of lying awake worrying about her toddler's hitting habit, she too will be close behind her. Probably armed with a bottle of Smirnoff for good measure. I'm not feeling quite that bleak, but I could certainly do with eight hours of shut-eye more nights than I'm getting it. Yes, please. Surely if we all try a few of these failsafe shortcuts we might be a step closer to that blissful natural slumber every single night of the week?

- You could try investing in a Sleep Cycle Alarm Clock, a cheap app for your iPhone that will monitor sleep patterns and tell you the perfect time to wake up. Great idea, but you've got to be able to fall asleep first, right?

- OK, so everybody I ask who sleeps well rates exercise high on their agenda. Not manic body-pumping until midnight, as this may well have the opposite effect and have you wired all night, but a healthy approach to lightweight exercise. Outdoor fitness came up trumps with the sleep-well tribe, a morning jog winning hands down. If getting Elle's body isn't reason enough to don lycra leggings, then pursuit of zzzzzs may well be.

- Cutting out caffeine and sugar after 2 p.m. is a common tip I half-hoped was a myth. I love a cup of instant and a chocolate HobNob to get me through the afternoon, but I now discover that it takes six hours for your body to dispel the speedy effects of caffeine. My Nescafé and handful of choccy biccies at 6 p.m. will still be running around my bloodstream at midnight. No wonder I'm still writing articles at the witching hour instead of cosying up with a goose-down pillow.

- Taking time to chill out is almost impossible for Nelly. She works late most nights and, failing that, eats supper with her BlackBerry beside her. I relate to this plight. I often find that once my children are in bed and the house is quiet (anytime after 9 p.m.), I use this time to work and catch up with emails. Not particularly conducive to chilling and relaxation. Nelly recommends downloading free, white-noise MP3s of ocean waves (www.cantonbecker.com/music/white-noise-sleep-sounds) or Paul McKenna's iPhone app complete with hypnotic soundtrack (I Can Make You Sleep) to play post final email while lying in bed. It worked for her. During a particularly bad sleep spell I try some MP3 meditative heartbeats, but Mr S says very politely that he feels like he's tapped in a day spa waiting for someone in a white coat to come along. It seems winding down is easier said than done.

- Lara complained of a similar fall-out – except her Mr M complained that he was falling asleep in an aquarium. Failing the muffled tone of dolphin calls under the duvet, she tried the old-fashioned, hot bath, dimmed lights, lavender on pillow technique. It works. Kind of. She goes to sleep at 10.30 p.m., is woken at midnight by her toddler's cries for 'miiiilllllk', and then wakes again at 2 a.m. on the button, worrying about said toddler and his stick-welding antics at day care. Her new technique is to cover her clock, so she can't see the time and get stressed as the minutes roll by. After about half an hour, if she's not asleep, she gets up and makes herself a cup of chamomile tea, while keeping the lights low. I still can't get my head around the lack of HobNobs with my hot drink, but I see what she's trying to do. Now she just needs to master the art of sleep-training her toddler and she'll have this slumber dilemma nailed.

Both Lara and Nelly agree that they're sleeping better (and, strangely enough, so is the sleep-walking toddler). They've saved time and money not having to check into a sleep clinic and don't need to worry about an imminent addiction to sleeping pills. I, on the other hand, still have the occasional night of not-quite-forty winks. It's hard to wink at all when you're stressing about 2000-word magazine features stuffed full of sparkling quotes and wisdom due *right now*. And I still haven't touched on our house's subsidence. I do hate the idea of popping a pill, so maybe next time I have a sleepless night I'll try to count sheep instead. I just won't get an MP3 of farm noises to listen to in tandem. Mr S will only complain that he feels like we're camping, and he hates canvas at the best of times.

Finding inner Zen when you can't afford to spend three weeks at a Balinese spa

Following my bout of dolphin noises and insomnia and a cold that left north London depleted of Kleenex, I started to ponder on the idea that what I needed, what I *really, really* needed, was some chill-out time. Forget pounding on a treadmill, forget crunching those abs, forget spinning until you can see stars – surely some form of serious relaxation would be a much better way of spending that sacred forty minutes 'off' a week. A DVD box set and a handful of Celebrations doesn't count.

The only slight glitch is that I'm not very good at the chilling out thing. I've accomplished the art of doing several things at once and if I sit down to do just one, I feel slightly, well, bored. Take being on holiday. Sun lounger, Ambre Solaire, stash of glossy mags, children catching the waves with Mr S. All I need to do is lie back and soak it all up. Simple, no? Ah, but here's the thing: being still is just so one dimensional. Within five minutes, I'm up, reapplying sun cream, scrabbling around in my beach bag looking for my sunnies, fetching water from the beach kiosk, scrolling my iPhone for any urgent texts. It's August, Grace, everyone is on holiday. Now why can't you just lie back and chiiiiiiilllllllll?

My attempts at yoga and meditation are sadly no exception to this rule. I tried yoga sometime between my no-longer-flash gym and decision to swim if and when I could. While all the other Zenners lay very still, breathed deeply and thought of 'ooooommmm', my mind just couldn't stop wandering to the October issue deadline, shopping list, dry-cleaning collection and youngest child's recorder practice. Every time a new essential thought popped into my head, I'd attempt to discard it and focus on silence. It's just, I knew that if I didn't remember to collect my dry-cleaning-by-noon-the-dress-wouldn't-be-ready-for-tomorrow-and-I-needed-that-special-dress-for-a-very-important-meeting-and . . .

Obviously, things would be different if I had a week-long pass for a very flash, very inspiring yoga retreat in the Swiss Alps. Oh yes, I'm sure they would. I would promise to leave both my iPhone and children behind and throw my entirety into one long week of silence. Alas, the Swiss Alps are unlikely and the three children are mine to keep, so what I need, what I *really*, *really* need, are some shortcuts to inner Zen. I know inner calm is almost the last thing in the world that you can rush, but honestly? With my busy life, in order to clinch even a morsel of relaxation, I need realistic shortcuts I'll stick to for more than just one week.

- What I'd like to do: yoga
  What I'll realistically do: swim and steam
  While I look on at yoga bunnies, with their perfect postures and rolled-up pink mats, with envy, however hard I try, it's just not me. Instead, once a week, I vow to finish off a swim with a sweat-sesh in the steam-room/sauna. As long as it's not packed with old men jabbering on about gardening, it's a great way to shut down, and comes with the added bonus of sweating out a weekend of overindulgence in good food and wine.

- What I'd like to do: pilates
  What I'll realistically do: go for long walk in the woods/ park/common (failing that, anywhere that evokes more of a relaxed vibe than your local high street)
  I know it's not the same as stretching those core muscles, but it's a peaceful way to get from A to B and comes with the added bonus of fresh air. Passable?

- What I'd like to do: meditation
  What I'll realistically do: DIY home relaxation
  I'm afraid no amount of incense-burning and meditation CDs playing in the background will convert me. What I will do is turn off my phone, run a hot bubble bath, light some scented candles and soak to the sound of silence for at least half an hour.

- What I'd like to do: indulge in a two-hour massage at my local spa
  What I'll realistically do: twist Mr S's arm and get a

sixty-second back-rub while watching telly. Maybe if I twist both his arms it might persuade him to buy me a professional massage voucher for Valentine's Day. I am off to perfect the art of a damn fine Chinese burn immediately.

- What I'd like to do: motivational workshops
  What I'll realistically do: positive affirmations and cutting myself some slack
  However much I try, I just can't imagine myself attempting a weekend of motivation with Tony Robbins. If I'm ever granted the luxury of a free weekend, I'd be more likely to stay with friends in the country. Or take out a loan and hit that Swiss spa I've read about in *Condé Nast Traveller*. But I do see the value of a space to refocus, motivate and remind yourself of your good traits, so I'll try a mantra of 'positive affirmations' whenever I'm feeling like the world's worst woman for screaming at my kids/burning the supper/missing a deadline. Say after me, 'I am a good mum, I am a nice colleague, I am patient . . .' Let's face it, we're all allowed a bad day. Or three.

In my mind, there'll always be the faint hope of a deep-tissue massage or a salutation to the sun, but in the meantime I'll run that hot bath, light a yummy smelly candle and attempt to silence the inner chatter. Cowshed's 'Knackered Cow' bubbles are, of course, an integral shortcut to long-term calm.

Life's too short to impersonate a headless chicken all the time.

DIY relaxation techniques

by **Tara Lee**, celebrity yoga teacher and probably the most chilled-out person you'll ever meet

Picture the scene. You've mislaid your car keys and you're running late. Within sixty seconds, your stress levels have soared through the roof, you're hyperventilating and are seriously considering killing your other half. Sound familiar? Thought so. Even if car-key loss isn't life-threatening, our frantic lives make it feel major. If we're honest, it's not the situation that is inherently stressful, but our reaction that gives a hernia. My shortcut to helping you cope better and remain calm? Deep breathing says it all. Try to focus your awareness on your breathing and slow it right down, lengthening your exhalation with each breath. Even if you haven't lost the car keys forever more, you might find this technique helpful when your mind's racing at night and you can't sleep.

I'm a massive convert to yoga, so I'm obviously going to say yoga, yoga and more yoga is the long-term shortcut to relaxation. But it's absolutely true! Check out Yoga Alliance UK (www.yogaalliance.co.uk) or British Wheel of Yoga (www.bwy.org.uk) for a qualified teacher in your area. I'd try to find a class that combines pranayama (breathing techniques), asana (postures), meditation and philosophy or philosophical readings. If you want a package that will help overall fitness *and* well-being, you want a class that doesn't just work the physical side of yoga. If yoga's not your cup of tea, adopting any exercise that includes stretching and strengthening will tick the same boxes. Swimming is one, pilates another. Taking an hour each day or week for yourself will give you buckets more energy and enthusiasm in the long run. I promise that if you don't attempt to master the occasional deep-breathing exercise or chilled exercise ritual, you'll end up drained, exhausted, running on adrenaline and probably killing your other half over the car keys.

Talking about your 'issues' without boring your friends to tears *(or driving them to drink)*

At a fortieth birthday bash recently, I bumped into a long-lost uni pal next to the Twiglets and tinned olives. She was looking extraordinarily calm and relaxed – very, very relaxed, in fact. In all honesty, said girlfriend had totally transformed from the scatty, neurotic London lass who bit her nails down to stumps and shared pints and tears over guys with me at the student union. The once nervous, stressed workaholic who was constantly trapped in a cycle of negative relationships and self-sabotage seemed to be juggling an array of work blips, marriage hitches, bereavement and young children with such maturity and balance she looked positively serene (her life story reads like the Christmas omnibus script for *EastEnders*, so this new-found serenity seemed even more remarkable).

After my second glass of wine and sixth tinned olive, I plucked up the courage to ask her if she'd:

1. Embarked on a fabulous guilt-free love affair.

2. Recently returned from a year out on a deserted island (drinking nothing but coconut water and communicating with dolphins).

3. Found the key to inner calm. In which case I needed her yoga teacher, now.

Her answer was quite simply: 'No, I've got myself a good therapist. It beats any of the above for transforming your life.'

Shell-shocked and still slightly in awe that she'd managed to achieve such admirable inner poise (when even my broken sat-nav can force me into a frenzied melt-down), I went home to ponder. So, it seemed that an unwavering devotion to therapy had helped her cope with the inevitable anxiety and stress of a massive marriage wobble and a recent redundancy and encouraged her to find inner confidence. Top this off with her enviable glow – noticeably absent in most of our tired, stressed, multitasking peer group, and sadly not something you can buy in a jar from Boots. Hmm, interesting. Ironically, this chance meeting coincided exactly with the buzz phrase 'thirty-something mid-life crisis' that seemed to be on everyone's lips. You couldn't open a women's magazine without the phenomenon cropping up. The following weeks bought a weird synchronicity of confessions. Three of my friends confided to being in unhappy marriages, two owned up to feeling 'disillusioned' and 'lost' and one fabulous girlfriend who never looks anything but on top of the world owned up to suffering regular anxiety attacks. All this and the success of *Eat Pray Love*, which says all that's needed about a desire to 'find oneself' and break free of the facade of perfection. Was all this evidence of a disappointed generation of women, brought up to believe we could have it all and now sorely let down? If your life wasn't as high-octane and glamorous as those depicted in the media (and don't forget you now have to be a yummy mummy too), you'd failed.

I'd always thought of therapy as a domain of the mentally ill or manically depressed. However, on closer inspection, I started to see why the idea was catching on. It seems we are a society of women in crisis, and therapy may well offer the perfect answer to the symptoms of living in this pressure cooker. When you're expected to cope with immense financial pressure, a hugely competitive job market, rising debt, a young family (often coming from a fractured family unit yourself or without any close relatives nearby to help), it makes therapy attractive, as a neutral place to unpack some of these issues in order to feel somewhat 'normal'. A support system, escape valve and place to offload and unpack issues that are starting to weigh you down. Wow!

When I raised this view, some of my friends openly shared their therapy stories. And there I was thinking they went to a Thursday night aqua aerobics class, when really they were seeing a counsellor to help them cope with everything from bereavement, relationship problems, parenting issues, fertility stress, trauma and addiction.

Seeing as therapy and the idea of a 'healthy body, healthy mind' is more topical than ever, I thought it wise to check out a few top tips and shortcuts to making it work for you. Let's face it, if we're going to break down the pressures of everyday life, we want to do it efficiently and somewhere near a Starbucks so we can sneak in a latte and comfort blueberry muffin afterwards.

I meet my dear friend Lesley, a psychotherapist and role model for self-awareness. We brainstorm. Not only do I leave wishing I was more like her (well-adjusted, peaceful, even-tempered), but I also glean masses of insight into successful therapy.

Choose the type of therapy well, otherwise you could end up wasting time or feeling despondent and misunderstood.

Behavioural therapy (better known as cognitive behavioural therapy – CBT)

A short-term method that focuses on specific problems and aims to change repetitive negative thoughts and behaviours and deal with phobias and sexual trauma. The downside of this therapy style is that it doesn't look deeply into the underlying issues causing you angst. While many GPs refer patients on for CBT as a quick-fix solution, it's this same popular fast-track tag that has gained it the reputation for being a 'band-aid' through a crisis (i.e. it doesn't heal the root cause). Limited sessions may not solve the cycle of anxiety entirely, but it's certainly worth a go in your attempt to ease areas of low self-esteem, anxiety or depression and get you up and running again. Goodbye, zoned-out space cadet; hello, world.

Solution-focused therapy

Often referred too as 'brief therapy', this method looks at the positives and to the future instead of dredging up the past. Your therapist will help you to construct a vision for your 'preferred future' and determine how you can achieve these goals. Sounds to me rather like one of those upbeat American motivational workshops – 'I am a success, I am a success, I AM A SUCCESS' – but goal-setting might well be your preferred therapy method if you don't fancy working your way through a family-size box of Kleenex weeping about the past.

Psychotherapy

This can be a long- or short-term therapy (you choose) and is more of a 'talking therapy' – a good vehicle for looking at the deeper issue behind your anxiety or depression. Brilliant if you want a client-led journey of self-awareness.

Couples therapy

Joint therapy will attempt to resolve conflict, improve your relationship and give you tools to communicate better, diffusing that heated domestic over mortgage repayments/washing-up/the in-laws before it bubbles to the surface and explodes over Sunday brunch. We like.

2 Be selective about your therapist. Always check that they're registered with the British Association for Counselling and Psychotherapy (BACP) – they now have 50,000 counsellors and therapists in the UK – and go for a trial session first. You could even book appointments with a couple of different counsellors, so you can compare and contrast. The aim should be to feel comfortable and safe. There's no point in wasting an hour staring at your feet wishing you were shoe shopping instead.

3 Consider location and timings when you embark on counselling. You may want a therapist close to work, which will make a pre-work session or lunchtime dash easy. However, think about the practicalities of this – my friend Natasha got fed up of hiding tear-stained cheeks and entering a targets meeting with her head full of dredged-up disputes with her estranged mother. A location close to home might be easier, but think about how it will work with all your other commitments. It's crazy to choose 3.30 p.m. if this is when you pick up the kids, or 9 a.m. if this is the time you should be en route to the office.

4 If you're investing in 'you', consider asking your therapist for relevant books and materials, or some tips about diary-writing, which might help you when you're not on the couch with them. Sure, you don't want to be a walking, talking self-help

book, but a little bedtime reading or writing might help you get the most out of therapy. And, let's face it, when fees can rise to £150 plus an hour, you don't want to be unravelling your relationship angst forever more.

To be honest, my eyes are still opening to this whole idea of 'generation perfection fallout'. I'm still weighing up the pros and cons of talking through these pressures and dredging up the past in the process. While I'm open to the idea of therapy (especially when life throws inevitable stress/anxiety/grief in your path and tests every morsel of your resilience), part of me also thinks that if we were all a little nicer to each other, a little more honest about the fact that we can't have it all and it's exhausting trying to pretend that we can, we'd be a lot happier. My *ultimate* shortcut to a happier body and mind then? Admit your imperfections and give yourself credit for the things you have achieved. Eat supper with people you love and let the good times roll. Not Manolo, flat-tummy and small-talk good times, but real, gritty, pasta-and-red-wine-induced honesty. We've all got baggage. No one's perfect. Be kind to yourself; you might just get used to it.

CHAPTER EIGHT

GLAM GLOBETROTTER

Selecting a holiday destination that's more chi-chi than chav

I know this chapter is all about travel, but indulge my shoe fetish a moment longer if you will. For in the mind of a Louboutin fetishist such as myself, holiday destinations are just like shoes. Before you scoff and skip on, think about it for a moment. Travel plans are not too dissimilar to those still-in-the-box three-inch wedges. They both a) promise the world but often deliver mozzies, rip-off batik sarongs, bunions and backache; b) cost anything from peanuts to a second mortgage; c) make you feel a million dollars but the moment you take them off/return home resign you to humdrum reality and the sad fact that you no longer feel like Sienna Miller; d) follow a trajectory of fun-loving, care-free adventurer (i.e. Terry de Havilland f-off wedges) to over-thirty, knackered, I-just-want-sun-and-a-half-decent-kids'-club (i.e. Birkenstocks).

Take my friend Lola. She's the perfect example of a full-of-promise stiletto and the mistress of mock chi-chi holiday destinations. She may live in a miniature one-bedroom flat off a dusty high street packed with pound shops, but when it comes to holidays, she morphs into a Heidi Klein-alike. Sure, she's not strutting her Liz Hurley two-piece down the white sands of Necker Island in June, St Tropez in September and the Bahamas in February (with mini-breaks in New York, Milan, Paris and LA in between, just for good measure), but she certainly ensures her Top Shop crochet stringkini gets a good airing in Rhodes every year.

The thing is, she'll obsess about the perfect fake tan, the ultimate-cleavage cossie and the ideal hotel for sun-worship and eye-candy, but every year it's the same. Too noisy, too quiet, too hot, too cold, too fish-and-chips, too halloumi. After all the anticipation, the holiday doesn't change her life. She's still Lola, the PA, returning to her one-bedroom flat, damp problem and on-off boyfriend whom she'd really rather dump. Remind you of when those high-street strappy stilettos don't transform you into a Kylie-stylie dancing queen the moment you don them and in actual fact just give you blisters by midnight?

I wouldn't say I could even screech in as an Office stiletto these days. I feel far more like a safe Converse baseball boot, possibly rather scuffed, certainly in need of a good washing-machine spin. Pre-kids, during the early stages of swooning with Mr S, our holiday choices would veer from the exotic to the extraordinary. A month of steam-training it around north India, two weeks of hitchhiking through Morocco, ten days of island-hopping in Greece. Oh yes, and Mount Sinai at dawn and deep-sea diving in Zanzibar at midnight. Now, however, we're lucky to venture further than a two-hour EasyJet flight to the Balearics, and even then we've sussed the best supermarket for the kids' Cornflakes and the best tapas joint for maximum under-tens-paella-hurling tolerance. We almost qualify for a loyalty card from both.

I'm almost certain that, whether you're a stiletto, a Converse, a Birkenstock or a Manolo, or whether you're a fortnight in Cornwall, Malaga, San Francisco or Koh Samui, what you'd like from either is a delicate combo of the fabulous and the feel-good factor. You'd like to feel comfortable and inspired, relaxed yet ready for fun, all with the bonanza bonus possibility that you won't need to sleep with your bank manager to fund it. My top tips to achieving all this in one simple transaction? Head straight to Selfridges' shoe gallery for the feet, then tick off the following to ensure boho beach luxe, not football-shirt-wearing lager louts.

1. It sounds obvious, but before you start to check out floor plans of the shabby chic bolthole in Bali, check the weather forecast for the time of year you want to go – www.internationalweather.net. My friend Josie spent thirteen days of her two-week September break in Florida sheltering from a hurricane. Her friend Samantha was equally unimpressed when her April holiday in Mauritius was spent reading Jackie Collins under the duvet while sheltering from torrential downpours. Who wants soggy pages just when you're getting to the juicy part?

2. Even if (like me) you've resigned yourself to being a Converse traveller rather than a Choo type – opting for ease, speed and familiarity over spicy curry and jet-lag – try to re-engage with your inner treacherous traveller every so often. Hard with three kids who ask, 'Are we nearly there yet?' on a two-mile drive, but not impossible. Get inspired by logging on to www.tripadvisor.co.uk, www.thebrief.org or www.thecoolhunter.co.uk during your lunch break or flicking through *Condé Nast Traveller* and *The Sunday Times Travel Magazine* on the Monday morning commute – a sure-fire way to dull the smell of that sweaty armpit shoved in your face between stops.

3 Sorted your dream destination? Don't you just love a long weekend in Morocco (and buying locally made bowls never carries the same style risks as a bronze dolphin with moving glass eyes)? Now to number-crunch a viable budget. I'm your first-class guilty party for tearing out pages of *Condé Nast Traveller*, convinced those white sandy beaches will be the answer to my January woes. Alas, Barclays may well say, 'Dream on!' No point in surviving off baked beans for a year just so you can live it up with the yacht set and eat caviar for elevenses for a couple of weeks. Unless you're going for an all-inclusive deal, the buck doesn't stop with the travel agent. You'll need cash flow for car hire, food, booze and spending money. Remember that you can save money by holidaying close to home, looking for special deals, travelling off-peak (a good tip if you're not bound to kids' school holiday dates), opting for not-so-popular travel times and exploring self-catering, which will save you a fortune in room-service Caesar salads. Even if you do stay at a hip hotel, nip to the supermarket en route and bulk-buy water. Guaranteed to piss hotel staff off but save you a small fortune.

4 Once you've been wooed by your Google search of 'Kerala', ensure you book with a reputable travel firm. Here are some of the best.

Loaded, with a suitcase full of Missoni

- www.scottdunn.com
- www.abercrombiekent.com
- www.i-escape.com

Ready to push the boat out, but not sell your body to fund it

- www.mrandmrssmith.com

- www.blacktomato.co.uk

- www.trailfinders.com

It's got to come in under £2.50 (well, almost)

- www.thomascook.com

- www.ebookers.com

- www.expedia.com

If you're a new mum (or, like me, part of the Swiss Family Robinson) you might find that villa holidays tick all the boxes. For starters, you can make as much racket around the pool as you like, and it saves all that nonsense about interconnecting rooms/climbing five flights of stairs to your bedroom when you forget your baby's sunhat/forking out for flash meals when the children only want pasta Bolognese. Good villa companies to choose from include www. jamesvillas.co.uk, www.gicthevillacollection.com and www. ownersdirect.co.uk. Just make sure you see detailed pictures of the interior and exterior of the property, ask about pool safety (until your children are competent swimmers, you need a gated-off pool), check out the local area for beaches/ restaurants/shops/supermarkets and hire a car. I always find the first day of swearing at the 'I can't bloody work it out' oven timer pretty stressful, but once you've located the good beach and the nearest supermarket and cheap-as-chips tapas joint (therefore bypassing the 1940s oven altogether), you're away.

6   Unless booking your hols is a last-minute job (cue Hannah and her book-a-week-before motto), take this chance to make sure passports are up to date. The IPS (www.ips.gov.uk) will answer all your passport questions. Check with either your airline or travel agent if any visas or vaccinations are required. Go to www.medicineplanet.com or www.traveldoctor.co.uk for specific immunisation advice.

7   Now you've had a tetanus shot in your bottom and a cheesy, non-smiley passport pic taken by Snappy Snaps, you can start indulging in the good stuff. 'What I will do on holiday and how it will change my life' is almost as sacrosanct as what wedding dress to choose and 'how this will transform me to love goddess and offer up my very own happy ever after'. Delusional, but part of the fun. Shortcut to avoiding disappointment? Aim to be a traveller, not a tourist. Steer clear of all-inclusive resorts, leave the hotel grounds at least once, and try to eat more than just Cornflakes.

I must confess, Converse trainer or not, the feeling of booking a good holiday is still like being asked out on that first date. My friend Cal says it's even better than a first date: no possibility of being dumped, take the right chick lits and you won't be bored, and minimal chance of bad sex or an STD either. You press the 'book' button and go forth with gusto to plan your outfit(s), wax your bikini line, eliminate Pinot in the hope of gaining that beach-buff flat tum. All this is done with the strong image imprinted in your mind of running into the crest of a wave à la designer fragrance advertisement. Just remember, that break in the South of France/Ibiza/New York/Goa may not change your life, but if you go prepared it will certainly invigorate it. We like invigorated. 'Change' might mean running into that crest of a wave with a rough and ready local yoga teacher. Mr S would be royally pissed off about that.

Packing without including the kitchen sink

It's true, I used to be a kitchen-sink packer. Until I reached my mid-twenties, the only time I'd ever managed to pack small and light was when I went to live and teach in China for a year. I took a small(ish) backpack for twelve full months. It goes without saying that by the end of the year I was so clothes-starved that I was squeezing myself into very small Hello Kitty dresses designed for petite Chinese women. I'm five-foot-nine. This and men's bamboo flip-flops, the only style I could find to fit my elephant size-seven feet. Mr S almost fainted when he collected me from Heathrow.

Maybe it was this backpack trauma that opened up the gateway for panic-packing. Never again would I be left to wear Hello Kitty viscose that would expose my navel to fellow BA passengers. Instead, I would stuff suitcases with all the essentials (a few wafty maxi dresses, one wedge heel, one pair of Havaiana's, a few bikinis, SPF and a stash of novels) before Hello Kitty panic would set in and the piles of T-shirts, denim shorts, extra shoes, bags, hats, saucepans and mugs would find their way in. I almost sank the little chug boat destined for our romantic honeymoon destination. It's just, you never know if you'll need a thick cashmere jumper, sieve, Scrabble set and hot water bottle on that remote island in Zanzibar . . .

Luckily for all concerned (Mr S, chug-boat drivers, BA baggage handlers etc), my job on a glossy fashion magazine soon whipped

Life's too short to book the identical package deal every year from now until your golden wedding anniversary.

my packing panic back into shape. When you're editing clothes for a 'nautical and neon' shoot in the South of France, only to get straight on a plane to shoot 'rock chic' in New York and then swing by Rio to snap 'carnival queen' on the beach, you really do need to pack ruthlessly. Either this or have a private jet at your disposal. When my personal luggage started to take up more room than the luggage needed for the job in hand, I really did need to worry. Minimal became my new mantra. OK, minimal and just one extra pair of Havaianas for good measure. Some shortcuts to practical packing are as follows:

- Check flight weight restrictions. We know the *aim* is to pack light, but it's good to know what we're up against.

- My friend Kate manages four diverse holidays per year (biatch) and swears by making lists prior to packing. She's ruthless and pens down what she expects to be doing each day and night and what excursions she'll be taking. She can then work out exactly what outfits she'll need day by day (gulp). It also helps you to see if you're missing that clear thong/white vest/beaded sandal, leaving time to nip to the shops to buy it. Kate goes as far as to photograph the outfits she's planned, alongside accessories, and stores these in a clear file to refer to at her destination. UNBELIEVABLE. I tell her there must be a money-making opportunity somewhere in here. I'm far too disorganised to get camera-happy, but for a two-week hol, I will select four or five key outfits for days and evenings and pack accordingly.

- If you're strapped for time and inspiration ('hello, flight to the sun leaves in a few days, there's not a Panama hat left in the shops and I'm so busy I can't leave my

desk even once before I check in'), look no further than
www.style-passport.com. In short, this is your one-stop
shop for absolutely everything you'll need for your hols. We
love the idea of nabbing a cheap-as-chips nail polish in
that perfect summer shade alongside a wafty après-beach
maxi dress and that all important sun hat – all delivered to
your door without you having to abandon those nagging
pre-holiday deadlines even once.

- Once you've sussed your holiday looks, you might come
  to realise that you have no viable suitcase (recycled
  Waitrose bags do not count), in which case buy one
  sharpish. For cheap-ish and practical, I'd suggest
  Antler (www.antler.co.uk), but if you want to channel the
  glam jet-set vibe, look no further than Globe-Trotter
  (www.globetrotter1897.com). If you do have suitable
  existing suitcases, you will then have to undertake the
  arduous job of fetching them from the loft/top of the
  wardrobe. Mine are always stuffed with old receipts, kids'
  beach toys and almost-empty mozzie repellents, and have
  old airline labels attached to the handles; if you're like me,
  now is a good time to spring-clean your suitcase. Check
  too if the wheels still work or got lost down the luggage
  shoot at Stansted.

- When packing, try to obey the three-shoe rule. One pair of
  flip-flops for the beach, one pair of heels for the evening
  and one pair of Converse or Bensimon pumps for travelling
  and day trips. This obviously doesn't apply for a ski-trip,
  but you get my gist. If you've got shoe bags, use them –
  that jagged heel can run riot with your flimsy chiffon maxi
  skirt – and pack your shoes at the bottom of your case.

- Remember, fewer clothes, more accessories. A great

pendant can change the look of a maxi dress, denim shorts or LBD. We love small but perfectly formed add-ons. As for the perfect boho-luxe holiday bag (that will instantly double up as your must-have, summer-in-the city companion too), one word: Buba. Total and utter fashion fabulousness in one beautiful beaded bag (www.bubalondon.com). Oh slow, my racing heart.

- Always take a pashmina. Great for the plane, cool evenings or wrapping around your toddler when the flight is delayed until 1 a.m. and you're in an air-conditioned café in Rome.

- If you've got any shoe bags spare, these are great for sorting underwear, swimwear and accessories. It will save you time unpacking and sorting at the other end, which we love because we'd rather be finding a Cornetto.

- I always leave buying toiletries until I get there, but in truth often forget and end up washing my hair with the kids' Johnson's Baby Shampoo or, worse, Fairy Liquid. Kate swears by taking all her toiletries from home. If it all seems too bulky, you could buy a travel kit with miniatures – Aveda is great (www.aveda.co.uk) – or just decant your existing lotions and potions into small plastic bottles from Boots (www.boots.com). Remember to cover toothbrushes with plastic cases (www.johnlewis.com) and check the seals of your creams are tight to minimise the risk of the Pantene-all-over-your-Pucci effect.

- If you want to be the ultimate packing goddess and save yourself any morsel of crease or fold in sight (hello, slightly scary), pack your clothes in tissue paper or on hangers in clear dry-cleaning bags, placing bulkier items at the bottom of the case and lighter ones on top. This is the quickest way of unpacking straight into your hotel/villa wardrobe without the hassle of searching for non-existent hangers. It may well illuminate the need for a travel iron too. I religiously used these shortcuts when packing for shoots, but now, to be honest, whether I'm packing for a writing assignment in New York or a family holiday in Cornwall, it's usually at midnight the night before we leave and clothes are lucky to get an 'are you clean?' check. No red wine down the front? You're good to go. Bundle, crease, shove.

- If you're taking paperwork/documents, keep them safe and dry in clear plastic pouches (www.paperchase.co.uk). Nothing like a smudged, soggy car-hire print-off when you need to collect that Fiat in the wee hours.

- Try to leave a little space in the suitcase for all those floral tiles that are essential buying after a few Sangrias. If you have to sit on your case to do up the zip, you may just need to buy an extra bag when you get there. Or stuff a lightweight bag in the side pocket for good measure.

- Once zipped-up and ready to go, tie a ribbon on the handle so you can spot it on the arrivals' carrousel. Don't choose red. I counted fifteen red ribbons in one go on a recent trip to the sun.

Now we've sussed simplicity-packing, all we need is to get rid of that five-fold tummy and make our toes look less Shetland pony and more Liz Hurley, and we'll be fit for public beach exposure.

Prepping that white, flabby body for beach glory

OMG, we now have ten days to transform our fluorescent white skin, Pringle-excess tum and scabby soles into string-bikini-wearing, buff body-beautiful. Either that or change our destination to the Isle of Skye and pack knits and thermals instead. Great for non-exposure of Quality Street sins, not ideal for boho beach-babe glory. Now is the time for major holiday-panic hyperventilating. Take your time. Once a semblance of calm has ensued, let's look at shortcuts for damage limitation.

- My pal Polly swears by cutting out all booze, sugar and refined carbs in the fortnight before a holiday. The aim? To flatten her tum and clear up her skin. Good idea in principle, but I tried it once and found that freshly baked croissants at Prêt became something of an obsession. A middle road is less booze and more salads. Bread too though, please.

- If you're serious about skin-care and want minimal burnt-lobster skin and maximum radiance on your return to the drab city, take a tanning supplement. It will protect your skin and boost bronzing potential. Pop to your nearest Boots and buy Imedeen Tan Optimizer tablets (www.boots.com). Take two a day from now until the suitcases go back to the loft.

- Scrub that lustreless body twice a week in the pre-hols lead-up. It will help give skin a good glow and prepare you for that pre-beach fake tan. Try Soap & Glory Scrub 'Em and Leave 'Em (www.soapandglory.com), and use it with an exfoliating cloth. You should aim to scrub your whole-body, including feet, in circular movements for five minutes and then blast it off with cold water. Slather on moisturiser afterwards. In a dream world, I'd use Dr Hauschka Rose Body Moisturiser (www.drhauschka.co.uk), but any thick, nice-smelling body butter will do the trick.

- Book yourself in for an eyelash tint – so much less hassle than wearing mascara on the beach. Two words: bad look.

- Unless you opt for tree-hugging, hairy glory, don't forget to de-fuzz your bikini line (and, if you're feeling organised, your legs and underarms too). Try not to leave DIY or salon waxing to the last moment; sore red patches on the beach will only have you swimming in your sarong. Or, worse, jeans.

- Every year in July, Zoe advises me to fake tan the week before my hols, so as not to blend into my white pool towel. She manages a 'slow build-up' a month before and then opts for a salon St Tropez tan at Dove Spa (www.dovespa.co.uk) the day before she flies. I, on the other hand, am busy trying not to stain my cuticles the night before. If you're still terrified your legs will look like milk bottles in that new French Connection sundress, pack some L'Oreal Glam Bronze for Legs (www.loreal.co.uk) and you'll have golden, glowing pins for the first-night-at-the-beach-bar razz.

- Restore toenails to their pre-winter-in-Uggs glory with a quick DIY or salon pedicure. If you want to minimise the effects of dance-floor chips and ocean fade, try Nails Inc's Three-week Manicure and Pedicure (www.nailsinc.com). A push at around £50, but it'll keep your nails looking gorgeous all the way through your hols and probably well into their return to those matted-up old Uggs.

- If all else fails, plonk your towel next to an obese, fluorescent-white-skinned holidaymaker. A sure-fire way to make you look slimmer and browner. Or you could wear very dark shades and hope that the rest of the holidaymakers do too. Even at night. Both are far cheaper and less hassle than exfoliating your skin to within an inch of its life when you could be watching *Episodes* instead.

Choosing beachwear that will transform you into a sexy surf-siren

by **Melissa Odabash**, ultimate boho beach babe

- Before trying swimwear on, it's important to be realistic about your body shape. If you want to disguise a large bum, go for a smaller bikini bottom. The temptation is to opt for a bigger size but, to the eye, more fabric equals more derrière and it will actually give an illusion of piling on the pounds.

- Go for tie-bottoms if you have a fuller figure. You can adjust the tightness on the hips, so there'll be no digging in. The aim is to have fabric lying flush with the body. Roughing, pleats and ruffles are also a good choice if you're trying to distract the eye away from folds, creases or muffin tops. If all else fails, go for a roughed black halter-neck bikini, the guaranteed way to make any woman look thinner and feel fabulous.

- Padded tops always help lift the bust and give the illusion of a fuller chest. Who doesn't want this on the beach?

Halter-necks are also brilliant at lifting the bust. Post-baby boobs? No problem. A halter-neck will make them perfectly pert.

- Make sure the suit is lined. Fabric changes a lot in water and a lining will help your bikini keep its shape. Unlined bikinis might be cheaper, but you may well end up throwing it away after the two-week break because it's sagging and bagging and the bottoms resemble a diaper. No style or economy in that!

- Every girl needs a few insider tricks to beachwear that is easy to pack, easy to sling on and easy to give that air of boho beach beauty. I always flat-pack everything, so I can fit more in my case. Without fail, I'll pack kaftans, belts that can be worn with different kaftans and metallic sandals, as they will match everything. Bring some cool chains to throw on top of the kaftans for after the beach, and maybe a pair of cut-off jean shorts to wear underneath.

- Go for beach accessories that look natural and not OTT. I love beach hats – Panama, floppy or cowboy – and gold, bronze and brushed-silver sandals, as they look great when your legs are tanned and basically go with every colour.

- If you know you'll fancy a few cocktails after the beach, choose a long silk kaftan that can later be added to with a belt, a few necklaces and some flat sandals. I'm not a fan of high heels with long kaftans, as it takes away the whole elegance of it and you'll end up looking tacky. If you want to tower above everyone else, wear a wedge.

- Bear in mind the big beach-goddess no-nos: lots of make-up, a G-string, too much bling all over the suit with a matching bling kaftan and shoes, bright nail polish on toes and fingernails (tacky), so tanned that you look orange, badly applied self-tanner (which, I must admit, has happened to me many times, so be very careful around ankles and knees) and bright prints that you can spot a mile away.

Now, feel free to go forth and conquer that beach.

Flying economy but looking like you turned left when boarding

I *have* flown first class. Twelve years ago. It was a total fluke. Not like I paid ten grand for the seat or anything. It was a total blag, masterminded by my travel editor colleague, who owed me a favour for sorting her out with some seriously discounted Jimmy Choo shoes and a handful of sample-sale Whistles dresses. It was what I call my 'A-list princess moment', so profound that I'm sure I still have the Virgin eye-mask in a drawer somewhere.

The only negative part about sampling the pleasures of hot towels, fully reclining seats, champagne on tap and sundried-tomato roasted peanuts is having to face turning right on your next, self-paid, flight. And probably every other flight for the rest of your life. Say goodbye to lovingly marinated olives and head rests you literally sink into like a goose-down pillow; on EasyJet to Rome you have to pay a small fortune for a miniature bottle of water and a head rest takes the form of Mr S's shoulder. And did I mention you may need to empty your supersaver account if you want to fund a hot bacon and egg toastie, and ask the person next to you if they mind you sitting on their lap every time you get up? Fly long-haul economy and you might save enough to pay for a week at the Ritz in Paris, but you'll feel as if you've been five rounds with Mike Tyson and then been tied up and left in an airless sealed box for twenty-four hours. Or a week. Try it with three kids, and you start to see why Valium was the 50s housewife's drug of choice.

Life's too short to kill yourself with a self-imposed bikini boot camp. A slattern's last resort is, of course, to buy a bigger size instead.

For some insane reason, when my daughter was one and I was pregnant with my second child, we booked a much-needed 'break' in Anguilla. One delayed long-haul flight, two missed connections, and a bus, boat and jeep later, we arrived in 'paradise'. I looked a wreck and felt worse. Louis Vuitton trunks would be hard pushed to match the size of the bags under my eyes. Forget stepping onto the beach looking uber-fabulous and ready for a non-alcoholic cocktail, I needed a week in bed. Minimum.

Over the years, however, I've grown very used to surviving airless, squashed box syndrome. In my staff-on-a-women's-glossy days, I'd fly long-haul at least once a month, always economy and always with a mammoth workload to complete in transit. The New York red-eye was my second home, and I became accustomed to dashing straight from JFK to a work assignment, grabbing a double espresso en route for good measure. I'm now more familiar with the 6 a.m. EasyJet one-stop to Ibiza, alarm clock bleeping at 2 a.m., so you make it to the departure lounge in time to buy Elizabeth Arden Eight Hour before boarding. I'm not sure what the seats on the flights are like; I'm always pacing the aisles with a strung-out toddler.

I'm pretty sure that, be it JFK, Ibiza or Timbuktu, I continue to look knackered on arrival. However, I never give up hope. For other hopeful travellers out there, here are the tricks to bear in mind.

- To avoid the chance of dud-seat syndrome, check out www.seatguru.com, which details almost all airline seat plans. There may not be a way of determining whether the person seated next to you will have bad breath/verbal diarrhoea/an errant toddler, but at least your legs will be happy. Although most airplanes charge you for reserving seats, Virgin are an exception to this rule and BA lifts the fee twenty-four hours before departure. At least this way you'll be able to avoid the dreaded back row.

- Forget the myth that you should drink tons of water on a flight. Yes, poorly humidified air in the cabin does lead to dehydration, but if you drink too much on the flight your stomach will swell (remember what happens to feet in the air). Aim to drink a litre of H2O before the flight and a litre after, and sip occasionally during. This trick will save you looking six months pregnant on arrival.

- As well as your small bottle of Evian, take a few healthy snacks to save you munching your way through a family tube of Pringles. Take some seeds, fruit or muesli bars instead. Oh yes, and some Maltesers for good measure.

- Avoid caffeine and alcohol. Obviously if you've been upgraded to business and the free Moet is flowing, it would be a cardinal sin not to indulge. Majorly. Just be warned, you will probably have a hangover on arrival at your destination, and it may well be only 10 a.m.

- I'll always remember the uber-chic flier next to me on my only first-class flight. She looked immaculate in black 'dressed-down' Prada and sipped Tea Palace Green Tea throughout. She even had her own tin; it was purple and matched her cashmere pashmina, natch. I've subsequently found out that green tea is the secret to flight de-bloating, so keep this in mind if you want your jeans to fasten once you've got rid of that long-haul cramp.

- To counteract the flight dehydration, slap on that moisturiser. Elave Dermo Intense Moisture Surge is thick and quenches thirsty skin, as does Bliss Triple Oxygen + C Energising Cream. Just remember to decant before you leave, or it will be nabbed by security and you'll be left fuming. If you want to make life really easy, opt for an all-in-one in-flight beauty essentials pack by This Works (www.thisworks.com) – each container is small enough to make it past airport security. The same extra-hydration rule applies for lips, so buy a tin of Vaseline in WHSmith when stocking up on mags. While passing duty-free, nab a Guerlain Super Aqua-eye Anti-puffiness Smoothing Eye Patch, which will deflate puffy eyes and leave you smelling like a rose garden. Delicious.

- Who hasn't had a post-flight cold and blamed it on the germs recycled in the cabin air-con? It's a yearly complaint in this house. My friend Susie is my unofficial alternative-medicine guru. She may be an artist, but these days she seems to know more about homeopathy, acupuncture and aromatherapy than she does about oil paints. She regularly flies to India and hasn't had a cold for five years. Yes, *five years*. Her secret? She puts a few drops of immune-boosting, antibacterial essential oils, such as lavender and tea tree, on her pashmina and inhales them during the flight. Bingly-bongly, you may say, but it's worth a try if you want to avoid post-hols mucus mayhem.

LIFE'S TOO SHORT

- If you're too posh to use the Singapore Airlines eye-mask, take your own. Clarissa Hulse makes lovely ones and you can buy them online at John Lewis (www.johnlewis.com). If you're feeling particularly flash and faux-first-class, invest in a cashmere travel set from Cowshed, which comes with matchy-matchy camel cashmere eye-mask, socks, mini hot water bottle and blanket (www.cowshedonline.com).

- My friend Zoe swears by good earplugs for flights. She hates the noise of screaming kids and giggling hen-night girlies in equal measure. Sony's MDR-NC300D are in-ear noise-cancelling earplugs and block out around 98 per cent of all noise (www.sony.co.uk). Bloody genius. Maybe I need these at home too.

- Never rely entirely on in-flight entertainment; you'll only fail to find the chick flick you want or yours will be the one screen to blow after the first hour. The iPad is obviously the dream ticket, as it doesn't weigh much more than your lip balm and allows you to watch films, listen to tunes or read that long-overdue novel. If you can't justify the expense, even if you will use it *all the time* (goodbye, beach; hello, surfing the net), go for an iPod Touch, which skids in at under £200. If even that eats up your holiday booze fund entirely, take your ancient walkman and that beach novel on loan from your best mate. Never fails.

- Just before you land, pop an au naturale David Kirsch Afternoon Energy capsule. Zing in a pill, and far more classy than downing a can of Red Bull. You could also spray yourself with Eau Thermale Avene Spring Water Spray, which costs under a fiver from Boots. Splashing tap water on yourself is less fancy-schmancy, but it's free and easy to do while having a pee, so we like.

I will endeavour to one day fly first class again, even if I have to 'accidentally' slip past the curtain while waiting for the loo and fall into the lap of passenger 1A. Even this swift act might give me the opportunity to spy on Tea Palace drinkers and nab those roasted cashews. Failing that, I will take my own designer nuts and flash my iPad around for all to see. Not forgetting to dramatically and liberally apply moisturiser. Economy may be my destiny but, my God, I'll attempt to do it in style.

Beating jet-lag and ridding those eyes of their excess baggage

If there's one thing worse than temporary insomnia, it's jet-lag. Not only will you sew name tags in all your children's clothes and hand-wash all your long-forgotten silk smalls at 3 a.m., but when you finally fall back asleep at 6 a.m., it'll be time to get up and go. I've spent many working years blighted by jet-lag and during my late twenties found short-term memory loss, mind-blanks in crucial meetings and washing silk smalls in the early hours 'normal'. I think I mentioned that I was on first name terms with all the cabin crew on the red-eye flight to JFK. I actually think Mr S suspected I was having an affair with the pilot.

Whether it's a work trip to the States or a 'find yourself' holiday in Thailand, the psychological dislocation of jet-lag is debilitating. There's also a limit to how many name tags you can sew on. The best shortcuts to avoiding jet-lag:

- If at all possible, book a night flight and try to catch forty or more winks before landing. The 'red-eye' to the States is called that for a reason. No one ever sleeps that much, but if you manage to make it through the next day and then crash early on the first night, you'll be on the right track to feeling semi-human.

- The moment your bottom touches the seat, set your watch to match your new time zone and adjust your meal times and sleep times accordingly. Your body clock should follow your wristwatch within the next few days. Or weeks.

- Keep busy on the first day at your destination and don't succumb to that 4 p.m. desire for a nap. It will be your ruin. Stay awake as long as you can, slugging water throughout, and if you feel really super-human, try a little exercise too. You know? A short walk around the block, or to the nearest coffee shop!

- If you can claim expenses for 'combating jet-lag', invest in some express preening care of a Clubhouse Lounge spa. The treatments offered by the Cowshed Spa at Heathrow's Terminal 3 are guaranteed to leave you so chilled out you'll forget you've been stuck in a cramped seat next to a snoring bloke with bad breath for ten hours plus. No use if you're arriving in Delhi or have maxed out your budget on swish bikinis. If this is the case, DIY your post-flight skin with Guerlain Issima Midnight Secret, which has been plugged as 'sleep in a bottle'. I've also been tipped off about Dior Hydra Life Beauty Awakening Rehydrating Mask. Cake it onto your face before you attempt sleep in the hope of plumped-up skin when you awake.

Buying local gems between soaking up rays

by **Kelly Hoppen**, MBE, interior designer and super-chic homes guru

When shopping abroad, it's important to keep in mind your own personal style, whether it be at local flea markets, furniture fairs or stores. Don't get swept away in the moment by the different styles and cultures that you aren't sure will fit with your rooms at home. Make sure that your home is a neutral palette and you adorn it with accessories and items that reflect your personality, and what you buy will be a reminder of your travels.

City-slicker chic

by **Sara Berman**, designer and reluctant fixture on the mwah-mwah Paris/Milan/New York/LA network

City breaks that mix tons of hard work with some seriously hard play are a firm fixture in my life. Given the amount I need to fit into my time, I've become an incredibly organised and pragmatic traveller. In stark contrast to the luxurious summer break, when I have a tendency to pack a different outfit for day and evening, plus beach options, spillage options and changed-my-mind options, for city breaks, I go the other way. It is all about taking as little as possible whilst providing for every eventuality – the working day, business dinners, fashion parties, a night out with the girls and even a romantic evening with my man.

There are three golden rules when it comes to the perfect work/play city wardrobe:

1   Versatility

2   Flexibility

3   Practicality

There is no point in taking an outfit for every eventuality if you can be a bit clever and take a few key pieces which can be worn in different ways. It is also worth remembering that you may well indulge in a little shopping in your city of choice, and you will need to either leave room in your case for your purchases or, at the very least, enough space to accommodate a rolled-up soft bag to transport your loot home.

Key pieces which can be dressed up or down but have some statement value are the key to having the right look for the right occasion. I have some sheer black sequinned leggings which I bought from Patrizia Pepe about five years ago and have stood me in great stead. I also have a full-bodied couture lace skirt which was made for me by a fellow St Martin's graduate called Arkadius about ten years ago, and this piece takes me everywhere. I will always, always take a Sara Berman leather jacket, which I can shove over everything for a bit of 'edge', and I never travel without a cocktail dress of some sort, which can take me anywhere either dressed down with a baggy cardigan or up with some mega costume jewellery. I am also pragmatic when it comes to shoes: 1 x uber-high stilettos, 1 x high-heeled boots, 1 x flats.

A few extra shortcuts to bear in mind when packing:

- Take a pair of cheap and cheerful high-denier tights. When they get dirty, cut the feet off and turn into leggings.

- Pack a pair of flat pumps. Carry them in your handbag for when feet give out, and use them as slippers in the bedroom. I love the French Sole low-cut black ones, as they are soft and light. Super simple, but super chic.

- Find a handbag that fits all. You want it light but large enough to fit a little shopping in alongside your laptop, purse and a mini bottle of Evian.

- Pack your make-up into a clutch bag, so you have an evening option. There's no point wasting space on non-essentials such as a make-up bag if you can use a clutch instead.

- Remember that simple black tops work under dresses, with jeans or leggings – I love T by Alexander Wang.

- Take a T-shirt dress in black to wear over everything.

- A silk, printed scarf always adds interest to a basic outfit and is light to carry. I'm loving our scarf collaboration with Dan Baldwin, full of colour and when folded even smaller than your BlackBerry.

- If you're going to a city in autumn or winter, take a beanie hat to shove in your handbag in case it rains. Lighter than an umbrella and saves hair. N.Peal do great ones.

- Take a silk camisole and kill two birds with one stone – it can double as a vest if it's chilly and sexy nightwear if your man is joining you. Zadig & Voltaire do lovely ones which are great worn as tops too.

- Stash a statement hairband and you'll have an instant tool to jazz up a basic outfit. Also useful for keeping your hair off your face when you're washing off your make-up. I love the Miu Miu ones.

- Packing a pair of great skinny jeans is a must for both work and evening. Topshop skinnies win hands down for comfort and style.

- Fill boots with tights and underwear to save space when packing.

- Take some emergency talcum powder and hair mousse to revamp tired hair.

- Pack five adaptor plugs. They're like socks and always go missing!

As glam as city travelling can be when you're on the move, a lot it can be discombobulating. I always do the following to make a place more home-from-home than desolate, twenty-four-hour-Sky-habit homesickness:

- I always travel with a set of three mini candles from Diptyque. They are expensive, but their scent is so rich and they smell of home.

- It's worth finding room in your case for a beautiful body cream. Whilst I'm a major fan of the little trinkets to be found in hotel bathrooms (OK, I confess, I'm obsessed with them and have been known to steal as many as is humanly possible), as a general rule these freebie body lotions never seem quite thick enough and unless you love the scent it can be off putting. A slap of thick, luxurious, 'scent of home' body cream can easily mask the stress of a hot, hideous working day and herald the start of a sexy city evening.

- If I'm in a city for some time (particularly Paris, where I enjoy my independence), I'll sometimes rent an apartment. The quick-fix to making it feel homely is to find a local florist and invest in flowers to brighten the room.

- Make the concierge your best friend. There are all the obvious reasons to do so – restaurant bookings, theatre tickets, the list is endless – but remember, this person will also make sure the rest of the staff help you out in a fix. Big hairy spider on your ceiling at 1 a.m.? No problem. Blocked toilet? Not an issue either. Nor is a request for white wine at midnight or Nurofen at dawn. I generally find the golden rule of concierge etiquette is to make a point of introducing yourself on arrival and make it clear that you would appreciate some special attention. Always tip at the beginning and the end of a stay.

Some tried-and-tested haunts when out and about

Paris is almost a home from home for me. I usually stay in a hotel I love called the Bourg Tibourg in the Marais, which is in easy reach of all my favourite hot spots. Comptoir de Thiou does great Thai fusion, or try the Feria Café in the Marais for the best people-watching-and-burger combo. Café Les Philosophes wins hands down for hot chocolate, and for romance I love Chez Paul, a traditional French bistro which is nearer to Bastille than the Marais, but the difference is only a brisk walk, which is always lovely in Paris. If you are eating alone in Paris, then be warned – the Parisians feel this is deeply un-chic. If you're British, you won't give a damn. I always carry a book – which doesn't add to the cool factor, but frankly I don't really care! I always do great shopping in Paris, and my top four are the Kooples, Swildens, Merci and a wonderful vintage shop called Delphine Pariente, just off Rue St Antoine near the Place de Bastille. Genius buying and crammed with a million little gems.

New York is another familiar stomping ground and there are two amazing vintage shops downtown on Thompson. I confess to an unhealthy obsession with Duane Reade! I always stay at the Four Seasons for work and Soho House for pleasure. My favourite eateries are Seraphina for Italian, Del Frisco's for seafood and the Mercer Kitchen for a daytime snack. Balthazar is great fun and Sunday brunch at Pastis is a must. If I am running around and need a quick something, then the Fig and Olive is perfect. I adore being downtown and enjoy the way Chanel rubs shoulders with Marc Jacobs and Anna Sui. I also love the random mix of fashion and lifestyle, which makes for a fun shopping experience.

Tokyo is a city that I know and don't know at the same time. I've spent a lot of time there over the last six years, but somehow the city keeps unfolding. I'll start my trip with a stroll down Cat St. This runs through Omotesando and has a mixture of Japanese designers, cult labels and design shops; such fun. I love the store Undercover as a designer concept store and my favourite Japanese shop is Opaque. I also love Aqua Girl, which has several stores and Allurville. Eat sushi at any good fast-food jaunt, and you're away.

I encourage any woman to drink hot chocolate in Paris, buy vintage in New York and eat sushi in Tokyo. Life's too short not to attempt just one of the three, at the very least.

Booking a mini-break when you can't afford that lusted-after fortnight in the Bahamas

All this talk about in-flight facemasks, kaftans and batique souvenirs is making me rather jealous. There's nothing neutral about it. Simply put, it's slow sun-deprived torture. I just want to be lolling on a beach sipping a Mojito right now, OK? The only snag is my overdraft is very likely to be at its max, the children are well into the swing of a new term, and a mound of work deadlines are clogging up my inbox. Not a bloody bottle of sun cream in sight. You get it, right?

So what does a girl do when she's got work commitments coming out of her ears, a pre-winter cold sore and major kaftan envy? Well, you have three choices:

1. Ditch the boyf and find yourself a very rich man immediately. He will sweep you off your feet and take you to his private island in the Maldives. You'll never have to look at another gas bill or empty fridge again. But there are major flaws here: he'll probably be over-controlling, bald, fat and very possibly have a small willy. Plus the fact we can earn our own money, thanks very much.

2. Wallow in self-pity, applying Zovirax to your cold sore while you're at it. Then take up 'holiday porn' in your spare time, which involves cruising travel websites with the same desperate, beady eyes as a sex-addict viewing call-girl sites.

3. Book a mini-break. In the UK.

I shall opt for number three and embrace it with the same vigour and excitement as if I were off to Mauritius. Well, almost. To cut through all the crap and find a weekend break that will be just that, a break, try Mr & Mrs Smith (www.mrandmrssmith.com). If you were to offer one to me now? Boy oh boy, I'd go for:

- Dean Street Townhouse in London, where you'll get a room for under a hundred quid and can walk to art galleries without giving yourself bunions. Great people-watching opportunities in the bar too – www.deanstreettownhouse.com.

- The Scarlet in Mawgan Porth, Cornwall. Unbelievable ocean views, seafood galore and canvas pods, suspended from great heights and ready to slip into when that lunchtime drinking gets a little too much – www.scarlethotel.co.uk.

- The Hoste Arms in Norfolk, which is home to retro decor, the biggest Aga in the world and an array of inexpensive holistic spa treatments. Fantastic value from £95 a night – www.hostearms.co.uk.

- Cowley Manor, in Gloucestershire or Babington House in Somerset. If not just to swim in a heated outdoor pool in December – www.cowleymanor.co.uk, www.babingtonhouse.co.uk.

- Delphi Mountain Resort, Ireland. Stunning views, wooden floors, cosy shagpile carpets and a spa with seaweed baths. Say no more – www.delphimountainresort.com.

When booking any much-needed mini-break, tell the receptionist you are celebrating a very important birthday or anniversary and if there is any chance of an upgrade you would be extremely grateful. Works for me every time, but only when I remember to follow through on arrival ('Oh, Mr S, has it really been ten years today since . . . blah, blah'). Unpack straight away and make yourself at home. My friend Sadie takes her favourite scented candle and lights it while she takes a long bath. She vows it's the best feel-good substitute when a Mediterranean ocean view is otherwise engaged with more fortunate occupants. Book spa treatments, sleep, read, go for long walks and, most importantly, eat your body weight in delicious food. Oh, and don't forget those Top Shop lacy undies. A sure-fire way to pass the time when the skies open outside.

Channelling an air of gorgeous glamper, not crusty camper

Just as I live in hope of being a sophisticated drinker, I also cling on to the slim chance I may one day be a camping connoisseur. It just hasn't happened. Yet. The thing is, when everyone else is hopping onboard BA and heading to Corsica and we've booked nada all summer and not even a chilled weekend at a UK bolt hole looks viable (three kids and two adults in one room with no TV, are you mad? Hello, torture chamber), the idea of camping can seem, well, rather romantic. I confess, I still harp after the one 'proper' camping trip I've experienced since I was about six. I was eighteen and spent four nights at Glastonbury. F-U-N encapsulated in one small tent with a short boho sundress and dangly bracelets to finish it off. Having said that, it was rather a haze of Becks beer, ProPlus and post A-level adrenalin, and I'm not quite sure if I actually slept in the tent much. Certainly zzzzzs were not a top priority.

A while back, during a phase of holiday desperation, I decided to take a fresh step into camping euphoria, just this time around delete the ProPlus and exam adrenalin. My one sacred shortcut? To take the most efficient and glamorous route available. And cheat. 'Glamping' it is then. No tent, no ground sheets, no pots and pans, no fire-lighters, no damp bottom. I like this a lot. There are so many options available for camping cheats, it's a surprise we even need EasyJet.

I'm a sucker for beautifully shot marketing material and immediately fell for Feather Down Farms (www.featherdownfarms.co.uk). It's very hard not to succumb to the hype. Canvas tents lit by oil lamp, sleepy children's faces peering over fluffy white double duvets, marshmallows toasting on campfires, the sun setting over farm gates. Who doesn't want to be that girl in the Hunters, striding arm in arm with a Barbour-wearing Jude Law lookalike? I'm such a sucker for the promise of a fantasy life that, within seconds, I'd booked a long weekend en famille on a farm in Hampshire. It only took a little twisting of Mr S's arm – 'This will be great British outdoor fun, you'll see' (what, no *Match of the Day*?).

I won't bore you at length with the gory details. Let's just say there were a few freezing-cold nights when even my warmest thermals felt like I was wearing ice blocks, 5 a.m. wake-up calls from children who weren't used to life without blackout blinds and swear words hurled when Mr S realised his 'beloved' had forgotten to pack bog roll and Nurofen. I won't bore you at length with the beautiful details either. Snap one: three blonde children fast asleep and entwined in one log bed. Snap two: middle son, who cares more about football than wildlife 99 per cent of the time, delivers newborn calf. Snap three: Mr S catches a fish from the pond, wearing Hunters and a Barbour. I kid you not. What I will say is that although wiping my bottom with leaves wasn't a highlight, there were enough laughs to make us re-book the last three years running.

I have to say, I haven't quite ventured into 'hardcore camping' yet (what, no double duvet or yurt in sight?) but I'm warming to the idea. Slowly. I have plenty of non-crusty camper friends who scoff at my glamping anecdotes. 'Freezing? You don't know the meaning of the word!' They regularly chide me by trying to shove tent pegs down my knickers. They rave about their faithful DIY canvas companion, and who can blame them? It's cheap, eco-friendly and rarely involves jet-lag or sunburn. You don't even need to get a mani or pedi to qualify.

I want to avoid starting a glamp v camp war, so my best bet is to pool shared knowledge to come up with the definitive list of sleeping outdoors shortcuts.

- Fforest in Pembrokeshire has a selection of wooden domes, teepees, nomad tents and cottage-like crog lofts to choose from. All have outdoor cooking areas and a sociable pub on site. Result! Check out www.coldatnight.co.uk.

- Feather Down Farms offer clusters of canvas tents based on farms all around the UK. Kitted out with duvets, log-burning stoves and cutlery and crockery, you can bypass soggy sleeping bags and 'Oh no, I forgot the corkscrew' and move straight onto that Boden-style family photo. Remember to ask what other bonus extras the farm has to offer and if you're lucky they'll have wood-burning pizza ovens, livestock, a play-park and chickens – www.featherdownfarms.co.uk.

- Yurtcamp near Exmoor offers yurts with accompanying beds, gas stoves and kitchen equipment. Not too dissimilar to Feather Down in the glamping stakes. They provide a great assault course too. Ideal for entertaining the kids while you crack open a bottle of red. Failing that, my friend Amie and her mates enjoyed it after a bottle of red. Minus any under-tens – www.yurtcamp.co.uk.

- Vintage Vacations is my friend Nell's idea of heaven. Restored aluminium trailers equipped with patchwork quilts, hand-knitted rugs and retro-print furnishings. She even insists on wearing 50s T-dresses for the entirety of the mini-break. The one 'glamping' choice where you don't need a car boot full of thermals to survive past day one of hyperthermia.

- If you wouldn't be seen dead sleeping under a teepee, then go forth with your two-man tent, but make sure you choose your campsite well. Smelly loos are only acceptable at Reading Festival – www.coolcamping.co.uk, www.pitchup.com, www.ayrholidaypark.co.uk and www.fishergroundcampsite.co.uk are all top sites to try.

- If you're camping under DIY canvas, invest in a good tent. Wailing winds we can deal with, wet bottoms we can't. I'm told by my seriously cool camping friends that www.tentipi.com and www.belltent.co.uk are the places to go to ensure your tent is the hottest on site.

- The usual camping suspects apply – sleeping bags, groundsheet, builders' buckets (dual-action ice-bucket/washing-up bowl), torch, bin bags, towels, tons of toiletries, pots, pans, knives and forks, a lighter, waterproofs, wellies, flip-flops (let's be hopeful), booze (screw-top wine essential), biscuits, baked beans and tons and tons of warm clothes. Even if you're living it up in a yurt and can omit the tent pegs, make your life easy and pack loo roll and Nurofen. It goes without saying that cotton pads intended for eye make-up removal and a stonking hangover at 6 a.m. just don't cut it when you're trying to relax.

- My friend Jodie swears by sourcing B&Bs local to the campsite prior to arrival. Contingency plans are always helpful in June when rain is predicted non-stop for a full week. And you already have a stinking cold. Now I think about it, luxe spa hotels within a fifty-mile radius are worth jotting down too.

Travelling anywhere with kids and not overdosing on their emergency Calpol

Travelling with kids is hazardous, full stop. I confess, at times I find 'travelling' with three kids just to get a pint of milk from the 24/7 poses a challenge on many levels. Patience, for one. Sanity, for another. Don't even get me started on the issue of volume control. Mine not theirs. Poor little blighters. When we do venture beyond the post box at the end of our road, I always take the following shortcuts:

- Take fewer clothes and more washable felt-tip pens. Forget diligently packing gorgeous boho beach looks for your children. Unless you're Suri Cruise, a matching floral dress and sun-hat combo for every day of the week, with a change for the evening, is a waste of time. All the children I know are very happy in a pair of Crocs and a hooded towelling dress. Boys too – www. thewhitecompany.co.uk. A few swimming cossies, and you're away. Substitute the clothes with story books, crayons, fantasy figures and sticker books. A Petite Bateau linen sundress won't kill an hour on the beach/ stuck in departures/ waiting for the paella to arrive; Usborne's dolly-dressing

Life's too short to lust after five-star glory when getting down and dirty can be just as much fun (well, almost, and that doesn't include The Necker island option). Just don't forget the bog roll and Becks.

books, with 400 stickers, or Rosie Flo's colouring books
will (www.usborne.com, www.rosieflo.co.uk).

- My friend Charlotte swears by taking a portable DVD
  player on all her family flights. Fireman Sam is her Sri
  Lanka/Sicily salvation. Useful too when the hotel TV only
  has two local channels.

- Loosen up about routines when you're abroad *en famille*.
  My friend Lotte is about to travel with nine-month-old twins
  and vows to stick to Gina Ford all the way to the sand
  dunes. I don't have the heart to tell her they may not have
  blackout blinds in Jaipur and Plum Organics pureed
  spinach might be tricky to source. It may be wise to
  embrace flexibility, just a tad. The same applies for older
  children. Just remember to keep them fed and watered,
  with the odd ice-cream thrown in now and then. My
  three have a bedtime of 8 p.m. during term time, but on
  hols they'll be skinny-dipping at midnight. We all generally
  pay for it the next day, but being a morning beach-grump
  is surely a rite of passage when you're four-foot-
  something?

- My friend Jessie only ever travels to places she knows
  she'll find other kids. She's a single mum with three
  under-sixes. Her best option for achieving a morsel of
  holiday wind-down is to source a hotel with a semi-OK
  kids' club, choose a destination where she can hook up
  with other families or head to areas/beaches/hotels with a
  guaranteed posse of under-tens. If she teams up with
  another family to hire a villa, they always insist on drawing
  up a rota on arrival. Sounds military if you ask me, but
  apparently, by dividing up jobs like cooking/shopping/
  babysitting, it diffuses any potential daggers-at-dawn

confrontations and means you'll still be on speaking terms by the time you return to Heathrow.

- If you've got young kids and can't face the thought of sterilising bottles in the dunes, you could consider sanitation and a semblance of sanity care of a holiday in the Med. Check out Kids In the Med (www.wandotravel. com/families), which also comes with the added bonus of a 'send-ahead service' that delivers nappies/food/wipes direct to your holiday door.

- Shite, forgotten your baby's passport photo and Snappy Snaps has closed for the night? Email a digital pic of your squidgy to Paspic and they'll whizz off a set of four passport-suitable photos – www.paspic.co.uk.

- Always take Marmite. You're a mum, and this comes with the job description.

- Don't expect to read a whole book, even on a two-week break. This is impossible. I think I managed fifty-two pages on my last holiday and this was a definite upgrade on the year before.

- If all else fails, drag your big kids off their DS and pack them off to PGL for a week (www.pgl.co.uk). Good old-fashioned pony trekking, leaving you to catch up on work, tidy the 'banned – do not enter' bedroom for the first time in six months and miss them dreadfully. Well, a bit.

I love my kids dearly. Oh yes, I do. I just wish they would leave me to read page fifty-three and beyond of my beach novel. I'll return the favour with double 99s, I promise.

OVER AND OUT

So, here I am, at the end of a hair-raising and often hilarious journey. I've been waxed to millimetre of my pubic life, forced to embrace a pink boa-less hen night, encouraged to sort out my finances and persuaded to abandon some of my hippy-luxe maxi dresses and dip my toe into the world of 'classic fashion staples' – all in the name of nailing a one-stop shop for busy, multitasking women such as myself.

My aim at the beginning of this project was, first and foremost, to ensure it was a good laugh to write and to make a silent vow to myself that I would never, ever take myself or my clutter-phobia too seriously in the process. I also wanted to attempt to compile a funny, gritty, anecdotal, no-holds-barred guide for readers like you and me, who need a million and one solutions, shortcuts, ideas and resources in one honest, easy-to-read package – in a nutshell, we just want an easy life, thanks very much. As I typed away, I felt myself becoming quite passionate about offering an antidote to all the preachy 'isn't my life perfect' literature that implies we just can't measure up. I figured life's far too short to feel a total failure racked with guilt about everything from your weight to your mothering skills all the bloody time. I hope I've pulled this off and produced a book that doesn't compound our endless feelings of inadequacy, but instead encourages us to feel that doing our best (cutting a few corners, taking a few shortcuts and slurping a few glasses of Pinot while we're at it) is more than enough.

Now, can we all raise that glass of Pinot in agreement that life's far too short to have sleepless nights about cellulite, how to home-make a complex cordon bleu starter from scratch after a long day in the office or how to be goddamn perfect from the second you open your eyes in the morning to the second your weary head hits that pillow at midnight? Hurray to that.

A million thanks to . . .

Mr S and my three little blondies for giving me the time and space to write. I know the fridge has been bare and the sound of typing has kept you up half the night, but I love you all – you're quite simply the foundations of my life.

Carly Cook, the only editor I know who can rival my speed of speech and shoe collection. You're quick, smart, funny and gorgeous, and I think I owe you a very large drink.

Jo Whitford, Helena Towers and Vicky Cowell at Headline – alongside Carly, surely the hardest-working team in publishing?

My brilliant agent Lizzy Kremer at David Higham Associates, another smart thinker, fast talker and shoe hoarder. We make a great team. A large glass of Pinot for you too?

My dear friend and confidante Ros, who bent over backwards and tied herself in knots to support this project. Your contacts book (which, by the way, should be diamond studded at the very least), loyalty and generosity are just three of the reasons I love you to bits.

Lovely Katie, who tirelessly shared top tips and suggested resources, while simultaneously teaching me to surf. Multi-tasking personified.

All my brilliant contributors and their willing agents/PRs. Denise Van Outen, Sam Roddick, Jools Oliver, Baukjen De Swaan Arons, Savannah Miller, Charlie Miller, Deborah Meaden, Sasha Speed, Serena Rees, Jasmine Birtles, Audrey Carden, Alice Temperley, Sheherazade Goldsmith, Sarah

LIFE'S TOO SHORT

Beeny, Pearl Lowe, Jane Clarke, Hannah Lanfear, Gaby Roslin, Jemma Kidd, Lisa Eastwood, Louise Redknapp, Nicky Kinnaird, Eliza Doolittle, Natalie Hartley, Beatrix Ong, Katie Hillier, Sophie Ellis-Bextor, Tess Daly, Tara Lee, Kelly Hoppen, Melissa Odabash, Sara Berman – your pearls of wisdom are spot on.

Sara M, Mel, Sue, Jo, Leigh, Gayle, Clare, Jennie, Lyn, Lesley, Jacky, Shazza, Lou, Lizzie, Lerryn, Rosie, Lucie, Paula, Missy, Amy, Rainbow, Maya, Jainey, Giselle, Annie, Flora, Nicola J, Isabel F and all my other wonderful friends who have contributed in some way to this book. Don't stop sharing your wise, inspiring, fabulous ways just because I've stopped emailing you at midnight for tips.

Lastly to my beloved family and biggest supporters – Mum, Dad, Sam, Fleur, Rocco and Will. Not even a passing interest in Bikram, boyfriends or bills between you. Thank goodness for that.

INDEX